PROFESSIONAL RESPONSIBILITY AND REGULATION

By

DEBORAH L. RHODE
Ernest W. McFarland Professor of Law
and
Director, Keck Center on Legal Ethics and the Legal Profession
Stanford Law School

GEOFFREY C. HAZARD, JR.
Trustee Professor, University of Pennsylvania

D1166157

CONCEPTS AND INSIGHTS SERIES

New York, New York
FOUNDATION PRESS
2002

Cover Design: Keith Stout
Cover Art: Yale Law School (with thanks)

Foundation Press, a division of West Group, has created this publication to provide you with
accurate and authoritative information concerning the subject matter covered. However,
this publication was not necessarily prepared by persons licensed to practice law in a
particular jurisdiction. Foundation Press is not engaged in rendering legal or other
professional advice, and this publication is not a substitute for the advice of an attorney. If
you require legal or other expert advice, you should seek the services of a competent
attorney or other professional.

COPYRIGHT © 2002 By FOUNDATION PRESS
     395 Hudson Street
     New York, NY 10014
     Phone Toll Free 1–877–888–1330
     Fax (212) 367–6799
     fdpress.com

For
Mary Tye

*

ACKNOWLEDGMENTS

We are deeply grateful for the superb research assistance of Stanford Law School students Joshua Klein and Angie Schwartz. And we owe equal debts to Mary Tye, to whom the book is dedicated, for her invaluable contributions in preparing the manuscript for publication.

*

TABLE OF CONTENTS

TABLE OF CONTENTS

*

PROFESSIONAL RESPONSIBILITY AND REGULATION

*

Chapter I

INTRODUCTION

A. The Concept of a Profession

In a book about the legal profession, it is appropriate to begin with an understanding of what membership in a profession implies. Occupations that we now consider "professional" have been in existence for well over 2000 years, although the term itself and the distinctive features of these vocational groups did not begin to emerge until the sixteenth century. "Profession" comes from the Latin term, "professionem," meaning to make a public declaration. The term evolved to describe occupations that required new entrants to take an oath professing their dedication to the ideals and practices associated with a learned calling.

Contemporary definitions of professions generally emphasize their special expertise and ethical responsibilities, which give rise to other defining features, such as self-regulation, prescribed qualifications, codes of conduct, occupational associations, and monopolies over certain work. American lawyers have long prided themselves on being a profession. According to a prominent report by the American Bar Association (ABA), professionals are those who are "pursuing a learned art ... in the spirit of public service."[1] By the same token, lawyers also have long been concerned about a loss of professionalism and the "decline of law into a business." Over a century ago, one American commentator captured widespread views in observing that the bar had lost its "fine sense of dignity" and had become "contaminated with the spirit of commerce."[2]

During the past two decades, expression of these concerns has intensified, fueled by increasing competition and commercialism in the market for legal services, and by a sense of decreasing professional control over the regulation of lawyers and the scope of their monopoly. To a growing extent, the bar shares its authority over lawyers' conduct with courts, legislatures, employers, and administrative agencies. The profession's efforts to prevent the "unautho-

1. American Bar Association (ABA) Commission on Professionalism, "In the Spirit of a Public Service:" A Blueprint for the Rekindling of Lawyer Professionalism 3 (1986).

2. American Lawyer, quoted in Deborah L. Rhode, In the Interests of Jus-

tice: Reforming the Legal Profession 1 (2001). See also Geoffrey C. Hazard, Jr. & Angelo Dondi, Legal Ethics: A Comparative Study, Chapter 1, at 45 (forthcoming).

1

rized practice of law" by nonlawyer competitors has been eroded by market pressures and technological advances. Increasing specialization within the profession has also raised questions about the usefulness of treating lawyers as a single unified group subject to the same education and regulatory standards.

The practice of law has traditionally been regulated at the state level rather than nationally or locally (as in Europe). In modern times, legal practice has increasingly crossed jurisdictional boundaries, both state and national. This growth of "multi-jurisdictional practice" has compounded other ambiguities in the boundaries of lawyers' work. In many nations, much of the work that American lawyers do in this country is not reserved to members of the bar or is divided among subgroups of the legal profession. For example, in European and South American countries, some types of legal documents are exclusively prepared by *notaires*, who have legal training and significantly more status and official responsibility than their American counterparts. And in Japan, a large number of individuals in business and the professions have legal education and perform legal tasks, but only about two percent of these individuals pass the bar and are able to represent litigants in court.[3] Other nations generally permit non-lawyers to give legal advice and to join with lawyers in multidisciplinary partnerships. As a consequence, multinational accounting firms have eclipsed law firms as the world's largest providers of legal services.

How the American bar is responding to these trends is addressed in Chapter IX. For present purposes, what bears emphasis is the challenge that they raise to traditional understandings of the profession. Those understandings have been subject to criticism on several levels. First, critics from both the right and left have questioned whether professions like law are qualitatively different in terms of expertise or public spiritedness from others that have not attained professional status. Not all legal practice requires greater skill and training than that of occupations not traditionally considered professions, such as investment banking or information technology. Nor is it apparent that lawyers have been more selflessly public-minded than other occupational groups in structuring their own regulation and policing their own membership. Popular opinion polls demonstrate considerable public skepticism about the profession's claims to public spiritedness. Fewer than a fifth of Americans view lawyers as "honest and ethical;" three-fifths view lawyers as "greedy," and four-fifths believe some of their work

---

3. See Rhode, supra note 2, at 119.

could be done as well with less expense by others.[4] To many observers, the bar's rhetoric about professionalism often serves as window dressing for economic protectionism and an inflated self-image.[5]

By contrast, bar leaders generally view recent market trends and opinion polls as a reason not to relinquish claims of special status, but rather to rekindle professional ideals. To that end, state and local bar associations have launched a broad range of professionalism initiatives, including conferences, commissions, centers, and civility codes. How much effect these efforts have on practice remains an open question. But the underlying aspiration is surely worth preserving. Whatever its other limitations, the bar's commitment to professionalism has made an enormous contribution to the rule of law and the pursuit of justice. Lawyers inspired by that commitment have been at the forefront of every major public interest cause in American history. Their efforts to provide pro bono assistance, to protect individual liberties, and to serve as an independent check on governmental overreaching have been models for other bars throughout the world. Many individuals choose law as a career at least in part out of a desire to advance social justice, and they seek a professional identity that will serve that end.

B. Professional Norms: Law, Morality, and Legal Ethics

A key concept in a book about the regulation of lawyers is "legal ethics." The term is often used interchangeably with "professional responsibility" to describe the bar's governing norms. A threshold question is what is the "ethics" in legal ethics, and how is it related to the law of lawyering.

As a definitional matter, most scholars trace *ethics* to the Greek words *ethikos*, which means pertaining to custom, and *ethos*, which refers to character. *Morality* comes from the Latin *mores*, which refers to character or custom and habit. In contemporary

---

4. Id., at 4; Gary A. Hengstler, "Vox Populi: The Public Perception of Lawyers: ABA Poll" A.B.A. J., Sept. 1993, at 60; Randall Samborn, "Anti–Lawyer Attitude Up," National L. J., Aug. 9, 1993, at 20; Stephen Budiansky, Ted Gest, & David Fisher, "How Lawyers Abuse the Law," U.S. News & World Report, Jan. 30, 1995, at 50; Gallup Poll Releases, Nov. 1999.

5. For the classic conservative position, see Milton Friedman, Capitalism and Freedom 144–149 (1962). See also

Richard Posner, Overcoming Law 37–38, 91–93 (1995). For criticisms from the left, see Rhode, supra note 1, at 1–22, 135–41, 207–08. Russell G. Pearce, "Law Day 2050: Post–Professionalism, Moral Leadership, and the Law-as-Business Paradigm," 27 Fla. St. U. L. Rev. 9 (1999); Richard Abel, American Lawyers 12 (1989); Richard L. Abel, "The Contradictions of Professionalism," in Lawyers and Society: The Common Law World 186–243 (Richard L. Abel & Philip Lewis, eds. 1989).

societies, both terms have become somewhat detached from their original meaning. Philosophers generally consider "ethics" to be the study of morality, or to refer to the customary norms in a given society (i.e., its *ethos)*, and "morality" to involve universal principles of right and wrong.[6] However, since philosophical moral theories overlap with customary norms, many contemporary theorists doubt the usefulness of any general distinction between ethics and morality.

In one sense, legal ethics is simply a form of legal regulation that incorporates mandatory rules of conduct adopted by courts, legislatures, and administrative agencies. In another, equally coherent sense, legal ethics is a branch of trans-legal norms that reflect and reinforce broader concepts of morality drawn from religious and philosophical traditions. On both these dimensions, legal ethics is central to the working lives of lawyers. The bar's code of conduct determines their continued eligibility to practice, and helps shape their moral identity as professionals.

The application of much contemporary moral philosophy to problems of legal practice is limited by two of its defining features: its commitment to universal principles and its assumption of knowledge about the facts on which normative judgments rest. Yet in the working lives of lawyers, knowledge is incomplete and context matters. Moreover, the very fact that legal ethics involves the practice of law is centrally important. "Lawyer" is not simply a job description but a legally defined occupation with legally prescribed powers and duties, such as the duty to keep a client's confidences. As a general matter, the dominant traditions of moral philosophy may help frame questions, but they do not supply determinate answers to the concrete dilemmas of practice.[7]

The two philosophical traditions generally viewed as most relevant for legal ethics are utilitarianism and deontology (or rights-based theory). In its classic form, utilitarianism holds that the morally right action is the one that produces the greatest good for the greatest number. Under this theory, each person's happiness is equally important. Deontology, a term derived from the Greek word "deon," or duty, holds that the morally right action is one that conforms to universal, generalizable principles of obligation. Immanual Kant, a leading deontological theorist, believed that ethically justifiable conduct must satisfy one ultimate moral principle, the categorical imperative. Kant gave this principle two

---

6. G.W.F. Hegel, Phenomenology of Spirit 266–94 (A.V. Miller trans., 1977); John Hartland-Swann, An Analysis of Morals (1960).

7. See Geoffrey C. Hazard, Jr., "Law Practice and the Limits of Moral Philosophy," in Ethics in Practice 75, 77 (Deborah L. Rhode, ed., 2000).

formulations. The first is that individuals are to "act only according to that maxim ... [which] should become a universal law." A second is to "treat others only as an end, and never as a means only."[8] In applying deontological theory, philosophers have attempted to identify obligations that would satisfy the requirements of universalization, generalization, and respect for others. Such obligations typically include duties of fidelity (keeping promises, avoiding deception), duties of benevolence (helping others and avoiding harm), and duties of justice (treating similar cases similarly). Because these obligations imply corresponding rights, deontological frameworks are often referred to as rights-based theories.

Each of these approaches has been applied to legal ethics issues, and each has been subject to criticisms that are relevant for such issues. One problem with utilitarianism is that is usually impossible to objectively identify, weigh, and compare the consequences of a particular act against all the alternatives. A further problem is that the theory provides no way of protecting individual rights against majority preferences, or of distinguishing qualitatively between preferences, such as between those founded on irrationality, bigotry, or addiction, and those founded on more benign values.[9] Deontological theories have been similarly criticized as indeterminate. Principles like the categorical imperative are of little assistance in resolving ethical dilemmas that implicate competing values such as fidelity to clients and benevolence toward third parties. A requirement that rules be generalized and that individual rights be respected is of little help when the issue is which rule we should generalize and whose individual rights should have priority.[10]

These limitations become even more apparent in the context of particular legal ethics issues. A representative example involves the classic dilemma, discussed more fully in Chapter VI, of whether lawyers should disclose a client's confidences in order to prevent serious harm to third parties. It is possible to justify broad protections for client confidences on both rights-based and utilitarian grounds; it is equally possible to critique such protections on similar grounds.

---

8. Immanual Kant, Foundations of the Metaphysics of Morals 46 (Lewis White Beck, trans. 2d ed. 1990).

9. See sources cited in Deborah L. Rhode, Professional Responsibility: Ethics by the Pervasive Method 20–23 (1998); Amartya Sen, Collective Choice and Social Welfare 118–48 (1970); J.J.C.

Smart & Bernards Williams, Utilitarianism: For and Against 33 (1973).

10. Rhode, supra note 9, at 23–24; Roberto Magabeira Unger, Knowledge and Politics 54 (1975); Alisdair MacIntyre, A Short History of Ethics 197–98 (1966).

The basic rights-based argument for confidentiality obligations builds on several assumptions about societal values and client conduct. The first assumption is that an overarching objective of the legal system is to preserve individual rights. In an advanced industrial society, people have an array of legal rights (due process, privacy, the right to contract, for example) that are vulnerable to infringement, either by the government or by other private interests. Preventing or redressing infringement often requires the assistance of lawyers. Lawyers cannot provide adequate representation unless clients feel free to provide all relevant information. Many individuals will be unwilling to seek legal assistance or to disclose essential facts without assurances that their communications will remain confidential. Protection of such confidences serves not only to safeguard legal rights in general, but also to preserve certain specific entitlements such as constitutional guarantees for criminal defendants. If lawyers could disclose inculpating client communications, persons accused of a crime could not fully exercise both their Sixth Amendment right to counsel and their Fifth Amendment privilege against self-incrimination.

Critics of broad confidentiality protections make several responses. First, they note that concerns about criminal defendants' constitutional rights do not justify sweeping protections in civil contexts. Nor do concerns about individual liberty and privacy explain the extension of broad confidentiality safeguards to corporations. It is also not self-evident why the rights of clients, especially corporate clients, should always take priority over the rights of others, particularly where individuals' health and safety interests are implicated. Moreover, current confidentiality mandates are subject to exceptions and indeterminacies; existing research leaves doubt whether some further limitations on the protection of confidentiality would significantly alter client behavior.[11]

An alternative utilitarian justification for broad confidentiality rules is that they promote the greatest good for the greatest number by facilitating compliance with legal norms. Lawyers who can acquire confidential information can counsel individuals about their legal obligations and encourage appropriate resolution of legal disputes. However, for all the reasons noted above, critics of broad confidentiality protections argue that allowing some disclosures in order to prevent injuries to third parties would not significantly intrude on the lawyer's counseling role. Exceptions to confidentiality safeguards already exist, most individuals are unaware of their

11. See the discussion in Chapter VI infra.

scope, and many clients have sufficient reasons to confide in their attorneys regardless of the precise scope of ethical obligations.

The merits of these arguments are explored more fully in Chapter VI. The point here is simply to underscore the contributions and limitations of ethical theory in addressing legal ethics issues. Abstract moral principles may help in framing the relevant inquiry. But the resolution will generally depend on concrete factual information about the effects of particular ethical decisions and contextual judgments about how to reconcile competing moral claims. In the confidentiality case just noted, it is important to know how different disclosure rules affect clients' behavior and how to weigh their interests against those of third parties affected by the rules. However, that kind of information is virtually unattainable. Debates over the issue necessarily proceed on a level of unsupported self-assurance on both sides.

It is, however, inappropriate to conclude that moral theory is useless and that an entirely relativist approach to ethics is appropriate. In its extreme form, relativism holds that there is no objective basis for justifying one set of ethical beliefs over another. Relativism is appealing because it combines a healthy skepticism towards universal truths and an equally healthy tolerance for cultural diversity. From a relativist standpoint, disagreements about facts look qualitatively different from disagreements about morality. On factual issues, as greater information becomes available, greater consensus becomes likely. On moral claims, valid and persuasive information is often unavailable: we lack an objective basis for determining how different confidentiality rules would affect lawyer-client relationships, or how to weigh the needs of clients against other individuals affected by the rules. Ethical judgments are generally "subjective" to a degree that factual judgments are not. Moreover, ethical convictions vary widely across cultures. To take only the most obvious examples, practices that contemporary Americans would find abhorrent–torture, subjugation of women, or infanticide–have been widely accepted in other societies.

However, as critics of relativism note, factual claims may also be subject to dispute, but few of us conclude that convincing answers are never available. Many societies long argued about whether the earth was flat; we do not therefore doubt the possibility of valid claims about geography. Moreover, few individuals are prepared to accept relativism in its most extreme form and conclude that actions like genocide and terrorism violate no universal moral principle.[12] Over time, substantial consensus has emerged on certain basic moral premises. Given full information and an opportunity for dispassionate and disinterested judgment, most individuals will agree about some essential principles, such as honesty, benevolence, and so forth. Although disagreements will remain about the application of those principles in particular cases, including those in legal ethics, some positions will often seem more persuasive than others–more rational, informed, and internally consistent.

In any event, however lawyers resolve the philosophical debate over relativism, they must make considered ethical judgments of the kind that are the subject of this book. The fact that individuals of good faith often differ in their judgments is an argument for tolerance of competing views. Even the most committed critics of relativism, who believe passionately in their position, need not always seek to impose their views on others. We can remain sensitive to the risks of moral arrogance without abandoning our moral convictions. On many issues of legal ethics, lawyers with high moral principles may disagree about what those principles require in hard cases. Particularly where competing values and factual uncertainties are involved, the most professionally responsible approach may require respect for differing views. How to arrive at well-considered judgments in the face of ambiguity is a key focus of the chapters that follow.

C. The Law of Lawyering

In the United States, law is a highly regulated profession. American lawyers are subject to a complex set of formal and informal norms that are largely under the influence of the profession but that are also affected by other forms of regulation. The most important sources of authority are as follows.

Courts

The judicial branch traditionally has asserted "inherent power" to regulate the practice of law, an authority rooted in the proposition that lawyers are officers of the court. In the American context, that judicial authority rests on constitutional provisions governing the separation of government power. Some exercises of the judiciary's oversight are simply instances of common law adjudication. For example, courts have applied contract, fiduciary, and

---

12. Morris Ginsburg, On the Diversity of Morals, in 1 Essays on Sociology and Social Philosophy 97–129 (1956); Michael Moore, "Moral Reality," 1982 Wis. L. Rev. 1061, 1088–1096.

related principles to govern lawyers in areas such as malpractice, fee disputes, and conflicts of interest.

In addition, the judiciary has asserted authority to adopt general procedural rules and ethical codes. Virtually every state supreme court has exercised control over bar admission, discipline, and unauthorized practice of law. Federal judges enjoy comparable inherent authority as well as statutory power to regulate admission, discipline, and trial conduct in their own court system. For substantive standards, federal courts generally rely on the ethical codes and common law of the jurisdictions in which they sit. To varying degrees, judges in both state and federal systems have enforced legislative regulation that they view as not inconsistent with their own oversight powers.

Bar Associations

In exercising their regulatory responsibilities, courts frequently have deferred or delegated authority to bar associations. About two-thirds of the states have "integrated" bars, which require lawyers to belong to state bar associations as a condition of practice. In some states, bar organizations largely administer admission and disciplinary structures, although the judiciary exercises nominal supervision. Other states have separate regulatory bodies that are subject to judicial review. In either case, although non-lawyers often have some representation on disciplinary committees, members of the profession exercise control. The organized bar generally has shaped the relevant ethical standards through committee recommendations and lobbying efforts.

In addition to state bar associations, many lawyers belong to national, local, or other bar organizations, including those structured around fields of practice, political and legal causes, or race, gender, and ethnicity. The largest of these organizations, representing almost half of the nation's attorneys, is the American Bar Association (ABA).

Ethical Codes

One of bar associations' most significant activities has been formulating ethical codes that are adopted by courts. The ABA is responsible for the two major model codes currently in use. The Model Rules of Professional Conduct were approved by the ABA in 1983 and have been adopted in whole or in part by about four-fifths of the states, usually through their supreme courts after advice from their bar associations. Other states, with the exception of California, have versions of an earlier Model Code of Professional Responsibility, initially approved by the ABA in 1970. California has a unique system that grants its Board of Bar Governors statutory power to promulgate rules directly, subject to approval by the California Supreme Court. These rules draw on the ABA Code but are in some respects different. The California legislature has also adopted a broad business and professions statute that has provisions applicable to lawyers.

In almost all jurisdictions, bar ethical codes have the force of law as a result of their adoption by state supreme courts. In a minority of jurisdictions, courts have ratified these codes only as guidelines, which can then be given force in judicial and bar disciplinary proceedings. Ethical codes are designed to set standards only for lawyer discipline and expressly disclaim any intent to establish a basis for civil liability.[13] However, most courts have relied on codified rules in malpractice cases. During the late 1980s and 1990s, many state and local bars also adopted codes of civility. For the most part, these codes establish voluntary standards, but several of them have been approved or adopted by a court.

D. Sources of Regulatory Authority

Other primary sources of regulatory standards include bar ethics committees, legislatures, administrative agencies, specialized bar organizations, and legal employers. Rulings by state, local, and national bar committees have played a significant, although declining, role in defining lawyers' ethical responsibilities. Traditionally, these opinions have responded to inquiries by attorneys and have claimed to interpret or amplify codified standards. However, as courts have grown increasingly active in disciplinary and malpractice proceedings, and as voluntary bar organizations have grown increasingly concerned about avoiding antitrust violations, ethics committee opinions have become less influential.[14]

At the same time, the role of legislatures and administrative agencies has expanded. Courts generally have allowed legislatures and agencies to define standards for parties appearing in administrative tribunals and to establish other rules of conduct as long as they are consistent with judicially approved rules. Some administrative agencies, for example workers' compensation boards and tax

---

13. The Preliminary Statement to the Code of Professional Responsibility makes clear that it does not undertake to define standards for civil liability of lawyers. The introductory provision governing the "scope" of the Model Rules of Professional Conduct similarly asserts that they are not designed to be a basis for civil liability.

14. Charles Wolfram, Modern Legal Ethics 65–67 (1986). In the aftermath of the settlement of a government antitrust suit against the ABA, its ethics committee issued an opinion declaring that its rulings were not binding on lawyers. ABA Comm. on Ethics and Professional Responsibility, Informal Op. 1420 (1978).

commissions, permit nonlawyers who meet specified qualifications to represent parties in their proceedings. Certain agencies such as the Securities and Exchange Commission and Internal Revenue Service also have power to impose sanctions for unethical conduct by those appearing before them.

The complexity of these overlapping regulatory structures is compounded in multi-jurisdictional practice. Much of lawyers' work cuts across state or national boundaries, and is therefore subject to more than one ethical code. Although the ABA's Model Rules establish principles for resolving conflicts between state codes, application of these principles can be problematic in practice.[15]

Other bar entities also play a significant regulatory role. State boards of bar examiners exercise authority over admission standards and procedures. These boards administer bar exams, moral character requirements, and the procedure for admission of out-of-state attorneys. Other professional organizations have promulgated standards for lawyers that can be an important source of guidance for practitioners, courts, bar committees, and drafters of ethical codes. The American Law Institute's Restatement of the Law Governing Lawyers is the most comprehensive and influential of these works. Other examples include the ABA's Standards Relating to the Administration of Criminal Justice, and the Standards of Conduct of the American Academy of Matrimonial Lawyers.

A final source of influence involves the formal and informal norms of legal workplaces. Some employers have specific policies, procedures, committees, or advisors concerning ethical issues. For example, large firms and corporate in-house counsel offices often have elaborate structures for dealing with potential conflicts of interest and other ethical issues. Many district attorneys' offices specify procedures governing plea-bargaining and press statements. Such procedures typically supplement as well as incorporate governing ethical codes, and often reflect other sources of authority, such as conditions imposed by insurance companies in malpractice liability policies.

Of equal or greater importance are the informal norms that attorneys observe among colleagues in their offices. In one of the few studies on point, lawyers ranked such collegial practices as the second most significant factor, after general upbringing, in helping to resolve questions of professional responsibility.[16]

15. ABA Model Rules of Professional Conduct, Rule 8.5. See Symposium, "The Multijurisdictional Practice of Law," 36 S. Tex. L. Rev. 657 (1995).

16. Fran Zemans & Victor Rosenblum, The Making of a Public Profession 172 (1984).

In this complicated regulatory environment with overlapping (sometimes competing) practice norms, "doing the right thing" both morally and legally can pose substantial challenges. Those challenges are the subject of this book.

Chapter II

THE AMERICAN LEGAL PROFESSION AND BAR REGULATORY STRUCTURES

A. The Origins of the Profession

The practice of law dates back over two millenia. By the mid-fourth century B.C.E. in Greece, advocates argued for parties at trial and legal counselors handled commercial matters and drafted legislative proposals. However, these individuals did not constitute a "professional" community in the contemporary sense of the term. Formal ethical standards were reportedly nonexistent, and systematic education and discipline were lacking. Payment for these law-related services was prohibited, but gifts may often have been expected.[1] Later Roman practice gave rise to a somewhat more professionalized culture of advocates and advisors. Between the first and third centuries A.C.E., associations of advocates with formal training and disciplinary standards emerged around the courts of major cities. However, with the fall of the Holy Roman Empire, the professional tradition also declined.[2]

In England, prior to the Norman invasion, disputes ordinarily were settled through communal adjustment or, more formally, through ordeal or trial by "compurgation." Ordeals were a form of adjudication based on divine intervention, in which the accused was placed at risk (such as by drowning or burning). Under an alternative trial procedure, a critical issue was the credibility of the accused, which was established through oaths by a specified number of compurgators. In order for their oaths to be valid, compurgators had to complete their recitation without any verbal slips. Tradition has it that the earliest Anglo–American legal practitioners were those who could be counted on to deliver their oaths without a sneeze or a stumble.[3]

---

1. See Thomas Holton, Preface to Law: The Professional Milieu 2–4 (1980); Douglas M. MacDowell, The Law in Classical Athens (1978); Robert J. Bonner, Lawyers and Litigants in Ancient Athens: The Genesis of the Legal Profession 200–13, 218–43 (1927).

2. J. A. Crook, Legal Advocacy in the Roman World 172–75 (1995); Wolfgang Kunkel, An Introduction to Roman Legal and Constitutional History 105–16

(J. M. Kelly trans. 1973); Hans Julius Wolff, Roman Law: A Historical Introduction 95–117 (1951).

3. S. F. Milsom, Historical Foundations of the Common Law 28 (1969); Marion Neef & Stuart Nagel, "The Adversary Nature of the American Legal System: A Historical Perspective," in Lawyers' Ethics: Contemporary Dilemmas, 73, 75–80 (Allan Gerson ed. 1980);

13

Over time, a more professional culture evolved. Church courts (which adjudicated various civil as well as religious matters) developed more rational procedures of factual and legal argument. The Normans who invaded England brought with them traditions of trial by combat, use of "juries" for investigation and trial, and expansion of church court jurisdiction. As the forms of adjudication became more sophisticated, a greater role for advocates developed.[4] And as the economy became more complex, a greater need also emerged for advisors who could provide assistance with legal documents, transactions, and commercial disputes. Practitioners in these matters evolved into two groups. Barristers provided trial representation and prepared for this role by attending one of four Inns of Court and then serving as apprentices to a practicing barrister. Attorneys and solicitors provided other forms of legal assistance and were governed by professional associations and rules of court, supplemented by legislative enactments.

Efforts to establish law as a "gentlemen's" profession resulted in restrictive entry practices. For a substantial period, barristers excluded certain presumptively unfit groups including Catholics, tradesmen, journalists, and women. Class also served as a filtering device; the costs of obtaining an education and establishing a practice limited access to those with substantial means. Although solicitors were less exclusive in their entrance standards, lengthy apprenticeship requirements and selective referral networks discouraged female applicants and candidates from economically and racially subordinate groups until this last century.[5] In recent years, the British profession has become much more diverse, and the differentiation between barristers and solicitors has been substantially reduced.

The colonists who settled America were generally not eager to import English legal traditions. Some colonies attempted to exclude lawyers entirely, either by barring them from courts or by prohibiting payment for legal services. This hostility had multiple sources. Many colonists had been victims of government persecution in England and retained a strong distrust of all officers of the court.

Henry S. Drinker, Legal Ethics, 12–14 (1953).

4. Theodore F. T. Plucknett, A Concise History of the Common Law 216–17 (5th ed. 1956). See also Herman Cohen, A History of the English Bar and Attornatus to 1450, 18–35 (1929); Roscoe Pound, The Lawyer from Antiquity to Modern Times (1953); J. H. Baker, "The English Legal Profession 1450–1550," in Lawyers in Early Modern Europe and America 16 (Wilfrid Priest ed. 1981).

5. Michael Birks, Gentlemen of the Law (1960); W. J. Reader, Professional Men: The Rise of the Professional Classes in Nineteenth–Century England (1966); Deborah L. Rhode, "Moral Character as a Professional Credential," 94 Yale L. J. 491, 494–95 (1981).

Merchants and landowners often wanted to run their own affairs without interference by intermediaries. And some religious and political leaders were wary of inviting legal limits on their authority or coping with the contentiousness that lawyers might encourage. Class prejudice was also at work. Lawyers were frequently tarred by their association with unpopular economically privileged groups.

Qualifications for the Bar and Discriminatory Practices

Yet as historian Lawrence Friedman concludes, "lawyers were, in the end, a necessary evil."[6] In a developing economy legal skills became increasingly useful, and a growing class of practitioners emerged. Their training was uneven and often slipshod. With a few short-lived exceptions, law schools were not available until the late eighteenth century. The dominant method of preparation during the bar's formative era was apprenticeship, which often left much to be desired. Many aspiring lawyers ended up as not very glorified clerks, with a heavy concentration of drudgery and little formal instruction.[7]

Admission standards were sporadically imposed, but until the twentieth century, they were seldom demanding. In 1800, most states required some brief preparatory period of study but even these minimal requirements largely vanished during the Jacksonian populist era. As Chapter XI indicates, bar exams were usually perfunctory. Many were oral, and involved only a few rudimentary questions and an exchange of pleasantries.[8]

Not all applicants benefitted from this open admission system. Although formal entry requirements were fairly lax until the late nineteenth century, informal screening occurred through educational, apprenticeship, and hiring practices. Such practices were strongly colored by class, racial, ethnic, and religious prejudices. The first black student graduated from law school in 1869, and a number of predominantly black institutions formed graduate programs in law around this same period, but few of the programs survived after the Reconstruction era. Estimates suggest that blacks constituted less than one percent of the profession at the turn of the century, and that they remained under two percent until the 1960s.[9] Other racial minorities were similarly underrepre-

6. Lawrence M. Friedman, A History of American Law 83 (1973).

7. James Willard Hurst, The Growth of American Law: The Law Makers 285–94 (1950); Friedman, supra note 6 at 96.

8. Len Yang Smith, "Abraham Lincoln as a Bar Examiner," 51 Bar Examiner 35, 37 (1982). See also Hurst, supra note 7, at 282.

9. Geraldine Segal, Blacks in the Law (1983); Walter J. Leonard, "The Development of the Black Bar," 407 Annals of the Amer. Acad. of Pol. and Soc. Science, 134, 136–43 (1973); Kellis E. Parker & Betty J. Stebman, "Legal Edu-

sented. In the 1930s, a series of legal actions began challenging segregation in legal education. This litigation initially forced establishment of "separate but equal" minority law schools, and eventually required integration of previously all-white institutions. However, even after changes in formal policies, the absence of financial aid, affirmative action, recruitment efforts, or supportive academic environments worked against minority admissions. Discrimination by employers, clients, and bar associations had comparable effects.[10]

Bias against religious and ethnic minorities was also common. During the late nineteenth and early twentieth centuries, some universities maintained quotas on Jewish applicants. Many bar leaders also spearheaded campaigns to upgrade entry requirements in the hope of screening out those with immigrant and lower class backgrounds. Antisemitic and nativist attitudes were similarly apparent among some state bar moral character committees and prominent law firms during this period.[11]

Discrimination against women was even more pervasive. In the Colonial period, a few women participated in legal transactions by acting as their husbands' representatives or obtaining powers of attorney.[12] However, the gradual formalization of bar entrance criteria in the late eighteenth century made it increasingly difficult for women to act as agents in legal matters. After the Civil War, the rise in female education, political consciousness, and reform activity sparked increasing challenges to sex-based admission standards. In 1867, Iowa became the first state to license a woman attorney, and, in 1872, Howard University conferred the first law school degree on a female graduate.

The reception for these women in practice was generally less than welcoming. In a celebrated 1873 decision, the United States Supreme Court affirmed Myra Bradwell's exclusion from the Illinois bar. The concurring opinions by Justice Bradley summarized prevailing assumptions about the sexes' "separate spheres:"

cation for Blacks," 407 Annals of the Amer. Acad. of Pol. and Soc. Science 144 (1973).

10. See sources cited in note 9 and Jerold S. Auerbach, Unequal Justice: Lawyers and Social Change in Modern America 106–07 (1976).

11. Robert Stevens, Law School: Legal Education in America from the 1850s to the 1980s at 100–01 (1983); Rhode, supra note 5, at 500–02.

12. Karen Morello, The Invisible Bar: The Woman Lawyer in America

1638 to the Present (1986); Deborah L. Rhode, Justice and Gender: Sex Discrimination and the Law 20–24 (1989); Deborah L. Rhode, "Perspectives on Professional Women," 40 Stan. L. Rev. 1163 (1988). See generally, Barbara J. Harris, Beyond Her Sphere: Women and the Professions in American History (1978); Marylynn Salmon, "The Legal Status of Women in Early America: A Reappraisal," Law and Hist. Rev. 129 (1983).

[T]he natural and proper timidity and delicacy which belongs to the female sex evidently unfits it for many of the occupations of civil life.... The paramount destiny and mission of woman are to fulfil the noble and benign offices of wife and mother. This is the law of the Creator.[13]

To many courts, the "peculiar qualities of womanhood" seemed ill-suited for "forensic strife."[14]

By the turn of the century, sustained political and legal challenges had secured women's formal right to admission in most states, but informal barriers remained substantial. Not until 1972 did all ABA-accredited law schools admit female applicants. Throughout the first half of the century, women constituted less than three percent of the profession, and women of color were even more underrepresented. Biases in salary, hiring, promotion, and placement were common.[15]

The Conditions of Practice

Until the beginning of the twentieth century, lawyers practiced largely in single-person offices or small firms. The nature of practice varied, and changed over time, partly because lawyers proved exceptionally "nimble in identifying new forms of work and new ways of doing it."[16] When edged out of one area by other service providers like realtors, accountants, or banks, attorneys generally found another. But obtaining paid work and restraining competition, both from within and outside the profession, were ongoing challenges. As one struggling mid-nineteenth century practitioner put it, "I wish the fees came in half as fast as the cases."[17]

Still, American lawyers were more successful in securing a strong market for their services than their counterparts in other nations. A primary reason was the centrality of the law in American society. The importance of the legal profession in public life prompted Alexis de Tocqueville's celebrated description of lawyers as the nation's "natural aristocracy." Compared with other countries, he noted, the United States had placed more power in the hands of lawyers and less in a hereditary class, or in the military, church, or civil service. That allocation of authority both reflected and reinforced the importance of law in American culture. As

---

13. Bradwell v. State, 83 U.S. 130, 141 (1872) (Bradley, J. concurring).

14. In re Goodell, 39 Wis. 232, 245 (1875).

15. See Rhode, Justice and Gender, supra note 12, at 23; Cynthia Fuchs Epstein, Women in Law 79–95 (1981).

16. Friedman, supra note 6, at 634.

17. See Maxwell Bloomfield, "The Texas Bar in the Nineteenth Century," 32 Vand. L. Rev. 261, 270 (1979).

Tocqueville also famously noted, "[s]carcely any political question arises in the United States that is not resolved, sooner or later, into a judicial question.... As most public men are or have been legal practitioners, they introduce the customs and technicalities of their profession into the management of public affairs." Another reason for the centrality of lawyers, according to de Tocqueville, involved their ability to serve as a "connecting link" between classes. They belonged to the "people by birth and interest" and to the aristocracy by "habit and taste." Their "love of order and formalities" aligned them with the upper class; their middle and upper middle class backgrounds aligned them with ordinary citizens and inspired the trust necessary for social influence.[18] As Supreme Court Justice Louis Brandeis noted in an influential 1905 address at Harvard Law School, during the nation's formative years, nearly "every great lawyer was then a statesmen, and nearly every statesmen, great or small, was a lawyer."[19]

The extent to which lawyers actually fulfilled the exalted role portrayed by de Tocqueville and other bar leaders is uncertain. The extent to which they can do so today is equally uncertain. As Chapter I noted, popular opinion surveys reflect little public confidence in attorneys' ethics and integrity. Lawyers still edge out used car salesmen, but not by much. Yet given the continued centrality of law in American public life, it seems likely that members of the profession will retain considerable influence in both public and private sectors.

B. Bar Regulatory Structures and Professional Associations

As soon as lawyers formed a critical mass in any local practice setting, they also tended to form professional organizations. After the Revolutionary War, the largest cities generally had voluntary bar associations, which served primarily social functions but sometimes played a significant role in admissions and discipline. During the early nineteenth century, as entry standards became more lax, these regulatory functions largely ceased. They resurfaced at the end of the century in response to several concerns. Leading lawyers saw bar associations as a way not only to socialize with other elite members of the profession, but also to raise ethical standards,

---

18. Alexis de Tocqueville, 1 Democracy in America 273–80 (H. Reeve trans., P. Bradley ed. F. Bowen rev. 1989) (1st ed. 1835). See also Geoffrey C. Hazard Jr., "The Future of Legal Ethics," 100 Yale L. J. 1239 (1991).

19. Louis D. Brandeis, "The Opportunity in the Law," in Business–A Profession 329, 330 (1914).

combat municipal corruption, curb unlicensed practice, and discourage competition.[20] One of the first undertakings of the American Bar Association, formed in 1878 at the Saratoga Springs summer resort, was to draft Canons of Ethics. The goal was both to promote integrity and to restrain overtly commercial activity. These Canons prohibited advertising, solicitation, and other related practices which, according to an accompanying report, had "debased [lawyers'] high calling in the eyes of the public." In the eyes of bar leaders, a growing number of new entrants, lacking "fixed ideals of ethical conduct," were threatening to reduce the profession "to the level of a trade." Sanctions were needed to stay their "itching fingers" in the "eager quest for lucre."[21]

However, as critics noted, the effect of these anticompetitive prohibitions was not so much to prevent the pursuit of profits as to restrict its methods and beneficiaries. Well-established members of the bar could attract clients through business and social connections without resort to overtly commercial forms of self-promotion. The bans on advertising and solicitation hindered less established lawyers from targeting their services to unsophisticated and low income clients, who lacked access to legal assistance and knowledge about how to obtain it.[22] Moreover, other early ethical rules, such as those requiring adherence to bar-established minimum fee schedules, were designed to reduce competition within the profession. The ABA's Practice Manual recommended presenting clients with lists of minimum charges in attractive folders suggesting a "degree of dignity and substance."[23]

Other bar activities were directed more toward the public interest. The profession promoted law reform and judicial independence; it sought to reduce corrupt or unduly partisan influences over governmental policy and judicial appointments; and it supported legal services for the poor and pro bono contributions by its members.[24] Lawyers were at the forefront of almost every major social reform movement of the last two centuries and many viewed public service as part of their professional responsibilities.

20. Hurst, supra note 7, at 286–289; Aurbach, supra note 10, at 62–67.

21. American Bar Association, Report of the Committee on [the] Code of Professional Ethics, 1906 American Bar Association Reports 600, 604.

22. Auerbach, supra note 10, at 64 ; Philip Shuchman, "Ethics and Legal Ethics: The Propriety of the Canons as a Group Moral Code," 37 Geo. Wash. L. Rev. 244 (1968).

23. Deborah L. Rhode, In the Interests of Justice: Reforming the Legal Profession 169 (2000).

24. Robert W. Gordon, "The Ideal and the Actual in the Law: Fantasies and Practices of New York City Lawyers, 1870–1970," in The New High Priests: Lawyers in Post–Civil War America 52–53, 56–59, 65–66 (G. Gawalt ed., 1984).

However, as the profession has grown larger, more specialized, more diverse, and more profit-oriented, it has faced greater challenges both in speaking with one voice and in playing a civic role. The assumption that inspired many early bar associations—that the profession was, and should remain "above trade"—is hard to sustain in today's legal market. Increasing competition and consumer activism have broken down many of the traditional restraints on commercialism and placed growing emphasis on earnings as a measure of professional achievement.

Yet lawyers also continue to be leaders in public interest movements. And on some issues, the increasing diversity within the profession has enabled bar associations to play a more informed role in public policy. One such issue involves equal opportunity and the elimination of bias in law-related contexts.

C. Diversity Within the Profession

Beginning in the late 1960s, the representation of women and racial and ethnic minorities in the legal profession began to increase substantially. Women's representation among new entrants to the bar grew from about three percent in the 1960s to fifty percent at the turn of the twenty-first century; minorities increased from one percent to twenty percent. Whether or not the proportion of gays and lesbians has changed remains unclear, given their traditionally closeted status, but the number who are able to be open about their sexual orientation has grown significantly.[25] Yet despite such progress, women and minorities remain overrepresented at the bottom and underrepresented at the top of professional status and reward structures. For example, women account for about thirty percent of the profession but only about thirteen percent of equity partners in law firms, ten percent of law school deans, ten percent of top in-house legal positions at *Fortune* 500 companies, and five percent of large firm managing partners.[26] Minorities account for about ten percent of the profession, but three percent of law firm partners, and two percent of general counsel at *Fortune* 500 companies.[27] Salaries are substantially lower for women, minority men, and openly gay and lesbian attorneys

25. "Los Angeles County Bar Association Report on Sexual Orientation Bias," 4 S. Cal. Rev. L. & Women's Stud. 297, 305 (1995).

26. ABA, The Unfinished Agenda: Women and the Legal Profession 14 (Report Prepared by Deborah L. Rhode 2001).

27. Elizabeth Chambers, Miles to Go 2000: Progress of Minorities in the Legal Profession 6, 10 (American Bar Association Commission on Racial and Ethnic Diversity in the Profession, 2000); Charisse R. Lillie, "ABA Commission Collects and Analyzes Data on Diversity," Metropolitan Corporate Counsel, June 2001.

than for other lawyers with comparable qualifications and positions.[28] Women are half as likely to achieve partnership as similarly situated men. And the limited data available on minority, gay, and lesbian lawyers document significant disparities in retention and promotion.[29]

Part of the discrepancy is related to historic patterns. Lawyers generally achieve higher positions in the profession as they accumulate experience in practice. There will be fewer law firm partners among those who have been admitted for five years compared with those admitted for 20 years, and 20 years ago the ratio of women and minorities graduating from law school was much lower than today. Another factor in the case of women is the difficulty that many face in accommodating family responsibilities with highly demanding practices.

However, other factors are also at work. Part of the problem is the lack of recognition that there is a serious problem. Ironically enough, recent progress has created its own obstacles to further change. A widespread perception is that barriers are coming down, women and minorities are moving up, and discrimination has largely been eradicated; whatever racial or gender disparities remain are often attributed to different choices and capabilities.

Yet much depends on how discrimination is defined and whose definition matters. To many attorneys, discrimination implies overt intentional prejudice, and the professional workplaces that they inhabit produce few clear examples. By contrast, other attorneys see bias in more subtle forms, such as unconscious racial and gender stereotypes, exclusion from informal networks of support, and inadequate work/family policies. From this perspective, most legal workplaces have ample room for improvement. Over the last two decades, some sixty studies have surveyed bias in the profession, and they consistently find substantial race and gender gaps in perceptions of discrimination. Between two-thirds and three-quarters of women report experiencing gender bias, while only a quarter

---

28. Chambers, supra note 27, at 5; David B. Wilkins & G. Mitu Gulati, "Why Are There So Few Black Lawyers in Corporate Law Firms? An Institutional Analysis," 84 Cal. L. Rev. 493, 503 (1996); Darryl Van Duch, "Minority GC's Are Few, Far Between," The National Law Journal, Oct. 18, 1999, at A1; "Study Shows Inequalities in Pay, Partnership," San Francisco Daily Journal, August 25, 1998, at 31; Kathleen E. Hull & Robert Nelson, "Divergent Patterns: Gender Differences in the Careers of Urban Lawyers," 10 Researching Law 3, 51 (American Bar Foundation News, Summer 1999); The State Bar of California, Report and Recommendations Regarding Sexual Orientation Discrimination in the California Legal Profession 2 (1996).

29. See sources cited in ABA Commission, supra note 27; Rhode, supra note 23, at 39; and in supra note 28.

to a third of men report observing it.[30] In the ABA's most recent survey, about two-thirds of blacks, but only about ten percent of whites, believe that minorities are treated less fairly in hiring and promotion processes.[31] A study by the National Association for Law Placement revealed similar race and gender gaps concerning selections for partnership.[32]

Both psychological research and empirical surveys suggest a strong basis for perceptions of differential treatment. Much of the problem involves the lingering, largely unconscious, influence of gender and racial stereotypes. Women and minorities often do not enjoy the same presumption of competence as their white male colleagues. Traditionally disfavored groups find that their mistakes are more readily noticed and their achievements more often attributed to luck or special treatment. So too, the mismatch between characteristics traditionally associated with women and those typically associated with professional success leave female lawyers in a persistent double bind. They are faulted as too assertive or not assertive enough and what is viewed as assertive in a man often is perceived as abrasive in a woman.[33]

The force of traditional stereotypes is compounded by other cognitive biases. People are more likely to notice and recall information that confirms their prior assumptions than information that contradicts them.[34] Attorneys who assume that their minority colleagues are beneficiaries of affirmative action, not meritocratic selection, will recall their errors more readily than their insights. Attorneys who assume that working mothers are less committed to their careers will remember the times that they leave early, not the

30. See sources cited in Rhode, supra note 23, at 39; and Deborah L. Rhode, "Myths of Meritocracy," 65 Ford. L. Rev. 585, 586 (1996).

31. Arthur S. Hayes, "Color-Coded Hurdle," 85 ABA Journal, 56 (1999).

32. Abbie F. Willard, Perceptions of Partnership: The Allure and Accessibility of the Brass Ring (Washington, D.C.: National Association for Law Placement, 1999) 33.

33. Bar Association of San Francisco, Goals 95 Report: Goals and Timetables for Minority Hiring and Advancement 14–15 (1996); Wilkins & Gulati, supra note 28, at 557, 571; Clear and Convincing Evidence: Measurement of Discrimination in America (Michael Fix & Raymond J. Struyk, eds., 1993); Kathleen E. Hull & Robert L. Nelson, "Gen-

der Inequality in Law: Problems of Structure and Agency in Recent Studies of Gender on Anglo-American Legal Professions," 23 Law and Social Inquiry 681, 688–91 (1998); see Willard, supra note 32, at 37; David A. Thomas & Karen L. Proudford, "Making Sense of Race Relations in Organizations," in Addressing Cultural Diversity in Organizations: Beyond the Corporate Context 51 (Robert J. Carter, ed. 1999).

34. Linda Hamilton Krieger, "The Content of our Categories: A Cognitive Bias Approach to Discrimination and Equal Employment Opportunity," 47 Stan. L. Rev. 1161 (1995); Federal Glass Ceiling Commission, Good for Business: Making Full Use of the Nation's Human Capital 26–28, 64–72, 93–96, 104–06, 123–25 (1995); Willard, supra note 32 at 93.

times they stay late. A related problem is that people share what psychologists label a "just world" bias.[35] They want to believe that individuals generally get what they deserve and deserve what they get. Perceptions of performance frequently are adjusted to match observed outcomes. If women and minorities are underrepresented in positions of greatest prominence, the most psychologically convenient explanation is that they lack the necessary qualifications or commitment.

However, a more adequate explanation would acknowledge that careers can also be waylaid by adverse stereotypes, race-or sex-based harassment, inadequate access to mentoring and client networks, and inflexible workplace structures. A wide array of research finds that people feel more comfortable with those who are like them in important respects such as race or sex, and are more likely to assist those with similar backgrounds. Women, minority men, and gay and lesbian attorneys frequently report being left out of the loop of advice, collaboration, and business development.[36] A significant number also experience race or sex-based harassment.[37] So too, because women generally bear a disproportionate share of family obligations, they pay a similarly disproportionate price for inflexible workplace structures. Although most legal employers in theory permit part time schedules, only about three percent of women and even smaller percentages of men feel free to take advantage of that option.[38]

These problems are compounded by the disincentives to challenge them. Most targets of bias are reluctant to appear confrontational, and discrimination claims are generally far too expensive to litigate in both personal and financial terms. Plaintiffs risk having all their deficiencies publicly aired, and the rare individuals who win in court may lose in life by being labeled as troublemakers.[39]

35. Melvin J. Lerner, The Belief in a Just World: A Fundamental Delusion vii-viii (1980)

36. Judith Lorber, Paradoxes of Gender 237–38 (1994); Federal Glass Ceiling Commission, supra note 34 at 552; Willard, supra note 32 at 54–58.

37. Deborah L. Rhode & Jennifer Drobac, Sex–Based Harassment: Workplace Policies for Lawyers (ABA Commission on Women in the Profession, 2002).

38. See sources cited in Deborah L. Rhode, Balanced Lives: Changing the Culture of Legal Practice (ABA Commission on Women in the Profession, 2001); Deborah L. Rhode, "Balanced Lives for

Lawyers," 70 Fordham L. Rev. 2207 (2002).

39. ABA Commission on Women in the Profession, "Greener Pastures," Perspectives 3, (Summer 1995); Special Committee on Lesbians and Gay Men in the Legal Profession, "Report of Findings from the Survey on Barriers and Opportunities Related to Sexual Orientation," 51 The Record 130 (Association of the Bar for the City of New York, 1996); Los Angeles County Bar Association Committee on Sexual Orientation Bias, "Report," 35 (June, 1994); Thomas & Proudford, supra note 33; Paul M. Barrett, The Good Black: A True Story of Race in America 59 (1998).

How best to respond to these problems is subject to dispute. One of the most controversial issues involves affirmative action, such as goals and timetables for minority hiring and promotion. The vast majority of lawyers of color favor affirmative action; most white lawyers do not.[40] Opponents view preferential policies as perpetuating a kind of color consciousness that society should be seeking to eradicate. They also worry that such treatment implies that women and men of color require special advantages, which perpetuates the problem. By contrast, supporters of affirmative action point out that the costs of inaction are also substantial. In their view, only by insuring a critical mass of minorities in top positions can we secure a workplace that is fair in fact as well as form. In some contexts, "special" treatment may be essential to counteract the special obstacles facing underrepresented groups.

Other disputed issues involve the need for special gender-related initiatives to counteract unconscious bias and exclusion and to accommodate family responsibilities. For example, lawyers differ over the value of diversity training, the appropriate terms of part-time policies, and the need for special women's networks.[41]

However these issues are resolved, most lawyers agree about the underlying goals. Difference in identity or background should not make a difference in professional opportunities. Full representation in the profession of those from diverse backgrounds is crucial to reflect diverse perspectives on legal issues; to create the fact and appearance of fairness in legal decision making, and to provide adequate legal services to all sectors of the American community. Policies that promote a balance between professional and personal lives generally prove cost-effective by improving recruitment and retention and reducing stress-related dysfunctions.[42] Diversity and equal opportunity in the profession are issues on which the entire profession has a stake.

40. See ABA Commission on Minorities, supra note 27, at 5–8; Rhode, supra note 23, at 44.

41. For discussion of such strategies, see ABA Commission, supra note 27; Rhode, supra note 38; and Rhode & Drobac, supra note 37.

42. David A. Thomas & Robin J. Ely, "Making Differences Matter: A New Paradigm for Managing Diversity," Harvard Business Rev., Sep.–Oct., 1996, at 79, 83; Rhode, supra note 38, at 20–21; Rhode supra note 23, at 41–44, 47.

Chapter III

THE FORMS AND ECONOMICS
OF LEGAL PRACTICE

A. The Structure of Practice

The term "law practice" is an abstraction that covers a wide range of professional activities whose only common denominator is that lawyers engage in them. Indeed, the variety of what attorneys do makes it difficult to identify shared experiences, besides the facts that almost all of those who are in active practice have graduated from law school and are members of a bar somewhere. Similarity of educational background and equality in formal status make for certain shared commitments and concerns, but these can often be eclipsed by the diversity in daily experience.

Lawyers' work varies along several dimensions: core functions, substantive fields, and practice contexts. A lawyer's minimal function, viewed analytically, is providing advice and advocacy concerning legal rights. From these core functions derive further specializations, cutting across substantive areas. The portfolio of required skills includes knowledge of substantive and procedural law, understanding of legal institutions such as courts and government agencies, and various interpersonal capabilities. It is conventional to classify lawyers according to which of these skills or substantive fields predominate in their professional repertoire. Thus, we speak of litigators and labor negotiators, or of tax and securities specialists.

Another variation involves "situation in practice." This concept can include locality (small town, metropolitan area, etc.), work context (solo practitioner, small firm lawyer, large firm lawyer, government lawyer, etc.) or professional experience and status (senior partner, junior associate, etc.). A different form of classification is premised on the attorney's primary clientele. Such distinctions depend on the proportion of professional assistance that involves indigents, individuals of modest means, small businesses, large corporations, governmental institutions, and so forth.

When considered along all these dimensions, the American legal profession is quite diverse, and it has changed significantly over the last half century. In 1950, the United States had about 200,000 lawyers, one for every 695 persons. At the turn of the twenty-first century, the number had grown to about 900,000,

25

roughly one for every 300 persons.[1] About three-quarters of todays' lawyers are in private practice, mostly in firms. About a third are solo practitioners, a significant decline since the 1950s. By contrast, the percentage of lawyers in large and midsize firms has increased, as has the size of the firms. In the 1950s, only about forty firms had more than fifty lawyers. Now seventy firms have more than five hundred.[2] Of the lawyers in firms, slightly over a quarter are in offices of two to five practitioners; another quarter are in offices of six to twenty, a quarter are in offices of twenty-one to a hundred, and slightly under a quarter are in offices of over a hundred.[3] About a third of the lawyers in firms are associates; the remainder are partners or lawyers in firms with no associates.[4] Of the lawyers not in private practice, about ten percent are in private industry, ten percent are in government, three percent are in the judiciary, one percent are in academia, and one percent are in legal aid, public defender, or public interest offices. Five percent are retired or inactive.[5]

The functions that lawyers perform are also quite diverse. They range from counseling ordinary citizens about ordinary legal problems to orchestrating "megalaw" mergers, litigating transnational disputes, and representing various client interests before governmental institutions. Over time, lawyers tend to specialize and, while they may move around in the system, most do not stray far from where they started.

The effect of such specialization is a pronounced stratification within the profession. In broad terms, that stratification corresponds to types of practice and, more particularly, to types of clientele. In a classic study, first conducted in the 1980s and then repeated in the late 1990s, John Heinz and Edward Laumann found a profession divided into two hemispheres. Clients in one hemisphere included individuals and small businesses; in the other were large organizations such as corporations, unions, or governmental entities. Few lawyers regularly crossed the equator, and those who served "corporate, wealthier, more 'establishment' clients" had greater status within the profession than those who

1. Clara N. Carson, The Lawyer Statistical Report 1 (American Bar Foundation, 1999).

2. Marc S. Galanter & Thomas M. Palay, "Why the Big Get Bigger: The Promotion-to-Partner Tournament and the Growth of Large Firms," 76 Va. L. Rev. 747, 749 (1990); David E. Rovella, "Living on the Edge: Growth Slows, Layoffs Begin & Salaries Are Flat. Soon, It May Get Even Worse," National L. J., Nov. 19, 2001, at A1.

3. Carson, supra note 1, at 8.

4. Id., at 9.

5. Id. at 7; "Lawyers in Profile: A Statistical Portrait of the U.S. Legal Profession," 10 Researching Law 1 (American Bar Foundation, Summer 1999).

served other clients.[6] The demand for services remained strongest in the corporate sector. About 60 percent of private practitioners' work is now devoted to corporate clients.[7]

Legal practice has changed in other important ways over the last half century. For most lawyers, the workplace has become more competitive, more commercial, and more time consuming. Close to half of private practitioners bill at least 1900 hours per year, and a substantial number, particularly at large firms, bill more.[8] Only about two-thirds of the time spent in the office can honestly be charged to clients; the remainder is taken up by personal and organizational needs such as dealing with internal firm matters and keeping current in areas of specialization. As a consequence, lawyers in private practice often work 60 hours or more per week. Technological innovations have also increased the pace of legal practice and encouraged expectations of constant availability and instant responsiveness. Many practitioners remain tethered to their worksites by cell phones, e-mails, faxes and beepers. Unsurprisingly, most lawyers feel that they do not have enough time for themselves, and close to half feel that they lack sufficient time for their families.[9]

Although the extent and causes of lengthening workweeks vary somewhat across practice contexts, some dysfunctional patterns are widely shared. One involves performance. Bleary, burnt-out lawyers seldom provide cost-effective services for clients, and overwork is a leading cause of lawyers' own disproportionate rates of stress, substance abuse, and other health-related disorders.[10] In addition, extended hours and inflexible schedules pose special problems for those with substantial family responsibilities. Because women assume a disproportionate share of those responsibilities, women lawyers pay a disproportionate price in professional opportunities. The lack of adequate alternative schedules and leave policies is part of the reason for persistent glass ceilings for women, and excessive attrition and recruitment costs for their employers.[11] Finally, as

6. John P. Heinz & Edward O. Laumann, Chicago Lawyers: The Social Structure of the Bar 319 (1982).

7. John P. Heinz, Edward O. Laumann, Robert L. Nelson & Ethan Michelson, "The Changing Character of Lawyers' Work: Chicago in 1975 and 1995," 32 Law & Soc. Rev. 751, 765 (1998).

8. See studies cited in Deborah L. Rhode, In the Interests of Justice 35 (2001).

9. See studies cited in Patrick S. Schiltz, "On Being a Happy, Healthy, and Ethical Member of an Unhappy, Unhealthy, and Unethical Profession," 52 Vand. L. Rev. 871, 888–95 (1999).

10. See Deborah L. Rhode, Balanced Lives: Changing the Culture of Legal Practice 21 (ABA Commission on Women in the Profession, 2002); Laura Gatland, "Dangerous Dedication," ABA J., Dec. 1997, at 28.

11. Rhode, supra note 10, at 21; Catalyst, Women in Law: Making the Case

Chapter IX notes, increases in billable hours have curtailed the time available for pro bono work.

The result is to deny lawyers valuable opportunities for training, trial experience, and community networks in the service of causes to which those practitioners are committed. Whatever their workplace setting, lawyers have a common stake in addressing issues concerning balanced lives and in designing appropriate responses. The increasing intensity of professional work is part of a larger similar phenomenon in all vocations in contemporary modern society. Many Europeans complain that it is an "American disease," but global competition is forcing millions of workers to adapt to the new regime. There are no signs of its abating. Individuals who are distressed by this environment, including lawyers, must make deliberate and systematic effort to reduce its adverse effects.

B. The Private Sector: Solo, Small Firm and Large Firm Practice

Over the last two decades, the proportion of lawyers in private practice has grown from about two-thirds to three-quarters of the bar.[12] As noted earlier, they practice in a range of different settings that carry distinctive rewards and challenges.

The third of the profession who work on their own generally are seeking advantages such as flexibility, independence, client contact, and escape from office politics.[13] Solo practitioners often can have more control over their caseloads and schedules than other lawyers. Some solo practitioners work out of home offices, which helps to reduce expenses and work/family conflicts. Yet the price for such advantages is often paid in greater isolation and economic instability, fewer intellectually challenging cases, and lower income and status.[14] Additional stress can come from the absence of mentoring and back-up support, and the complexities of running a small business while also serving current clients and developing new ones. Cooperative office sharing arrangements and

(2001); ABA, The Unfinished Agenda: Women and the Legal Profession (Report Prepared by Deborah L. Rhode 2001).

12. "Lawyers in Profile," supra note 5, at 6.

13. Carroll Seron, The Business of Practicing Law: The Work Lives of Solo and Small–Firm Attorneys 12, 79–80

(1996); Sherri Kimmel, "Alone and On Your Own: The Growing Allure of Solo Practice," Pa. Lawyer, July/Aug. 1997, at 12.

14. Seron, supra note 13, at 80; Kimmel, supra note 13, at 12–13; Clyde Jay Eisman, "The Ups and Downs of Practicing Alone," N.Y. L.J., Nov. 12, 1999, at 24.

referral networks with other lawyers can help minimize some of these difficulties. An increasing number of bar associations have also established support groups and educational materials specifically designed for solo practitioners.[15]

At the other end of the spectrum is the third of the profession that is in large firms of over fifty lawyers. As noted earlier, the number and size of these firms has increased dramatically over the last half century; the largest now has over two thousand attorneys spread across over thirty-five countries. That increase may be partly attributable to the pyramid structure of most law firms, which has a built-in growth imperative. In this structure, partners at the top profit from their skills, experience, reputation, and relationships by supervising and marketing the work of associates. Junior lawyers accept salaries that give the firm a surcharge for their labor in exchange for training and for the chance to compete for partnership.[16] Growth is inevitable unless the firm permits promotions only to fill the positions of departing partners. Such a limitation on size is generally unappealing to associates, because it provides inadequate assurance about opportunities for advancement. In order to recruit and retain qualified junior attorneys, many firms feel the need to promote a certain percentage of candidates whatever the vacancies left by partners' departure.

This growth pattern is further encouraged by the cultural tendency to view size as a measure of status and to assume that the largest firms are also the leading firms. Large firms also can achieve substantial competitive advantages and economies of scale by providing full service for clients needs that cut across substantive fields and jurisdictional boundaries.

Lawyers choose such settings for a variety of reasons. In general, large firms offer high incomes and status, generous benefits and support services, rewarding pro bono opportunities and the possibility of working on intellectually challenging cases under the supervision of talented senior lawyers. Many new entrants to the profession accept such positions, despite the limited prospects for advancement, in order to pay off law school debts and to acquire valuable training and credentials. However, the price for these advantages may be extended hours, inflexible or unpredictable schedules, lack of caseload control, and an excessive share of routine work. In firms with high associate/partner ratios, inadequate supervision, limited mentoring and client contact, and re-

15. Jill Schachner Chanen, "Solace for Stressed Solos," ABA J., Aug. 1999, at 82.

16. Carson, supra note 1, at 8–9; Marc Galanter & Thomas Palay, Tournament of Lawyers: The Transformation of the Big Law Firm 94–100 (1991).

stricted promotion opportunities can result in substantial rates of dissatisfaction and attrition, which are costly for all involved.[17]

Increases in size also can carry a cost in terms of bureaucratization, impersonality, and pressure to generate business for additional attorneys. Particularly in the largest firms, which have hundreds of lawyers spread across multiple offices with high turnover rates, a sense of collegiality and institutional loyalty becomes harder to sustain. However, many firms and bar associations are now making increased efforts to address such concerns and to improve lawyers' quality of life, particularly among junior associates. Many offices have added flexibility to the traditional two-tiered up-or-out system by creating multiple statuses, such as permanent associates, nonequity partners, "of counsel" positions, and temporary contract lawyers. In general, the demand for such positions and the profitability of large firms remain strong.

A final group of private practitioners are in small firms (two to twelve lawyers) or in midsize firms (twelve to fifty lawyers). These vary considerably in scope and structure. The smallest generally resemble solo practice; a few lawyers join together to share space, staff, and support services, and to provide backup caseload coverage when necessary. By contrast, many midsize firms resemble, and aspire to become, large firms. Other small and midsize offices are local affiliates of nationally franchised firms, which specialize in providing low-cost routine services to individuals of modest means.[18] Another group of small to midsize firms offer specialized "boutique" services in restricted fields, or provide general services but maintain a commitment to limited growth and a high quality of life.

How the structure of private practice will evolve over this next century remains an open question. Most experts predict a period of continued fluidity and experimentation, as firms adapt to an increasingly competitive and global market. As Chapter X notes, the current erosion of disciplinary and jurisdictional boundaries is likely to encourage further growth and diversity of organizations providing legal services. However, constraints imposed by conflict of interest rules impose some ceilings on size. Concerns about bal-

---

17. Rhode, supra note 10, at 35–37, 41–42; Boston Bar Association Task Force on Professional Challenges and Family Needs, Facing the Grail: Confronting the Cost of Work–Family Imbalance (1999); National Association of Law Placement, Keeping the Keepers: Strategies for Associate Retention in Times of Attrition (1998); Debra Baker, "Cash-and-Carry Associates," ABA J., May 1999, at 40.

18. For an overview of these firms see Seron, supra note 13. See also Jerry Van Hoy, Franchise Law Firms and the Transformation of Personal Legal Services (1997).

anced lives are also likely to affect the structure of workplaces, and to introduce greater flexibility in schedules and status.

C. Legal Counsel to Organizations

Although the percentage of lawyers working for private industry has remained fairly stable over the last half-century, the absolute number and status of those lawyers has grown substantially. Since the 1980s, in-house counsel have increasingly assumed responsibility for providing corporate clients with an array of basic legal services, as well as selecting and monitoring outside attorneys, implementing legal compliance programs, and preventing legal difficulties. Departments range in size from one to hundreds of attorneys and perform a wide variety of tasks that reflect the organization's nature and scope. The needs of small real estate companies may rarely extend beyond routine property, contracts, and taxation issues; a multinational corporation will encounter practically every kind of legal problem at one time or another.

A number of factors have accounted for the increased role of lawyers for organizations. From the standpoint of individual attorneys, positions in a client's law department hold several appeals. The time demands tend to be more manageable than in many private practice settings, and inside attorneys can avoid the pressures of juggling the needs of multiple clients while attempting to attract new ones. From the standpoint of organizations, it is often possible to achieve substantial savings by relying on inside attorneys who are familiar with their structure, employees, and objectives; who do not need to divide their attention among other clients; and who do not have incentives created by hourly fee structures to bill for unnecessary work. During the 1980s and early 1990s, many companies began to reserve routine work for their own legal departments, and to rely on outside firms for more episodic or specialized needs. However, that trend has slowed somewhat in recent years, as outside firms have grown increasingly competitive in their fees, and as corporations have faced pressure to downsize staff and outsource non-core functions.[19] One obvious disadvantage of corporate employment for individual lawyers is the dependance on a single client whose attitude toward legal services may shift with different management and economic conditions.

19. See John E. Morris, "Five Questions to Ask Yourself Between Crises," American Lawyer, June 1996, at 5; "Counseling in a Dangerous Time," House Counsel, Spring 1996, at 23–24; Peter D. Zeughauser, "The Revolution is Over," House Counsel, Spring 1996, at 32.

In-house counsel is the client's employee. In that sense, the attorney's role appears to lack the autonomy that is a defining feature of professionalism. But in practice, the degree of independence exercised by in-house counsel can vary widely. If the organization is itself complex–a multidivision multinational corporation, for example–its lawyer-client relationships can be as diverse as those of an outside law firm. Given the diffusion of power and competing interests within many organizational structures, one of the lawyer's most critical tasks may be determining who speaks for the client.[20] This fragmentation of authority often gives in-house counsel considerable flexibility and bargaining leverage. Although they lack some of the autonomy of outside counsel, their greater familiarity with the client often expands opportunities for influence.

The role that in-house lawyers play in particular organizational settings reflects a complex mix of personal preferences and situational factors. A recent empirical study of corporate law departments found that their lawyers generally clustered into three basic roles. About a fifth described their function as largely gate keeping; their work was highly "rule-based" and focused on assessing legal risks, monitoring legal compliance, and approving legal transactions. A second group, about half the sample, described their role as predominantly counseling; their work involved not just keeping corporations within legal bounds, but also looking for ways to maximize business profits through creative legal strategies. A final group of lawyers, about a third of the sample, identified themselves as entrepreneurs; their emphasis was on assisting with business planning, particularly in areas with legal implications.[21]

Whatever role they choose, in-house counsel often face special challenges in protecting the organization's legal interests while also protecting their own relationships with other employees. These challenges play out in a number of settings involving confidentiality and conflicts of interest, discussed in Chapters VI and VIII below.

20. See, e.g., Brian D. Forrow, "The Corporate Law Department Lawyer: Counsel to the Entity," 34 Bus. Law. 1797 (1979); Robert Eli Rosen, "The Inside Counsel Movement, Professional Judgement and Organizational Responsibility," 64 Ind. L. J. 479 (1989); Ted Schneyer, "Professionalism and Public Policy: The Case of House Counsel," 2 Geo. J. Legal Ethics 449 (1988).

21. Robert L. Nelson & Laura Beth Nielsen, "Cops, Counsel, and Entrepreneurs: Considering the Role of Inside Counsel in Large Corporations," 34 Law & Soc'y Rev. 457 (2000).

D. The Public Sector: Government Service, Legal Aid, and Public Interest Law

The roughly ten percent of lawyers in government provide a range of services as diverse as those in private practice, such as counseling, litigating civil and criminal cases, and implementing legislative and administrative regulations. These tasks cut across a variety of substantive areas, encompassing most private law specialties.

All government lawyers have the same "situation in practice" in that they are all public employees. Behind this resemblance lie many significant variations. For example, district attorneys in sparsely populated rural jurisdictions may handle all the public legal work in the area, often on a part-time basis, including criminal prosecutions, indigent child support claims, and representation of county commissioners. On the other hand, the district attorney's office in a large metropolitan center may have hundreds of lawyers, diversified across many specialties. In addition to such variations at the state and local level of government, some twenty-five thousand federal employees perform virtually all kinds of legal tasks.

Although the government lawyer's client is usually the agency for which he or she works, this is not always the case; public defenders and civil legal aid attorneys owe traditional duties of loyalty to the individuals they assist. However, when lawyers represent "the government," their relationship with the client ordinarily is not the same as in a private context. The legal agency itself will often have independent authority over matters within its jurisdiction. Thus, a district attorney has discretion over whom to prosecute without being answerable to any other public official. Prosecutors have no clients except in the metaphorical sense. Or, to put it differently, they have the authority of both client and lawyer in the representation. This independence is, of course, by no means complete. Government lawyers are responsible for implementing legislative and executive policy with which they may not agree. High-level officials are accountable to those who elect or appoint them. Junior lawyers are also subject to direction from supervisors, whose policy interpretations may appear problematic at best. Many government attorneys are employed in agencies with specialized subject matter, such as public hospitals or universities, where their relationship to higher authority in the organization is similar to that of in-house lawyers in the private sector.

Nonetheless, relative independence is one of the attractions of government service, along with its tendency to offer generous benefits, manageable schedules, and freedom from competitive and business development pressures. The price is paid in lower salaries and limited opportunities for advancement. As Chapter VIII notes, these counterveiling costs and benefits have led to a revolving door between public and private sector employment. That structure has its advantages in keeping government accountable as well as attractive to talented attorneys, but it also poses special challenges concerning loyalty and conflicts of interest that will be explored in the chapters that follow.

As noted at the outset of this chapter, approximately one percent of the profession works in legal aid, public defender, and public interest organizations. The term "public interest" is relatively new, but the concept has its origins in earlier movements concerning civil rights, civil liberties, and legal services for the poor. The Council for Public Interest Law defines the term to include "tax exempt non-profit groups devoting at least 30% of their resources to representing previously unrepresented interests on matters of public policy."[22] By that standard, the Council has identified some 200 centers employing slightly over a thousand attorneys.[23] In addition, a substantial number of private firms that are not tax exempt provide representation on such matters. A growing number of conservative legal foundations also consider themselves to be public interest organizations, although they may not satisfy the Council's definition because they often take positions that are already well represented by their corporate funders.[24]

Most public interest organizations emerged during the last quarter century, funded by a mix of foundation grants, membership fees, and private contributions. Their work spans a broad array of substantive fields, including environmental, consumer, poverty, civil rights, and civil liberties issues. Despite their modest numbers, public interest lawyers have had a significant social impact, in part through careful marshaling of resources, and in part by enlisting assistance from the private bar as well as various non-legal organizations and coalitions.

Government-subsidized legal aid programs have a longer history, although their numbers and mission expanded dramatically during the 1960s and 1970s. Like public interest lawyers, civil legal aid attorneys confront a highly expandable universe of legal needs, and often exercise considerable discretion in allocating their assistance. As the materials in Chapter IX reflect, the appropriate exercise of that discretion remains a subject of continuing controversy. Ironically enough, the effectiveness of legal aid lawyers in court has had the opposite consequences in legislatures. During the

---

22. Nan Aron, Liberty and Justice for All: Public Interest Law in the 1980's and Beyond (1989).

23. Id.

24. Aron, supra note 22, at 78; Roger K. Neuman, "Public Interest Firms Grow Up on the Right," National L. J., Aug. 26, 1996, at 1, 22.

Reagan administration, Congress imposed the first of a series of budgetary cutbacks and restrictions on the cases and clients eligible for federally-funded legal services, and a further wave of restrictions followed in the late 1990s.[25] The result has been to curtail salaries and support services, and to prevent much of the impact litigation that attracts attorneys to poverty law.

Public defender services have been subject to similar budgetary constraints for similar reasons. In many offices, lawyers' salaries are low and caseloads are high. Some defenders handle as many as 500 felony matters per year, and few have adequate time or resources for factual investigation and trial preparation.[26] The problems are compounded in the growing number of jurisdictions that rely on competitive bids to award indigent defense. The underpricing of services that is often necessary in order to win contracts also undercuts effective representation.[27]

Despite these challenges, many public defenders and legal aid organizations, like their public interest counterparts, manage to sustain high levels of professionalism and commitment. Financial rewards may be low, but psychic income is high. Lawyers in these organizations generally take considerable satisfaction in representing clients and causes that would otherwise lack representation in the justice system.

25. See discussion in Chapter IX infra.

26. Rhode, supra note 8, at 61; David Cole, No Equal Justice: Race and Class in the American Criminal Justice System 83–85 (1999).

27. See sources cited supra note 26.

Chapter IV

THE "CONSTITUTIONAL" FUNCTIONS
OF THE LEGAL PROFESSION

A. The Rule of Law and Individual Rights

As an historical fact, the legal profession has most fully evolved in political regimes based on the "rule of law," including legal guaranties of civil rights and rights of individuals and corporate entities to own and manage property. The rule of law signifies legal mandates that are prescribed in advance and applied impartially. No legal system is perfect in fulfilling these requirements, but the modern industrialized systems more or less approximate doing so.

The concept of individual rights generally is understood to include protection of free speech and freedom of conscience, freedom from arbitrary imprisonment and unfair searches and seizures, due process and fair trials, and, in more recent times, freedom from discrimination based on race, gender, religious affiliation, or national origin. An extension of these individual rights is the right to form organizations, such as religious congregations, private nonprofit institutions, and political parties. Individual rights also are understood—perhaps less generally—to include the right to own property and to engage in contractual transactions for employment, goods, and services. An extension of these property and transactional rights is the right to form organizations to pursue economic activity, specifically business partnerships and corporations.

B. Lawyers and Individual Rights

Individual rights are merely formal guarantees unless there are adequate procedures for recognizing and enforcing them. Although there remain regimes that view competent judges as a sufficient safeguard of individual rights, all regimes professing the rule of law recognize the right to legal counsel in court and the right to consult a lawyer in out-of-court matters. Individuals who can afford a lawyer exercise these rights; those who cannot often depend on access to subsidized legal assistance. Governments also rely heavily on lawyers in law enforcement and administrative agencies. As a practical matter, legal services are highly useful and often essential in achieving adherence to the rule of law and protection of individual rights.

This functional relationship between the rule of law and the role of counsel poses a constitutional question of major and continuing importance: To what extent should there be public subsidies to provide legal aid for people who cannot afford a lawyer? That question is addressed in Chapter IX. But another, perhaps less visible constitutional issue is involved in debates over the lawyer's role. What is the legitimacy of legal representation for individuals and organizations that can afford assistance of counsel, particularly the high-priced legal talent engaged by business corporations and wealthy individuals?

C. Lawyers for Business Enterprise

It is accepted in modern political regimes that a business corporation can employ lawyers to further its operations. Virtually all corporations of any size regularly engage lawyers to assist in minimizing their tax obligations, monitoring their regulatory obligations, and protecting their interests in relationships with employees, customers, suppliers, creditors, stockholders, and the government. All large corporations have sizable staffs of in-house lawyers. Most large, independent law firms are primarily engaged in corporate law practice. A substantial part of the practice of most smaller law firms deals with matters of property and business.

Nevertheless, in the modern era, ethical discourse about the legal profession has involved criticism of lawyers' disproportionate assistance to business organizations and wealthy individuals. A main theme of the profession's own pronouncements has been the assertion of independence from client interests and a distinction between legal practice and commercial activity, as in the often-repeated statement that "the practice of law is a profession, not a business."[1] Yet a large fraction of lawyer's work, especially in prestigious firms, has always been in the service of business. Eminent leaders of the profession, such as Alexander Hamilton, Daniel Webster, and Abraham Lincoln, all obtained most of their income from business clients.

D. The Critique of Corporate Capitalism

Underlying much of the traditional criticism of corporate law practice is a critique of corporate capitalism and its constituent

1. See American Bar Association Commission on Professionalism, In the Spirit of a Public Service: A Blueprint for the Rekindling of Lawyer Professionalism (1986); see also sources cited in Deborah L. Rhode, In the Interests of Justice: Reforming the Legal Profession 1 (2000).

legal institutions, including private contracts (particularly the adhesion contracts that pervade modern commerce) and the aggregation of power in large business organizations. In the public domain, the critique is symbolized in the demonstrations against corporate capitalism that have now become a common world event and that periodically break out in times of popular frustration and despair. Not far underneath is the critique of modern capitalism that emerged in the eighteenth century and was given strongest voice by Marx and other socialists in the nineteenth century.

The critiques are familiar: Corporate capitalism involves relentless competition, "commodification" of labor, preoccupation with "the bottom line" at the expense of broader values, domination by bureaucratic hierarchies, and manipulation of legal rules for the benefit of wealthy owners and overly powerful business interests.

Much in these critiques still needs to be taken seriously by the legal profession. Highly respectable national leaders such as Louis Brandeis and Harlan Fiske Stone have leveled such criticisms at American law practice.[2] Similar concerns have been raised by a broad range of contemporary commentators within and outside of the bar.[3] Lawyers who do not understand the critiques of corporate practices do not fully understand the profession in which they are engaged.

A full response to such critiques is beyond the scope of this volume (and our own expertise). However, the outline of such a defense on constitutional grounds is fairly straightforward: individuals have rights to own property, to enter contracts and to engage in economic production; individuals have a right to legal assistance in pursuing their objectives; the right to legal assistance includes the right to seek out the most competent available legal assistance; an effective means of implementing individual objectives is through cooperative activity in the form of organizations; the business corporation is a well-developed form of cooperative organization; as such, a corporation is entitled, on behalf of its owners and managers, to employ competent legal assistance.[4]

2. Louis D. Brandeis, Business: A Profession 329–43 (1914), discussed in Chapter II; Harlan Fiske Stone, Law and Its Administration (1924).

3. For a representative sampling, see Ralph Nader & Wesley J. Smith, No Contest: Corporate Lawyers and the Perversion of Justice in America (1996); Richard L. Abel, American Lawyers (1989); Jimmy Carter, Speech to the Los Angeles Bar Association, May 4, 1978.

4. The opinion in Upjohn Co. v. United States, 449 U.S. 383 (1981), the leading American case recognizing the attorney-client privilege for a corporation, essentially tracks this analysis.

However, each step in this constitutional logic is open to debate. The right to own a house does not entail the right to own or manage corporate entities in their current form; the right to enter contracts does not legitimate adhesion contracts dictated by the stronger party; the right to engage in cooperative activity does not entail the legitimacy of all practices by multinational corporations, and so forth. The gaps in the logic can be illustrated by comparisons. Compare, for example, the ownership of tangible property such as a plow, with the ownership of stock or a debt, which is an abstract right to require someone else to act in a specified way. Or compare the enforcement of a contract that is mutually agreed upon by equal bargainers, with enforcement of a form contract prepared by lawyers for one party that is unread and unreadable by the other party. These comparisons reflect deeper debates in contemporary politics over how modern society should be structured and how power should be exercised.

At the same time, the economic logic of global corporate enterprise is demonstrated by its pervasive scope and influence. Multinational organizations have achieved their dominance because they have developed efficient ways of satisfying market demands. International experience suggests that the corporate form permits the most disciplined coordination of cooperative effort; such disciplined coordination permits the most cost-effective matching of labor, components, and intelligent direction; and maximum cost-effectiveness in production results in more abundant goods and services, whatever their eventual distribution. However, granting these advantages still leaves open the questions of how such activities should be regulated and how their profits should be distributed. On these questions, lawyers for both the private and public sector have always played a highly influential role.

E. The Plausibility of Alternatives

In considering the legitimacy of corporate practices, and the role of lawyers who assist them, the critical question is always: compared to what? The alternatives seem to reduce themselves to three basic options. One would be to return to small scale enterprise and face-to-face dealings. A second would be to establish state ownership of major enterprises, i.e., some form of socialism. A third would be to implement more pervasive and effective regulation of corporate enterprises.

The first alternative seems to most knowledgeable observers to be simply wishful thinking. If it could be somehow achieved, it would result in a massive reduction in the material standard of living for most of the world's population. The second alternative generally has not to date proved compatible with a healthy and constitutional economic structure. Under socialism, those in control have a monopoly of economic as well as political power and have typically proved incapable of resisting the temptation to co-opt, manipulate, or suppress criticism, opposition, and innovation. A chief virtue of capitalism is that economic power is more decentralized, and governmental power is more constrained.

However, a major problem in regimes professing the rule of law has been the extent to which business has been able to capture its regulators. "Crony capitalism" is all too pervasive and is a corruption of constitutional systems. A genuine issue about capitalism–perhaps *the* fundamental issue–is whether government can be effectively independent of domination by corporate interests. In more pragmatic terms, the most crucial issue involves the third option, the proper extent of government intervention. Of particular concern are interventions to protect individuals' rights from corporate overreaching, and interventions to redirect or redistribute some of the profits of commercial activity.

In a constitutional regime, those issues are posed, debated, and resolved in terms of legal rules. Attorneys are involved in all aspects of the process. On one side are lawyers for government: in the legislatures drafting statutes; in administrative agencies formulating and implementing regulations; and in the courts enforcing the law through criminal and civil prosecutions. On the other side are lawyers for business in private firms or in-house counsels' offices. These roles involve complex symbiotic relationships. Some lawyers over their careers serve on both sides, and may pass through the "revolving door" on multiple occasions. However, whatever their position, lawyers generally share a commitment to the rule of law even while disagreeing about specific interpretations and applications. After all, a lawyer's vocation and livelihood depends on maintaining that commitment to legal principles and procedures.

Chapter V

BASIC PROFESSIONAL NORMS

The ethical rules governing American lawyers express several core values that guide legal practice. Those values and their corresponding obligations include independence, competence, loyalty, confidentiality, candor, and integrity in personal and professional conduct. These obligations extend to clients, courts, and the system of justice. Similar responsibilities are required in other legal systems throughout the world, although their implementation takes somewhat different forms and reflects different priorities.

A. Responsibilities as a Profession: Independence in Professional Regulation and Professional Judgment

The first basic norm of professional ethics is independence. It has two dimensions. The first involves the importance of preserving the bar's independence from government and preventing inappropriate interference by the judiciary. As the Preamble to the ABA's Model Rules of Professional Conduct notes, "An independent legal profession is an important force in preserving government under law, for abuse of legal authority is more readily challenged by a profession whose members are not dependent on government for the right to practice." Experience under totalitarian regimes makes clear that a bar that is overly subject to state regulation and control will be unable adequately to protect individual rights, check official misconduct, or insure due process. Lawyers defending unpopular clients and causes require some protection from political backlash.

To preserve professional independence, American courts have asserted inherent authority to regulate legal practice, and have permitted further legislative or administrative regulation only to the extent that it is consistent with judicial supervision of the bar.[1] In the exercise of their inherent authority, courts have delegated much of the day-to-day control over admission and disciplinary systems to the organized bar, or to agencies that are nominally independent but closely aligned with bar associations.

This structure of self regulation imposes corresponding obligations. As the Model Rules Preamble notes:

---

1. Charles W. Wolfram, Modern Legal Ethics 32–33 (1986). For a critical historical overview of the inherent power doctrine, see Charles W. Wolfram, "Toward A History Of The Legalization Of American Legal Ethics–II The Modern Era," 15 Geo. J. Legal Ethics 205, 210–18 (2002).

The legal profession's relative autonomy carries with it special responsibilities of self-government. The profession has a responsibility to assure that its regulations are conceived in the public interest and not in furtherance of parochial or self-interested concerns of the bar. Every lawyer is responsible for observance of the Rules of Professional Conduct. A lawyer should also aid in securing their observance by other lawyers. Neglect of these responsibilities compromises the independence of the profession and the public interest which it serves.

How well the profession has discharged its regulatory responsibilities is a matter of differing views, which subsequent chapters will explore in the context of specific rules and oversight structures. For present purposes, it simply bears note that critics of the current system question whether the existing degree of professional autonomy effectively serves societal interests. From some commentators' perspective, the bar's lack of public accountability inevitably compromises the performance of its regulatory process.

The problem is not that bar policies are baldly self-serving. Lawyers and judges who control regulatory decisions generally want to advance the public's interest as well as the profession's. Rather, the difficulty is one of tunnel vision, compounded by inadequate accountability. No matter how well intentioned, lawyers and former lawyers who regulate other lawyers cannot escape the economic, psychological, and political constraints of their position. Without external checks, these decision makers too often lose perspective about the points at which occupational and societal interests conflict.... Protecting the bar from state control clearly serves important values, and nations that lack an independent profession have had difficulty safeguarding individual rights and checking official misconduct. But professional autonomy and government domination are not the only alternatives. Many countries with an independent bar impose far more checks on its self-regulatory powers. Governmental efforts to increase lawyers' accountability do not necessarily pose significant risks of retaliation or threats to the proper administration of justice.[2]

Whether our legal system should build more external oversight into current bar regulatory processes will be a focus of the chapters that follow.

---

2. Deborah L. Rhode, In the Interests of Justice: Reforming the Legal Profession 143–45 (2000).

A second dimension of professional independence involves lawyers' capacity to exercise judgement on behalf of clients free from improper external influences. These influences include: pressure from judicial or government officials; the interests of other clients or potential clients; the concerns of colleagues, legal employers, or third parties who are subsidizing representation; and the lawyer's own financial, ideological, or reputational interests. Of particular concern is the influence of those clients who want their lawyers to "bend" the law in their favor–a euphemism for ignoring or concealing the clients' legal obligations. Attempts to prevent such interference have generated an extensive body of ethical requirements and legal doctrine. Rule 2.1 of the ABA's Model Rules of Professional Conduct sets forth the basic standard: "In representing a client, a lawyer shall exercise independent professional judgment and render candid advice." The Model Rules and Model Code also include more specific mandates governing conflicts of interest, discussed in Chapter VIII.

However, some influences do not readily lend themselves to specific regulations or external enforcement. Lawyers almost always want to continue in good standing with their clients. Lawyers also generally want to remain in good working relationships with others whose concerns do not necessarily coincide with those of their clients. The biases that may arise from such relationships are often difficult to prevent or police. For example, judges or supervisors may sometimes pressure lawyers to settle cases for reasons that run counter to their clients' best interests. In-house lawyers may face particular difficulties maintaining their independence, because their reputations and livelihoods are tied to a single client. For that reason, some countries such as Germany have rules on professional independence that prohibit members of the bar from working as corporate employees.[3] By contrast, American ethical rules have fewer categorical prohibitions and more context-specific requirements designed to minimize inappropriate external influences.

B. Responsibilities to Clients: Loyalty, Competence, and Confidentiality

The legal relationship between lawyers and clients is one of agency. An agency relationship entails several basic responsibilities:

---

3. German Code of Legal Ethics, "Protection of Professional Independence," Richtl § 40. Individuals with legal training who work in-house form a separate profession–Syndikusanwalte–and cannot join the bar. See David Luban, "Asking the Right Questions," 72 Temp. L. Rev. 839, 853 (1999).

loyalty, competence, and confidentiality. As agents, attorneys often occupy positions of knowledge and influence that present opportunities for exploitation, coercion, and paternalism. Maintaining loyalty to the client's interests as the client defines them requires a measure of self-restraint that is central to the lawyers's role.

Of course, lawyers can play an important part in helping clients identify their interests. One of the most valuable functions of a loyal advocate is to provide advice on the full range of considerations, moral as well as legal, that should inform a client's decision making. That counseling process will often prompt clients to reassess their short term desires in light of their long term objectives and ethical commitments. But ultimately, as ABA Model Rule 1.2 makes clear, a lawyer generally "shall abide by a client's decisions concerning the objectives of representation ... and shall consult with the client as to the means by which they are to be pursued." If the client "insists upon pursuing an objective that the lawyer considers repugnant or imprudent," then Model Rule 1.16, along with settled case law, permits the lawyer to withdraw. If the client is seeking assistance in a criminal or fraudulent act, or in other conduct that would violate rules of professional conduct, the lawyer must withdraw.

As a practical matter, withdrawal is an unattractive option. Terminating representation is likely to result in acrimony and loss of fees, and may have other costs in terms of reputation, and contractual disputes, or malpractice claims. To avoid such difficulties, lawyers generally try to screen out clients, cases, and work assignments that may pose ethical difficulties. When such screening processes are successful, the obligation of loyalty to clients generally will be consistent with lawyers' own financial and reputational interests in providing effective assistance.

In representation of individuals, the client-lawyer relationship is usually face-to-face, and many ethical problems are more or less obvious. For example, a lawyer may have direct information about whether a document provided by the client is authentic or was contrived after the fact. Some individuals, of course, deceive their lawyers, but seldom easily. More complications arise, however, where the client is an organization or a group whose members have competing concerns and it is unclear who speaks for the client. In organizational settings, as Chapter VII notes, lawyers are normally accountable to management, but their ultimate obligation is to the entity. Under Model Rule 1.13, if the lawyer knows that the organization's employees are engaging in illegal conduct that may be attributable to the organization, then the lawyer has an obligation to act in the organization's best interest. That obligation may include attempts to force reconsideration of the conduct, notification of its highest authority, or withdrawal from representation. When the organization is a governmental entity, as the Comment to Model Rule 1.13 notes, lawyers may have even more extensive responsibilities to prevent or remedy wrongful conduct because their obligation runs to the government as a whole, rather than to specific officials or agencies. When the client is a group, as in a class action lawsuit, lawyers' responsibilities run to the entire membership. Significant conflicts of interest among individual class members ordinarily should be brought to the presiding court's attention; separate subclasses with separate representation may be necessary.

Loyalty to a client's interests also entails competence in representing them. Model Rule 1.1 of the ABA's Model Rules sets forth the basic mandate: "A lawyer shall provide competent representation to a client. Competent representation requires the legal knowledge, skill, thoroughness and preparation reasonably necessary for the representation." The Comment to the Rule adds that "[a] lawyer may accept representation where the requisite level of competence can be achieved by reasonable preparation." Chapter XII explores what this requirement demands in specific circumstances. For present purposes, the important point is that lawyers have an ethical obligation to undertake only those matters that they have sufficient expertise to handle effectively, unless they can acquire the necessary competence without undue expense to the client. This obligation assumes special force where the client is an individual with limited ability to evaluate the lawyer's qualifications for the services required. Three years of law school and passage of a bar exam does not endow a lawyer with the diversity of skills and substantive knowledge that may be needed for effective representation in every context. In an era of increasing specialization, one important dimension of competence is lawyers' ability to recognize the limits of their own expertise.

A closely related professional norm is confidentiality. A commitment not to disclose information acquired during the course of representation is a central aspect of loyalty to the client and a prerequisite of competent assistance. A basic expectation of privacy is essential to ensuring trust and candor in the lawyer-client relationship. Model Rule 1.6 defines the basic obligation: "A lawyer shall not reveal information relating to representation of a client unless the client consents after consultation, except for disclosures that are impliedly authorized in order to carry out the representation." The Rule also provides some important exceptions, discussed more fully in Chapter VI. Lawyers may reveal information to the extent that they believe necessary "to prevent the client from committing a criminal act that the lawyer believes is likely to result in imminent death or substantial bodily harm." Disclosure of confidences is also permitted to prevent fraud on a tribunal, or to establish a claim, or defense in a dispute with the client.

The appropriate scope of confidentiality rules is one of the most controversial issues in American legal ethics. The ABA has frequently divided over proposals to alter Rule 1.6, and almost all states have adopted provisions with more exceptions than the current Model Rules provide. For example, some jurisdictions require lawyers to disclose information necessary to prevent life-threatening or fraudulent criminal conduct, and most expressly permit such disclosures.[4]

Issues concerning confidentiality are more controversial in the United States than in other nations. One reason involves the centrality of lawyers in American life, and the extent to which confidentiality obligations run counter to generally accepted values of openness in public affairs. In a society in which freedom of information is prized and official records are presumptively available for inspection, lawyers' broad claims of confidentiality are a jarring exception. In nations without such traditions of openness, nondisclosure is less controversial. A second reason for the exceptional levels of controversy over confidentiality in this society involves the exceptional frequency of malpractice claims against lawyers. The bar has often resisted even discretionary disclosure provisions for fear that failure to reveal questionable client conduct will subject them to civil liability.

Because the stakes in the confidentiality debate are substantial for both the profession and the public, the proper scope of confidentiality rules is likely to remain contested. But while the scope of provisions will be subject to dispute, the general commitment to maintain client secrets will not. To provide effective representation, lawyers need access to potentially compromising information. And to gain access, they need to provide assurance that such information generally will not be disclosed without the client's consent.

C. Responsibilities to the System of Justice: Lawyers as Officers of the Court

The Preamble to the Model Rules of Professional Conduct defines lawyers' basic obligations as officers of the court:

---

4. See Deborah L. Rhode & David Luban, Legal Ethics 227 (3d ed. 2001).

A lawyer's conduct should conform to the requirements of the law, both in professional service to clients and in the lawyer's business and personal affairs. . . .

A lawyer should demonstrate respect for the legal system and for those who serve it, including judges, other lawyers and public officials. . . .

As a public citizen, a lawyer should seek improvement of the law, the administration of justice and the quality of service rendered by the legal profession.

Model Rule 8.4 elaborates these obligations:

It is professional misconduct for a lawyer to:

(a) violate or attempt to violate the Rules of Professional Conduct . . . ;

(b) commit a criminal act that reflects adversely on the lawyer's honesty, trustworthiness or fitness as a lawyer in other respects;

(c) engage in conduct involving dishonesty, fraud, deceit or misrepresentation;

(d) engage in conduct that is prejudicial to the administration of justice;

(e) state or imply an ability to influence improperly a government agency or official; or

(f) knowingly assist a judge or judicial official in conduct that is a violation of applicable rules of judicial conduct or other law.

Model Rule 3.3 also impose specific obligations of candor to the tribunal:

A lawyer shall not knowingly:

(a) make a false statement of material fact or law to a tribunal;

(b) fail to disclose to the tribunal legal authority in the controlling jurisdiction known to the lawyer to be directly adverse to the position of the client and not disclosed by opposing counsel; or

(c) offer evidence that the lawyer knows to be false.

In addition, as Chapter VI notes, many jurisdictions have established voluntary civility codes specifying further responsibilities for lawyers as officers of the court. These codes range from matters of decorum (such as dress and punctuality) to trial tactics (such as bullying witnesses or opposing counsel). How much effect these aspirational standards have on behavior is an open question. But they clearly serve an important symbolic function in reaffirming the bar's commitment to basic professional norms of propriety and integrity.

Chapter VI

THE ADVERSARY SYSTEM, CONFIDENTIALITY, AND ALTERNATIVE DISPUTE RESOLUTION

A. The Premises of an Adversary System

The American system of justice is adversarial. The term "adversarial" has several connotations. A narrow connotation is that our litigation system depends on opposing parties to investigate, organize, and present the evidence and legal arguments in a dispute that goes to court. This contrasts, to some extent, with the "inquisitorial" model of civil law systems in Europe, most notably in France, Germany, Italy, and Spain. In those systems, the judge has greater control over a case after the pleading stage, particularly in questioning witnesses.

A broader connotation of "adversarial" is that our system places high priority on individual adversaries' legal rights. That priority is apparent not only in litigation (as in the right to take discovery, or to cross-examine opposing parties and witnesses) but also in legislative and administrative proceedings and in contractual negotiations. Thus, American legislative hearings sometimes look more or less like courtroom trials, and administrative agency procedures are often based on the litigation model. In contractual negotiations, particularly major business transactions, lawyers in our system generally play a far greater role than in other countries. A still broader connotation of "adversarial" is that interactions among American lawyers are frequently intensely contentious, in contrast with the more formally polite relationships among lawyers elsewhere.

As a general matter, the American public has deep faith in its system of justice; the vast majority believe that, despite its flaws, it is the best in the world.[1] That faith rests on two central premises. The first premise, drawing on utilitarian principles, is that an adversarial presentation is the best available way to discover the truth. A second premise, drawing on deontological rights-based principles, is that an adversarial process provides the most effective protection for individual rights.

---

1. American Bar Association, Perceptions of the U.S. Justice System 59 (1999).

The argument that the adversary system is the best available means of discovering truth depends on several core assumptions. Their fullest elaboration appears in an influential report by Lon Fuller and John Randal for a joint conference by the American Bar Association and Association of American Law Schools. In essence, these assumptions are that:

- The prospect of victory will motivate adversaries to put maximum effort into developing their case, while in inquisitorial systems, adjudicators lack such competitive incentives;

- Proof requires hypotheses and, if adjudicators develop the proof, their preliminary hypotheses will too easily bias their final decision;

- Reliance on an independent legal profession for developing the record provides a check on official power; and

- The advantages of competitive, party-controlled processes outweigh their costs.[2]

This faith in partisan processes is part of a broader world view that underpins America's basic social and economic institutions. Robert Kutak, chair of the ABA commission that drafted the Model Rules of Professional Conduct, observed that our commitment to an adversarial framework reflects "the same deep-seated values we place on competition" in other contexts.[3]

This truth-based justification for adversarial processes has, however, attracted considerable criticism. First and most obviously, as Plato pointed out centuries ago, the advocate is not a seeker of truth but a producer of belief.[4] Presentations by opposing counsel intent on victory rather than justice will not necessarily produce justice. Marvin Frankel, a former federal court judge and member of the ABA's Model Rules Commission, has argued that in practice, if not principle, our adversarial model ranks truth too low:

> Despite our untested statements of self-congratulation, we know that others searching after facts–in history, geography, medicine, whatever–do not emulate our adversary system. We know that most countries of the world seek justice by different routes. What is much more to the point, we know that many of

---

2. Geoffrey C. Hazard, Jr., Ethics in the Practice of Law 120–35 (1978); Samuel R. Gross, "The American Advantage: The Value of Inefficient Litigation," 85 Mich. L. Rev. 734 (1987).

3. Robert J. Kutak, "The Adversary System and the Practice of Law," in The Good Lawyer: Lawyers' Roles and Law-

yers' Ethics 172, 174 (David Luban, ed., 1983).

4. Plato, Gorgias (T. Irwin trans., 1979), discussed in Anthony T. Kronman, "Forward: Legal Scholarship and Moral Education," 90 Yale L.J. 955, 959 (1981).

the rules and devices of adversary litigation as we conduct it are not geared for, but are often aptly suited to defeat, the development of the truth.... Employed by interested parties, the process often achieves truth only as a convenience, a byproduct, or an accidental approximation. The business of the advocate, simply stated, is to win.... His is not the search for truth as such. To put that thought more exactly, the truth and victory are mutually incompatible for some considerable percentage of the attorneys trying cases at any given time.[5]

As the discussion below reflects, common techniques of discovery, witness preparation, and cross-examination often serve to obfuscate rather than reveal relevant information.

Moreover, in an adversarial model, the merits will be more or less likely to prevail only if the contest is a balanced one. As critics note:

The conventional paradigm presupposes combatants with roughly equal incentives, resources, and capabilities. How frequently those suppositions hold is open to question in a social order that tolerates vast disparities in wealth, renders most litigation enormously expensive, and allocates civil legal assistance almost entirely through market mechanisms. Under these circumstances, one would expect that the "haves" generally come out ahead.[6]

Marc Galanter's classic account of why the "haves" end up ahead identifies certain systematic advantages enjoyed by "repeat players" [RPs] who frequently engage in similar litigation against "one shot" [OS] adversaries.[7] Although acknowledging that these characterizations are somewhat oversimplified, Galanter finds them useful to illustrate the advantages available to frequent litigators such as prosecutors, creditors, or insurance companies:

(1) RPs, having done it before, have advance intelligence; they are able to structure the next transaction and build a record. It is the RP who writes the form contract, requires the security deposit, and the like.

(2) RPs develop expertise and have ready access to specialists. They enjoy economies of scale and have low start-up costs for any case.

5. Marvin E. Frankel, "The Search for Truth: An Umpireal View," 123 U. Pa. L. Rev. 1031, 1036–37 (1975).

6. Deborah L. Rhode, "Ethical Perspectives on Legal Practice," 37 Stan. L. Rev. 589, 597 (1985).

7. Marc Galanter, "Why the 'Haves' Come Out Ahead: Speculations on the Limits of Legal Change," 9 Law & Soc'y. Rev. 95, 97 (1974).

(3) RPs have opportunities to develop [helpful] relations with institutional [players such as court clerks or police].

(4) [The RP's] interest in his "bargaining reputation" serves as a resource to establish "commitment" to his bargaining positions. With no bargaining reputation to maintain, the OS has more difficulty in convincingly committing himself in bargaining.

(5) RPs can play the odds ... [and] adopt strategies calculated to maximize gain over a long series of cases, even where this involves the risk of maximum loss in some cases.

(6) RPs can play for rules as well as immediate gains. First, it pays an RP to expend resources in influencing the making of the relevant rules by such methods as lobbying. (And his accumulated expertise enables him to do this persuasively.)

(7) RPs can also play for rules in litigation itself, whereas an OS is unlikely to.... Since they expect to litigate again, RPs can select to adjudicate (or appeal) those cases which they regard as most likely to produce favorable rules. On the other hand, OSs should be willing to trade off the possibility of making "good law" for tangible gain.

(8) RPs, by virtue of experience and expertise, are more likely to be able to discern which rules are likely to [make a tangible difference] and which are likely to remain merely symbolic commitments.[8]

Given these limitations in the truth-based rationale for an adversarial process, its defenders often rely on an alternative justification: the system's capacity to protect individual rights and the underlying values of autonomy and dignity that such rights preserve. Allowing parties to shape the agenda of their "day in court" also fosters a sense of self-expression and self-respect; it gives individuals a sense of "hav[ing] their wills 'counted' in societal decisions."[9] A wide range of research indicates that, for most people, an opportunity to be heard under a procedurally fair process is more important than the outcome of that process in shaping their judgement about whether justice has been done.[10]

8. Id. at 98–103. See Marc Galanter, Farther Along, 33 Law & Soc'y Rev. 1113 (1999).

9. Frank I. Michelman, "The Supreme Court and Litigation Access Fees: The Right to Protect One's Rights, Part I," 1973 Duke L.J. 1153, 1172; Geoffrey C. Hazard, Jr. Ethics in the Practice of Law 120–35 (1978).

10. E. Allan Lind & Tom R. Tyler, The Social Psychology of Procedural Justice, 64–67 (1988).

This rights-based rationale for an adversarial system assumes special force in criminal cases. Individuals whose lives, liberty, and reputation are at risk are especially deserving of an advocate without competing loyalties to the state. The consequences of an alternative model are readily apparent in many totalitarian countries that lack an adversarial process and an independent profession. Where defense lawyers' role is to "serve justice," rather than their clients, what passes for "justice" often is simply deference to prosecutorial authority.[11] Without the prospect of a vigorous defense, government officials may have inadequate incentives to respect constitutional rights or to investigate facts thoroughly. In the long run, providing adversarial protections for individuals who are guilty also protects those who are not.

Yet how well the current adversary system serves these goals is open to question. As critics note, the rights-based rationale for adversarial procedures fails to address why the rights of a particular client should trump those of all other parties whose interests are inadequately represented. In a system in which not everyone can afford effective advocacy, adversarial models may leave many individual rights unprotected.

Critics also question whether the justifications for adversarial norms in criminal defense extend to civil contexts. Criminal proceedings account for a relatively small portion of lawyers' work and are distinctive in several respects: their reliance on state power, their potential for governmental oppression, and their impact on individual life, liberty, and reputation. Correlatively, our constitutional traditions impose special protections for criminal defendants, such as proof beyond a reasonable doubt and the privilege against self incrimination; the justifications for adversarial procedures are, accordingly, strongest in that context.[12] Of course, some civil matters raise concerns about abusive power or fundamental rights that are analogous to those at issue in criminal proceedings. But such cases do not constitute the mainstay of legal work. And, as discussion below reflects, for many ordinary civil disputes, some qualification of adversarial norms or resort to alternative dispute resolution procedures might yield significant benefits.

In civil disputes in today's world, another factor should be taken into account in the distinction between Repeat Players and One Shot adversaries. This is the emergence of a highly competent and generally well organized plaintiff's bar–lawyers who bring cases

11. See the cases discussed in Deborah L. Rhode, In the Interests of Justice: Reforming the Legal Profession 54 (2000).

12. See id. at 54–55; Richard Wasserstrom, "Lawyers as Professionals: Some Moral Issues," 5 Human Rights 1 (1975).

such as personal injury, financial fraud, racial and gender discrimination, and "mass torts." The individual plaintiffs in these kinds of cases are One Shot litigants but the lawyers on their behalf are distinctly Repeat Players. Their primary professional organizations are the American Trial Lawyers Association and its local counterparts. These groups have become very influential not only in litigation as such, but also in legislative drafting, lobbying, and judicial elections. As a consequence, trial lawyers' associations more or less counterbalance business and industry lobbying on the same fronts. The political battles over "tort reform" are a highly visible manifestation of this pattern.

Given all the limitations in conventional rationales for adversarial processes, some commentators argue that the current system is justifiable only on weak pragmatic grounds: it is not demonstrably worse than other systems, the costs of radical restructuring would be substantial, and the devil you know is better than the devil you don't.[13] However, these commentators join other critics in suggesting that lawyers should help to address, not exploit, the weaknesses in existing structures.

B. Litigation Tactics and Adversarial Abuses

The last quarter century has witnessed increased concerns about frivolous and abusive adversarial practices. A number of factors have contributed to these concerns:

- The growth in substantive rights that can give rise to legal claims;

- The growth in scale and complexity of some forms of litigation;

- The growth in size and competitiveness of the bar; and

- The related decline in informal community relationships of social control.

Yet, while perceptions of "the problem" have clearly heightened, the scope of that problem remains open to dispute. Whether "frivolous" cases have increased is particularly hard to measure, given inherent difficulties in defining frivolity. Available data indicate that the United States' current litigation rates are not exceptionally high, in comparison either with prior historical eras or with other western nations not known for undue contentiousness.[14]

---

13. David Luban, Lawyers and Justice: An Ethical Study 92–93 (1988).

14. Marc S. Galanter, "The Day After the Litigation Explosion," 46 Md. L. Rev. 3 (1986); Marc Galanter, "The Life

Many arguments about America's "legal hypochondria" or "hyperlexis" rest on largely anecdotal evidence of trivial cases: football fans suing referees, suitors suing dates, and beauty contestants suing each other.[15] However, examples such as these do not of themselves establish that America has exceptional problems with frivolous suits or that they occupy an undue amount of judicial time. The issue is always: compared with what?

Historical and cross-cultural research reveals similar examples of trivial claims, and what qualifies as frivolous is often in the eye of the beholder. Consider, for instance, one example of an "inappropriate" claim once cited by a prominent law school dean: sex discrimination suits against Little Leagues.[16] It is not self-evident that such claims are a "waste" of judicial resources, given the importance this nation attaches to sports, the longstanding inequalities in male and female athletic opportunities, and the gender stereotypes that such inequalities reinforce. Some substantial number of complaints about litigiousness may, in reality, be complaints about the reach of the substantive law; the "line between vindictiveness and vindication is often difficult to draw."[17]

Yet although the exact scope and nature of adversarial abuse is subject to dispute, there is little disagreement that some problems exist. Over 90 percent of bar leaders view incivility as a serious concern.[18] In large, complex cases, there are chronic difficulties with discovery. Although most litigation involves relatively few pretrial problems, high-stakes lawsuits often result in excessive costs, evasion, and delay.[19] In some significant percentage of such suits, material information is never discovered by opposing parties.[20]

and Times of the Big Six; or, the Federal Courts Since the Good Old Days," 1988 Wis. L. Rev. 921; Lawrence M. Friedman, Total Justice 15–23 (1985).

15. Lori B. Andrews, "Suing as a First Resort: A Review of Mark's, The Suing of America and Lieberman's The Litigious Society," 1981 Am. B. Found. Res. J. 851; Bayless Manning, "Hyperlexis: Our National Disease," 71 Nw. U.L. Rev. 767 (1977).

16. Manning, supra note 15.

17. Rhode, supra note 11, at 121.

18. Id. at 82.

19. James S. Kakalik, et al., Discovery Management: Further Analysis of the Civil Justice Reform Act Evaluation Data xx, 55 (1998); Austin Sarat, "Ethics in Litigation," in Ethics in Practice, (Deborah L. Rhode, ed. 2000); John S.

Beckerman, "Confronting Civil Discovery's Fatal Flaws," 84 Minn. L. Rev. 505, 506 (2000); Jeffrey W. Stempel, "Ulysses Tied to the Generic Whipping Post: The Continuing Odyssey of Discovery 'Reform'," 64 Law & Contemp. Problems 197, 219 (2001); Thomas E. Willging et al., "An Empirical Study of Discovery and Disclosure Practice Under the 1993 Federal Rule Amendments," 39 B. C. L. Rev. 525, 540 (1998).

20. See Wayne D. Brazil, "Civil Discovery: How Bad Are the Problems?," 67 A.B.A.J. 450, 451–56 (1981); Wayne D. Brazil, "Views from the Front Lines: Observations by Chicago Lawyers About the System of Civil Discovery," 1980 Am. B. Found. Res. J. 219 (1980); and sources cited in note 19.

Catalogues of discovery abuse abound. Common techniques for evading or exhausting an adversary include:

- Overuse of depositions and interrogatories;

- Abusive scheduling practices, such as arranging depositions in order to impose maximum inconvenience and expense, and refusing to acquiesce in reasonable requests for extensions of time;

- Objectionable questioning techniques, such as seeking embarrassing but unnecessary information, objecting to reasonable inquiries, or inappropriately coaching witnesses or instructing them not to answer;

- Evasive strategies, such as promising to answer at a later date; recycling vague allegations of a complaint or answer; reshuffling documents so that an adversary has little sense of how files are kept and how relevant materials can be located; or burying the "smoking pistol" where it is almost impossible to locate ("dump truck discovery").[21]

These practices arise from a complex set of economic, social, and psychological factors. By prolonging proceedings, some clients can continue to engage in legally dubious but financially profitable activity, avoid publicizing unfavorable facts, or buy time to prevent adverse events such as a corporate acquisition. By turning litigation into an expensive war of attrition, parties may also be able to force a favorable settlement, discourage other potential adversaries from filing suit, or retaliate for perceived abuses.

Lawyers' own incentives also contribute to procedural problems. Attorneys seeking to maximize billable hours have an obvious interest in meter-running, a practice that litigators frequently report having experienced, although they do not acknowledge having committed.[22] Many litigators are understandably risk-averse, and leaving no stone unturned has obvious advantages "if you can charge by the stone."[23] Prolonging pretrial maneuvers to force settlements can also avoid the risks of defeat and the loss of reputation that it might entail. Finally, lawyers as well as clients can easily become used to a combative approach, and retaliation has its own rewards.

---

21. Beckerman, supra note 19, at 525; Frank F. Flegal, "Discovery Abuse: Causes, Effects and Reform," 3 Rev. of Litig. 1, 21–22 (1982); Alex W. Albright, "Waging Unconditional Warfare: An Ex- asperated Court Speaks Its Mind," Tex. Law. Newspaper, Sept. 5, 1988, at 18.

22. Brazil, "Views from the Front Lines," supra note 20.

23. Rhode, supra note 11, at 61, 84.

There are, however, significant countervailing interests. In the short run, abusive behavior can be counterproductive if it provokes retaliation or sanctions and undercuts constructive settlement efforts. In the long term, such conduct can compromise a lawyer's reputation for integrity and reasonableness. The result is likely to be less credibility and fewer referrals from courts and opponents, as well as more acrimonious working environments. Relations with clients may also suffer. Many individuals recognize that when litigation becomes an arms race, the major beneficiaries are often the lawyers; the parties pay an undue price in aggravation, acrimony, and legal bills.[24] Moreover, the costs of procedural abuse are not borne by the litigants alone. Legal costs are passed on to consumers in the form of higher prices, and subsidized by taxpayers through public funding for the courts and tax deductions for business expenses. How to modify the incentive structures that contribute to abusive tactics is a matter of public as well as professional interest.

Bar disciplinary agencies rarely impose sanctions for litigation misconduct. Rather, the principle legal means of regulating procedural misconduct has been Rule 11 of the Federal Rules of Civil Procedure, and its state court analogues. The rule provides that lawyer's signature on any filing signifies that: "to the best of the [signer's] knowledge, information, and belief, formed after an inquiry reasonable under the circumstances;" the filing has "evidentiary support" or is likely to have such support after a "reasonable opportunity for further investigation;" the filing is "warranted by existing law or a good faith argument for the extension, modification, or reversal of existing law or the establishment of new law;" and is "not being presented for any improper purpose, such as to harass or to cause unnecessary delay or needless increase in the cost of litigation." When parties move for sanctions, their opponents have a 21–day "safe harbor" interval, during which they can withdraw the offending papers without penalty. A court that finds a Rule 11 violation may impose an "appropriate sanction," which may include monetary or nonmonetary remedies. Absent special circumstances, a law firm can be held jointly liable for violations committed by its partners, associates, or employees.

The terms of this Rule and its state court analogues have been a matter of ongoing controversy. Until its amendment in 1983, Rule 11 sanctions were discretionary with the court rather than mandatory. The Rule imposed no requirement of reasonable inquiry by

---

24. Rhode, supra note 11, at 85. Robert N. Sayler, "Rambo Litigation: Why Hardball Tactics Don't Work," ABA Journal, March 1, 1988, at 79; Bartlett H. McGuire, "Rambo Litigation: A Losing Proposition," The American Lawyer, May 1996, at 39–40.

the lawyer. In effect, this earlier version was violated only on a finding of subjective bad faith, and that standard was almost never met. The 1983 amendments required a reasonable inquiry, made sanctions mandatory if a violation occurred, and permitted fines payable to the opposing party. As a result, Rule 11 enforcement escalated rapidly. Motions for sanctions became a standard part of the advocate's arsenal and generated some of the harassing litiga-tion that it was meant to deter. The problem was exacerbated by the ambiguity of standards governing "reasonable inquiry," "good faith," and "well grounded in fact." In one study, almost 300 judges divided almost evenly about whether to impose sanctions in six out of ten hypothetical cases.[25] According to some studies, courts also disproportionately exercised their discretion to penalize civil rights plaintiffs.[26]

To address such concerns, the Rule was again amended in 1994. These amendments once again made sanctions discretionary, imposed a safe harbor option, and made financial penalties normal-ly payable to the court, unless payment to the adversary was warranted for purposes of deterrence.

This history is instructive in several respects. First, it helps to explain why bar ethical codes have been so ineffectual in response to procedural abuse. The Code and Model Rules both enjoin lawyers from asserting frivolous positions or taking positions merely to harass. However, like Rule 11 before its 1983 amendment, these provisions have proven largely unenforceable in practice. Not only is the burden of proving a violation unrealistically high, but liti-gants have little if anything to gain from referring the case to bar disciplinary agencies. Those agencies generally will not act during the pendency of litigation, will not impose fines that compensate complainants, and, except in the most egregious cases, will not expend scarce resources on matters where an alternative judicial remedy is available.

Moreover, judges are generally reluctant to impose sanctions for any but the most egregious instances of litigation misconduct. Sorting out who is at fault in pretrial disputes is a time-consuming and frequently thankless enterprise. It often requires more knowl-edge than overburdened judges would otherwise need to acquire, particularly on matters that are unlikely to require trial or that do

25. Saul M. Kassin, An Empirical Study of Rule 11 Sanctions ix, 17–29 (Federal Judicial Center 1985).

26. See id., at x, 38–39; Mark Spie-gel, "The Rule 11 Studies and Civil Rights Cases: An Inquiry into the Neu-trality of Procedural Rules," 32 Conn. L. Rev. 155 (1999); David B. Wilkins, "Who Should Regulate Lawyers?," 105 Harv. L. Rev. 799, 869, n. 308 (1992).

not involve clear villains and victims.[27] Most judges also dislike antagonizing lawyers by imposing sanctions, since that can interfere with facilitating settlement, risk reversal on appeal, or make the proceedings even more contentious. If counsel cannot manage to behave civilly toward one another, a traditional judicial response has been to let them pay the price.

In response to such weakness of enforcement, over a hundred bar associations have adopted voluntary civility codes.[28] The reason for their appeal is obvious; they are a concrete response at little cost. Lawyers who oppose such adversarial constraints can simply ignore them. Yet without enforcement mechanisms, the effectiveness of civility standards is questionable. The bar's current enthusiasm for such standards rests on no evidence that they significantly influence behavior. A few jurisdictions require lawyers to certify that they have read the applicable civility code; none have attempted to assess compliance or even to measure awareness of its requirements. Yet it seems doubtful that voluntary codes will be sufficient to cope with lawyers most likely to violate them.

An effective response to adversarial abuses requires multiple strategies. One obvious priority is to strengthen penalties. Other options include publicizing sanctions, improving disciplinary agencies' responses, and requiring legal employers to institute educational and monitoring programs in their organizations. More resources could also be available for oversight, not only by trial courts but also by magistrates, special masters, and volunteer referees from local bar associations.[29] Other commonly proposed responses to procedural abuse include law firm policies and training programs; more disciplinary measures directed against entire law firms; replacement of hourly billing structures with flat-fee rates that would reduce incentives for over-discovery; and orders that parties who make burdensome discovery requests subsidize their opponents' compliance.

Nevertheless, it seems evident that formal sanctions of any kind will have limited effect, and that sometimes the effect will be counterproductive. There are, however, informal sanctions operating beneath a formal system that are often more influential. The primary informal sanctions are retaliation and "bad-mouthing," as

27. Stempel, supra note 19, at 209–10; Arthur R. Miller, "The Adversary System: Dinosaur or Phoenix," 69 Minn. L. Rev. 1 (1984).

28. ABA, Promoting Professionalism 53 (1998); N. Lee Cooper, "Courtesy Call," ABA J., March 1997, at 8.

29. Rhode, supra note 11, at 95; Wilkins, supra note 26, at 835–39; Stempel, supra note 19, at 239–41.

opposed to cordial, professional relations. Retaliation includes refusal to cooperate, insistence on formalities, refusal to overlook an
opponent's blunders, or unwillingness to accommodate special
needs. Bad mouthing invites other lawyers to extend similar treatment to the offender. On the other hand, cordial professional
relations enable lawyers to trust each other, even when on opposite
sides of intense legal controversies. Relationships of trust almost by
definition arise only among groups that have continuing interactions with each other. Opposing specialists in any practice locale or
niche often have relationships so cordial as to excite suspicion on
the part of clients. There is, of course, no necessary contradiction
between cordiality to a fellow professional and effectiveness on
behalf of clients. However, some lawyers evidently think that they
must prove their "zeal" by making life unpleasant and burdensome
for their adversaries. To counter such perceptions, many professional organizations attempt to institutionalize forms of approval
for appropriate conduct, such as election to bar association office
and appointment to desirable committees. These longstanding professional activities can play an important part in encouraging high
standards of behavior and repairing frayed relationships.

C. Candor and Confidentiality

Rules governing candor and confidentiality in lawyer-client
relationships must balance several, sometimes competing, concerns.
One is to provide sufficient protection for confidential communications to ensure candor and trust in lawyer-client relationships. A
second concern is to prevent lawyers from assisting criminal or
fraudulent conduct or withholding information necessary to protect
innocent third parties and promote legal compliance. A third concern is to preserve some incentives for parties to prepare their own
cases adequately without freeloading on their opponents' efforts.

These concerns have shaped both bar ethical obligations and
evidentiary rules governing the attorney client privilege. The privilege protects confidential client communications from disclosure in
legal proceedings. The duty of confidentiality set forth in bar
ethical codes is broader than the privilege in two primary respects.
This duty encompasses information from any source, including, but
not limited to, clients. The ethical obligation also applies in all
contexts, not just to lawyers as witnesses in legal proceedings.

The lawyer-client privilege arose in the seventeenth century as
an outgrowth of the general principle that it is dishonorable to

reveal another's confidence.[30] Originally, the privilege belonged to the lawyer. During the eighteenth and nineteenth centuries, the rationale gradually shifted to the needs of a proper functioning legal system, and authority to assert or waive the right shifted to the client. In its traditional formulation, the law of privilege holds that:

(1) Where legal advice of any kind is sought (2) from a professional legal adviser in the lawyer's capacity as such, (3) the communications relating to that purpose, (4) made in confidence (5) by the client, (6) are ... permanently protected (7) from disclosure by [the client] himself or by the legal adviser, (8) except [if] the protection be waived.[31]

The attorney-client privilege as now understood also includes communications from the lawyer to the client if they explicitly or implicitly, refer to communications originating from the client. An auxiliary rule extends protection against disclosure to the attorney's "work product," i.e., information assembled in anticipation of litigation and lawyers' analysis of that information.[32]

Application of the privilege has generated an extensive body of case law and several important exceptions. Among the most significant qualifications are those governing waiver. The privilege is inapplicable if the communication takes place in the presence of a third party, if the client discloses the communication to a third party, or if the client or his agent implicitly or explicitly consents to disclosure. The privilege also does not apply to disclosures by jointly represented clients in any subsequent dispute arising between those clients. Other significant exceptions to the privilege involve information regarding client identity, future crimes, and continuing frauds.

Attorneys' confidentiality obligations are also defined by bar ethical codes. These codifications are more recent in origin than the lawyer-client privilege. They are generally traced to David Dudley Field's 1849 Civil Procedure Code, which was later incorporated in bar ethical regulations. Both the ABA Model Code and the Model Rules impose broader obligations that not only prohibit lawyers

30. Geoffrey C. Hazard, Jr., "An Historical Perspective on the Attorney–Client Privilege," 66 Cal. L. Rev. 1061, 1069–73 (1978); John H. Wigmore, 8 A Treatise on the Anglo–American System of Evidence in Trials at Common Law § 2290 (John T. McNaughton ed., rev. ed. 1961).

31. Wigmore, supra note 30, § 2292.

32. The original formulation of the privilege appears in Hickman v. Taylor, 329 U.S. 495 (1947). Exceptions to the privilege include statements given by a litigant or independent witness to an opponent's investigator, and experts who will be called as witnesses. See Fed. R.Civ.P. 26(b)(3).

from offering evidence about confidential communications with clients but also enjoin revealing confidential information from any source in any setting in or outside the courtroom. Disciplinary Rule 4–101 of the Code protects both "confidence(s)," which encompass any information protected by the attorney-client privilege, and "secret(s)," which encompass "other information gained in the professional relationship that the client has requested be held inviolate or the disclosure of which would be embarrassing or would be likely to be detrimental to the client." Model Rule 1.6(a) states simply that "[a] lawyer shall not reveal information relating to representation of a client."

These ethical mandates also are subject to exceptions. Both the Code and the Model Rules permit lawyers to reveal confidences if the client consents. Disciplinary Rule 4–101 of the Code allows lawyers to reveal confidences if required by law or court order. Model Rule 1.6(a) similarly exempts from confidentiality "disclosures that are impliedly authorized in order to carry out the representation." Most authorities agree that disclosures required by law are so authorized. Finally, both the Code and the Model Rules allow lawyers to disclose information to protect themselves or third party interests in certain circumstances. Disciplinary Rule 4–101(C)(3) permits but does not require a lawyer to reveal "the intention of his client to commit a crime and the information necessary to prevent the crime." One version of DR 7–102(B), applicable in some states, obligates lawyers to rectify frauds perpetrated during the course of representation. Model Rule 1.6(b)(1) permits but does not require a lawyer to disclose confidential information "to the extent the lawyer reasonably believes necessary ... to prevent the client from committing a criminal act that the lawyer believes is likely to result in imminent death or substantial bodily harm." Both DR 4–101 and Model Rule 1.6 also allow lawyers to reveal information necessary to establish their own claims or defenses in a controversy with the client or in proceedings concerning their representation of the client.

These exceptions in effect allow a lawyer to "blow the whistle" on the client in a transaction in which the lawyer's services have been used if that transaction turns out to involve crime or fraud. Under Model Rule 1.2(d), a matter that plainly involves crime or fraud is not one in which a lawyer should be involved in the first place. However, determining whether a transaction is fraudulent can be difficult, because clients in such a situation will usually make every effort to conceal its character from their lawyers. Where lawyers manage to discover such misconduct, they should attempt to dissuade the client or otherwise to abort the transaction before withdrawing from the matter or revealing confidential information. It should be expected that a confrontation with a client over such issues may be disagreeable, going on ugly. Lawyers don't like to talk about such a situation, and many of them don't even want to think about it. Professional discussions are larded with euphemisms.

In addition, the Code and Model Rules impose obligations of candor toward tribunals. Model Rule 3.3 provides:

A lawyer shall not knowingly:

> (1) make a false statement of material fact or law to a tribunal;
>
> (2) fail to disclose a material fact to a tribunal when disclosure is necessary to avoid assisting a criminal or fraudulent act by the client;
>
> (3) fail to disclose to the tribunal legal authority in the controlling jurisdiction known to the lawyer to be directly adverse to the position of the client and not disclosed by opposing counsel; or
>
> (4) offer evidence that the lawyer knows to be false. If a lawyer has offered material evidence and comes to know of its falsity, the lawyer shall take reasonable remedial measures.

DRs 7–102 and 7–106 include comparable provisions. Model Rule 3.4 also prohibit lawyers from unlawfully obstructing access to evidence or unlawfully destroying or concealing material of evidentiary value. DR 7–109 includes analogous prohibitions.

Many legal ethics experts have criticized the bar's confidentiality obligations as overly broad. As they note, Model Rule 1.6(b) does not require disclosure of confidential information in any circumstances except those involving fraud on a tribunal, and does not even permit such disclosure to prevent noncriminal but life-threatening acts. Nor does the rule ostensibly permit disclosures to prevent financial rather than physical injuries. In general, the lawyer's only recourse is to withdraw from representation and disavow any prior opinion that might assist criminal or fraudulent conduct. Rule 1.6, Comment. In representing organizations, a lawyer may, and in some contexts must, report legal violations internally, Model Rule 1.13b; Sarbanes-Oxley Act of 2002. Almost all state ethical codes, however, impose greater disclosure obligations than the Model Rules prescribe. A small minority require disclosure in certain circumstances, such as those involving death or substantial bodily injury, crimes and frauds, or criminal conduct in which the lawyer's services have been used. The vast majority permit disclosure under such circumstances, and all do so for death or substantial bodily harm.[33]

The justifications for broad confidentiality protections closely parallel the justifications for the adversary system. One rationale rests on the value of individual legal rights and the importance of confidentiality in securing them. A second rationale focuses on the instrumental value of confidentiality in promoting just resolution of legal issues and in encouraging compliance with legal obligations.

The rights-based argument for confidentiality obligations builds on several assumptions about societal values and client conduct. First, an overarching objective of the legal system is to preserve individual rights, which often requires legal assistance. Lawyers cannot provide adequate assistance unless clients feel free to communicate relevant information. Many people will be unwilling to consult lawyers or to disclose essential facts without assurances that the information will not be used against them. Confidentiality obligations serve not only to safeguard legal rights in general, but also to preserve certain specific entitlements such as those of privacy, effective assistance of counsel, and the protection against self-incrimination. In the absence of confidentiality safeguards, clients who are unaware of legal defenses might withhold helpful information. A commonly cited example is the battered wife who is afraid to acknowledge shooting her brutal husband because she does not realize that her act would qualify as self-defense.[34]

A second justification for broad confidentiality protections is that they promote just outcomes. By encouraging individuals to seek legal advice and to disclose all relevant information, the attorney-client privilege and related ethical rules facilitate compliance with legal norms. Lawyers can counsel individuals about their legal obligations and encourage appropriate resolution of legal disputes. To perform this function, attorneys need a level of trust that is incompatible with whistle-blowing obligations.

Whether these arguments justify the current scope of confidentiality protections is subject to dispute. Critics of broad confidentiality rules note that concerns about criminal defendants' constitutional rights do not justify sweeping protections in civil contexts.

---

33. Deborah L. Rhode & David Luban, Lethal Ethics 227 (3rd ed. 2001). The Restatement of the Law Governing Lawyers (Third), §§ 66 and 67, permits lawyers to disclose confidences to prevent reasonably certain death or serious bodily harm, or to rectify client crimes or frauds threatening substantial financial loss if the lawyers' services have been used in that matter. See the discussion in the text accompanying notes 44–45.

34. Monroe H. Freedman, Lawyers' Ethics in an Adversary System 4 (1975).

Nor is it self-evident why the rights of clients should always take priority over the rights of others, particularly where the client is an organization and other individuals' health and safety interests are implicated.[35] Similarly, critics also challenge the implicit hierarchy in current bar codes, which require disclosure to prevent fraud on a tribunal but not to save a life, and which permit disclosure to enable lawyers to collect their fees but not to prevent fraud against innocent investors. On general legal principles, a preference for lawyers as compared with third party victims is difficult to justify, since the lawyer is likely to be in a better position than others to prevent the wrong or to mitigate its impact.

Some commentators also challenge the effectiveness of broad confidentiality protections in safeguarding legal rights. As they note, many individuals are reluctant to confide in lawyers who might have competing loyalties, whatever the rules on confidentiality. Moreover, those rules are riddled with exceptions and indeterminacies that few clients now comprehend.

Available research leaves doubt whether different rules would significantly alter client behavior. The most systematic studies reveal only a tenuous connection between confidentiality rules and the willingness of clients to reveal sensitive information to their lawyers.[36] For example, one study of New York lawyers and clients, produced findings that: lawyers almost never inform their clients about the duty of confidentiality; clients substantially misunderstand the scope of confidentiality; and only about a third of former clients said that they gave information to their lawyers that they would not have given without a guarantee of confidentiality.[37]

So too, historical, cross-cultural, and cross-professional research makes clear that practitioners can provide effective assistance with more qualified confidentiality safeguards than now prescribed in ABA rules.[38] For that reason, many states have enacted mandatory or discretionary disclosure provisions beyond those that Model Rule 1.6 prescribes. Hence, the scope of confidentiality protections is likely to be the subject of continuing debate. Controversy is also likely to persist about the application of existing confidentiality rules in particular circumstances. Subsequent chapters will take up lawyers' obligations of candor and confidentiality in specific contexts such as negotiation and counseling. For present

35. See sources cited in Rhode, supra note 11, at 110–12.

36. Rhode & Luban, supra note 33, at 190–91; Fred C. Zacharias, "Rethinking Confidentiality," 74 Iowa L. Rev. 351, 382–83 (1989).

37. Zacharias, supra note 36, at 379–86.

38. Rhode, supra note 11, at 111.

purposes, two general issues merit particular attention: client perjury and client fraud.

How lawyers should respond to client perjury has generated considerable controversy, particularly in the context of criminal defense. In his influential treatment of the subject, Monroe Freedman analyzes what he labels the "perjury trilemma," which arises from competing ethical obligations.[39] It is said that, in order to provide effective advocacy, the criminal defense attorney must learn all the significant facts. At the same time, the attorney has obligations of confidentiality to the client and a duty of candor to the court. The trilemma arises if the client demonstrates an intent to give false testimony from the witness stand. There is often quibbling over whether a lawyer ever can "know" with certainty that the client's testimony is untrue, but in some situations a lawyer could not "know" otherwise in the ordinary sense of the term. One of our colleagues remembers a client accused of felonious assault who wanted to claim innocence in his testimony without disclosing the reason; he had used a hot branding iron on the victim only three times, not six or seven as the prosecution alleged.

According to Freedman, attorneys confronting client perjury can fulfill at most two of their three obligations. If they have acquired all relevant information, they will know that the testimony is perjurious, and then must breach either their duty of confidentiality or the duty of candor. Those duties can be reconciled only if lawyers remain selectively ignorant, which compromises their ability to provide effective advocacy. Freedman argues that in cases of conflict, the obligation of candor to the court must give way. In his view, the duties of confidentiality and zealous advocacy are of paramount constitutional and moral significance in criminal cases, for they are essential to the Fifth Amendment privilege against self-incrimination and the Sixth Amendment right to representation. A 1992 ethics opinion of the National Association of Criminal Defense Lawyers came to a similar conclusion on similar reasoning.[40]

By contrast, the Comment to Model Rule 3.3 summarizes the ABA response to the client perjury problem as follows:

> While it is agreed that the lawyer should seek to persuade the client to refrain from perjurious testimony, there has been dispute concerning the lawyer's duty when that persuasion fails [and when withdrawal is not possible]. . . .

39. Freedman, supra note 34, at 27–41.

40. The Ethics Advisory Committee of NACDL, Formal Op. 92–2, reprinted in The Champion, March 1993, at 23.

Three resolutions of this dilemma have been proposed. One is to permit the accused to testify by a narrative without guidance through the lawyer's questioning. This compromises both contending principles; it exempts the lawyer from the duty to disclose false evidence but subjects the client to an implicit disclosure of information imparted to counsel. Another suggested resolution, of relatively recent origin, is that the advocate be entirely excused from the duty to reveal perjury if the perjury is that of the client. This is a coherent solution but makes the advocate a knowing instrument of perjury.

The other resolution of the dilemma is that the lawyer must reveal the client's perjury if necessary to rectify the situation. A criminal accused has a right to the assistance of an advocate, a right to testify and a right of confidential communication with counsel. However, an accused should not have a right to assistance of counsel in committing perjury. Furthermore, an advocate has an obligation, not only in professional ethics but under the law as well, to avoid implication in the commission of perjury or other falsification of evidence....

If withdrawal will not remedy the situation or is impossible, the advocate should make disclosure to the court. It is for the court then to determine what should be done–making a statement about the matter to the trier of fact, ordering a mistrial or perhaps nothing. If the false testimony was that of the client, the client may controvert the lawyer's version of their communication when the lawyer discloses the situation to the court. If there is an issue whether the client has committed perjury, the lawyer cannot represent the client in resolution of the issue and a mistrial may be unavoidable.... However, the definition of the lawyer's ethical duty in such a situation may be qualified by constitutional provisions for due process and the right to counsel in criminal cases. In some jurisdictions these provisions have been construed to require that counsel present an accused as a witness if the accused wishes to testify, even if counsel knows the testimony will be false. The obligation of the advocate under these Rules is subordinate to such a constitutional requirement.

After the ABA's adoption of the Model Rules, the Supreme Court largely removed constitutional objections to disclosure of client perjury, at least under the U.S. Constitution. In *Nix v. Whiteside*, 475 U.S. 157 (1986), the Court held that a lawyer did not provide ineffective assistance of counsel by discouraging his client from giving what the lawyer believed would be false testimony. However, the *Nix* decision did not directly overrule lower court holdings that disclosure of perjury violated a client's due process rights.[41] Nor did *Nix* clarify what level of knowledge is necessary to trigger disclosure obligations. Under the Model Rules' somewhat circular standard, "knowingly" means "actual knowledge of the facts in question . . . [which] may be inferred from circumstances." The Commentary to former ABA Criminal Defense Standard 4–7.7 interpreted "knowledge" to require a defendant's admission of inculpatory facts to his lawyer that are corroborated by the lawyer's own investigations.[42] Some jurisdictions have imposed similar standards concerning the lawyer's knowledge, while other courts have proceeded with less rigorous requirements.[43] At a minimum, it would seem appropriate for trial courts to make some factual inquiry into the basis of lawyers' judgements about the falsity of their clients' testimony.[44]

In most cases, however, it is in the lawyer's own interest to resolve doubts in favor of their clients and avoid information that would unequivocally establish perjury. The main check against false testimony is not fear of disciplinary charges (which would generally be extraordinarily difficult if not impossible to prove) but concerns about effectiveness. That is, if the advocate for the accused is convinced that testimony will be false, judges and jurors also are likely to be convinced. The lawyer can advise the client accordingly.

A related set of issues involves client fraud. As noted earlier, most states permit disclosure of client frauds in at least some circumstances, and a small number require it. About two thirds allow lawyers to divulge confidences to prevent frauds that constitute criminal conduct, and another quarter allow disclosures if the lawyers's services are used in that matter. Section 67 of the Restatement of Law Governing Lawyers permits disclosure to prevent or rectify client crime or fraud involving "substantial financial loss" in which the lawyers' services are used. The ABA's Ethics

---

41. See, e.g., Lowery v. Cardwell, 575 F.2d 727 (9th Cir.1978).

42. That standard was withdrawn in 1979 on the understanding that it would be supplanted by the Model Rules ABA Standards Relating to the Administration of Criminal Justice 4.94–4.95 (2d ed. 1980) (Editorial Note to deleted Standard 4–7.7).

43. Compare In re Grievance Committee of U.S. Dist. Court, Dist. of Connecticut, 847 F.2d 57 (2d Cir.1988) (requiring acknowledgments of perjury and corroboration) with People v. Bartee, 566 N.E.2d 855 (Ill.App.1991) (holding that lawyer need not have a firm factual basis for believing a client would lie; a good faith determination would be sufficient). See Developments, "Client Perjury and the Duty of Candor," 6 Geo. J. Legal Ethics 1003, 1008–1009 (1993) (discussing appellate cases).

44. See cases summarized in Norman Lefstein, "Client Perjury in Criminal Cases: Still in Search of an Answer," 1 Geo. J. Legal Ethics 521, 538–41 (1988); Monroe H. Freedman, "Client Confidences and Client Perjury: Some Unanswered Questions," 136 U. Pa. L. Rev. 1939 (1988).

2000 Commission proposed such a provision for the Model Rules of Professional Conduct, but the proposal was narrowly defeated in the House of Delegates.

Opponents of such provisions for permissive disclosure worry that lawyers who fail to take advantage of them will be held liable in litigation by defrauded parties. By contrast, a categorical prohibition is assumed to protect lawyers against such suits. However, as legal ethics experts have noted, this protection is often illusory: third parties can claim that lawyers aided and abetted the fraud, and jurors will often be sympathetic to such claims whether or not they are supported by direct evidence. Even if lawyers ultimately can establish their lack of complicity and persuade decision makers that ethics rules demanded confidentiality, the financial and reputational costs of litigation are likely to be substantial. And even in the absence of third party claims, lawyers whose services are implicated in fraud may suffer a loss of credibility with judges, regulatory officials, colleagues, and the broader legal community. Prudent attorneys generally want the ability to prevent the fraud in the first instance, and rules allowing disclosure are necessary to that end. It bears note that loss prevention specialists in malpractice insurance companies typically support discretionary disclosure rules.[45]

From a societal standpoint, there is also a strong case for mandatory disclosure of frauds involving substantial financial loss, particularly those in which lawyers' services were used. Honest clients have little to fear from such requirements; dishonest clients have no right to secrecy, and innocent third parties could benefit from early warnings. Although systematic data are lacking, no evidence suggests that mandatory disclosure rules have proven unworkable in the jurisdictions that have adopted them.

Whatever the formal ethical rules concerning disclosure, lawyers have an interest in creating safeguards against involvement in client fraud. Workplace structures are often necessary to counteract financial temptations, peer pressure, diffusion of responsibility, and psychological predispositions that encourage see-no-evil, hear-no-evil attitudes toward client misconduct. Individuals generally tend toward reduction of "cognitive dissonance"; they are especially likely to register and retain information that is compatible with established beliefs or earlier decisions, and to suppress or reconstrue information that casts doubts on those decisions.[46] Once

45. Geoffrey C. Hazard, Jr., "Lawyer as Whistleblower," National L. J. March 5, 2001, at A19.

46. Thomas Gilovich, How We Know What Isn't So: The Fallibility of Reason in Everyday Life, 30–36 (1991); Deborah L. Rhode and Paul Patton, Lawyers,

lawyers have determined to represent a particular client, they may become less sensitive to ethical problems arising from that choice. Crafting internal reporting structures and external regulatory systems that will address such biases is an ongoing challenge for the profession and the public.

A final issue concerning confidentiality obligations involves the lawyer's role in crafting litigation settlements that include secrecy clauses. Clients who are permitted to agree to confidentiality have something of value that can increase the settlement. But the benefits to the clients and defendants carry a cost for other claimants and third parties. Many unsafe practices would come to light sooner if there were more legislative or ethical prohibitions on such secrecy clauses. Recent highly publicized examples involve cases of defective tires, exploding gas tanks, and sexual abuse by Catholic priests.[47]

A proposal to the Ethics 2000 Commission supported by many legal ethics professors would have amended the Model Rules to prohibit lawyers from facilitating such agreements. The proposed addition to Model Rule 3.2 provided:

> A lawyer shall not participate in offering or making an agreement, whether in connection with a lawsuit or otherwise, to prevent or restrict the availability to the public of information that the lawyer reasonably believes directly concerns a substantial danger to the public health or safety, or to the health or safety of any particular individual(s).[48]

The Ethics 2000 Commission rejected the proposal on the grounds that the appropriateness of such provisions was a policy decision that should not be resolved by ethical codes.[49]

Several states have addressed that policy issue with "sunshine in litigation" legislation, and others are considering such reforms.

Ethics, and Enron, Stan.J. Law, Bus. & Finance (2003, forthcoming) Deborah L. Rhode, "Institutionalizing Ethics," 44 Case Western L. Rev. 665, 685–86 (1994); Donald C. Langevoort, "Where Were the Lawyers? A Behavioral Inquiry Into Lawyers' Responsibility for Client Clients' Fraud," 46 Vand. L. Rev. 75 (1993).

47. See Ralph Nader & Wesley Smith, No Contest: Corporate Lawyers and the Perversion of Justice in America 72–73 (1996); Davan Maharaj, "Tire Recall Fuels Drive to Bar Secret Settlement," L.A. Times, Sept. 10, 2000, at

A1; Richard Zitrin, "The Fault Lies in the Ethics Rules," National L. J., July 8, 2001, at A25; Adam Liptak, "A Case that Grew in the Shadows," N.Y. Times, March 24, 2002, at D3.

48. Richard A. Zitrin, "The Case Against Secret Settlements (Or, What You Don't Know *Can* Hurt You)," 2 J. Inst. for the Study of Legal Ethics 115, 116 (1999).

49. Kevin Livingston, Open Secrets, The San Francisco Recorder, May 8, 2001, at 1 (quoting Nancy Moore, reporter for the Commission).

These statutes prohibit courts from granting secrecy orders in cases involving public hazards, such as product defects, medical malpractice, or environmental dangers. A few judicial decisions have also restricted the use of confidentiality agreements.[50] By contrast the ABA Section of Litigation has proposed Guidelines for Negotiation of Settlements in Litigation that expressly recognize the legitimacy of secrecy provisions, including provisions for turning over discovery products such as inculpatory documents.[51] The organized bar, at least at the national level, thus appears opposed to restrictions on confidentiality. Opponents generally claim that such restrictions are unnecessary and unwise; public risks eventually come to light despite settlements incorporating secrecy provisions, and preventing such provisions will deter settlements, fuel lengthy discovery fights, and encourage frivolous copy cat claims.[52] Proponents respond that such adverse consequences have not been demonstrated in states with legislative prohibitions and that substantial harms often occur before certain risks become public.[53] Whether the bar should act in the absence of such legislative prohibitions is likely to remain an issue of ongoing professional debate.

D. Alternative Dispute Resolution

Lawyers have always been involved in dispute resolution processes apart from the adversary system. The vast majority of legal controversies that reach lawyers eventually settle rather than go to trial. Negotiating settlements is therefore a major part of every advocate's undertaking. What distinguishes contemporary practice is a formalization of "ADR" and an emergence of specialists in mediation and arbitration. Interest in these processes has grown rapidly over the last quarter century. A broad range of factors fuel that interest: dissatisfaction with the expense, delays, and contentious nature of adjudication; concerns about undue litigiousness and unequal access to justice; desires for increased client participation, community empowerment, and remedial flexibility; heightened interest in preserving relationships and exploring root causes

---

50. See Martha Neil, "Confidential Settlements Scrutinized," ABA J. July 2002, at 20–21; Eric Frazier, "Judges Veto Sealed Deals," Natl L.J. Aug. 12, 2002 at A1; David Luban, "Settlements and the Public Realm," 83 Geo. L.J. 2619, 2651 n. 126–29, 2652–59 (1995).

51. See ABA/BNA Lawyers' Manual, June 5, 2001, at 346.

52. Frazier, supra note 50, at A11 Arthur R. Miller, "Confidentiality, Protective Orders and Public Access to the Courts," 105 Harv.L.Rev. 427, 480–82 (1991); Reynolds Holding, "Lawyers vs. Businesses: Battle Over Court Settlement Secrecy," San Francisco Chronicle, March 19, 1992, at A1.

53. Frazier, supra note 50, at A11 Luban, supra note 50, at 2652–59.

as well as legal symptoms of problems; and perceived inadequacies in other family, religious, and community institutions for mediating grievances.[54]

Advocates of ADR typically advocate "fitting the forum to the fuss."[55] Their approach assumes that different types of disputes and dispute resolution procedures have distinctive characteristics and should be matched accordingly. Lon Fuller, one of the principal architects of this framework, argued that adjudication was appropriate for cases implicating fundamental rights or unsettled legal principles but that other procedures might be more suitable for routine matters, for parties with ongoing relationships, or for grievances that affect multiple individuals and that do not lend themselves to principled win-lose decisions.[56]

A range of processes has emerged. Some ADR procedures have evolved through private initiatives, while others have developed under federal and state legislation or judicial decrees. For example, the Federal Judicial Improvements Act (Civil Justice Reform Act) of 1990 requires every federal district court to study its caseload and to develop a plan to "facilitate . . . adjudication of civil cases on the merits . . . and ensure just, speedy and inexpensive resolutions of civil disputes."[57] Among the strategies that courts are required to consider is referral of appropriate cases to alternative dispute resolution.

ADR procedures vary along several dimensions:

- *The role of the decision maker or facilitator.* Who selects that individual and by what criteria? What expertise is required?

- *The enforceability of the outcome.* Is the outcome advisory (mediation) or is it binding (arbitration) and, if the latter, is it subject to review?

- *Consent.* Is the procedure voluntary or mandatory?

---

54. See Susan Leeson & Bryan Johnston, Ending It: Dispute Resolution in America (1988); Carrie Menkel-Meadow, "Many Doors? Closing Doors? Alternative Dispute Resolution and Adjudication," 10 Ohio St. J. on Dispute Resolution 211 (1995); David D. Hechler, "ADR Finds True Believers," Nat'l L. J. July 2, 2001, at A1; Lisa Brenner, "What Lawyers Like: Mediation," Nat'l L. J., Nov. 15, 1999, at A1. For a review of issues surrounding ADR, see Rhode & Luban supra note 33, at 751–61.

55. Frank E. A. Sander and Stephen B. Goldberg, "Fitting the Forum to the Fuss: A User–Friendly Guide to Selecting an ADR Procedure," 10 Negotiation J. 49, 67 (1994) (crediting the phrase to Maurice Rosenberg).

56. Lon L. Fuller, "The Forms and Limits of Adjudication," 92 Harv. L. Rev. 353 (1978); Lon L. Fuller, "Mediation—Its Forms and Functions," 44 S. Cal. L. Rev. 305 (1971).

57. 28 U.S.C. § 471. See Federal Judicial Center, Guide to Judicial Management of Cases in ADR (2001).

- *Relationship to the adjudicative system.* Is the procedure connected to a state or federal court system, and if so, does it rely on in-house staff or outside experts who are trained and subsidized by the system?

- *Relationship to the community.* Is the procedure part of a religious or ethnic community's traditional method of dispute resolution?

- *Formality.* Is the procedure formally structured by fixed rules or by agreement of the parties, or is it relatively informal and flexible?

The most common forms of ADR are as follows.

Arbitration. In arbitration, parties submit their dispute to a neutral decision maker, often someone who has particular expertise in the matters at issue. Typically, the arbitrator is chosen by mutual agreement of the contending parties from a list of professionals. Some consumer agencies and industry groups such as the Better Business Bureau also have systems for arbitrating claims. Most states have statutes modeled on the Uniform Arbitration Act, 7 U.L.A. 5 (1985), which govern enforcement of arbitration agreements. Enforcement may also be available under the Federal Arbitration Act, and the Labor Management Relations Act of 1947. Arbiters' judgments are usually final; review is available only in limited scope, generally involving procedural violations. A number of federal and state courts require submission of certain cases to court-annexed arbitration, although parties typically have a right to trial de novo.

Private Adjudication. Some statutes and rules of court permit referral of cases to privately selected and compensated adjudicators, often retired judges. These referral programs, sometimes labeled "rent-a-judge," authorize the private adjudicator's decision to be entered as the judgment of the court. Unlike an arbitrator's award, such a judgment is normally subject to appellate review.

Summary Jury Trials. Under this procedure, lawyers give a summary of their trial presentation to a jury, usually without witnesses or exhibits. The jury then renders a verdict that is not binding, although the jurors are not informed of this fact before reaching their decision. This verdict can assist parties evaluate their claims and negotiate a reasonable settlement.

Mini-trials. Mini-trials, or "structured settlement" negotiations, offer opportunities for lawyers to present an abbreviated version of their case to a decision-making panel. In one common variation, the panel includes a neutral advisor and executives of the opposing parties. The aim is to enable the parties to hear a forceful presentation of their adversary's case. The advisor predicts what would happen if the case were litigated, and the principals then attempt to negotiate a settlement. In some mini-trials, the neutral advisor will render an advisory opinion only if the parties initially fail to reach an agreement.

Early Neutral Evaluation or Expert Evaluation. This technique, which is used both in private dispute resolution and in court-annexed programs, involves reliance on a third party neutral with relevant experience or expertise to evaluate a case. After summary presentations by counsel and the parties, the evaluator assesses the issues in dispute in an effort to facilitate settlement negotiations.

Mediation. Mediation is an informal process in which a neutral third party helps the parties resolve a dispute or structure a transaction. Ordinarily, this third party facilitates but does not impose a solution, and the parties voluntarily choose the mediator. However, some courts require mediation for certain types of cases, such as child custody disputes, and provide a panel of mediators for those cases.

Ombudsperson. Ombudspersons are officials appointed by organizations to prevent, investigate, and informally resolve disputes. In the private sector, ombudspersons function primarily in employer/employee relations, but in the public sector their role is often broader.

Neighborhood Justice Centers. Neighborhood justice centers, citizen complaint bureaus, and other community-based centers function as free-standing institutions or court-affiliated agencies. These organizations typically receive referrals from courts, prosecutors, police, or other community agencies, as well as walk-in clients. Professional mediators or community volunteers with mediation training handle a variety of disputes, including landlord-tenant, family, and neighbor relations.

At the most abstract level, supporters of such alternative dispute resolution share certain common objectives. They join in what then Chief Justice Burger summarized as the true goals of the legal profession: "to gain an acceptable result in the shortest possible time with the least amount of stress and at the lowest possible cost to the client."[58] At the concrete level, however, what constitutes "acceptable" remains a matter of some disagreement, and ADR goals are not always consistent. Conflicts may arise

58. Commission on Professionalism, American Bar Association, In the Spirit of Public Service: A Blueprint for the Rekindling of Lawyer Professionalism 41 (1986) (quoting Chief Justice Warren Burger).

between cost and quality; between enhancing access and reducing congestion and delay; and between facilitating party objectives and societal interests.

These tradeoffs have sparked criticism along several lines. Alternative dispute resolution has been faulted for being both too available and not available enough. Some commentators complain that options such as rent-a-judge or mini-trials are accessible only to the wealthy. In their view, such a market-based structure institutionalizes "legal apartheid"—convenient, speedy justice for the haves and cumbersome, inefficient processes for the have-nots. The existence of a two-track system may reduce pressure to reform the judicial system that makes such alternatives necessary.

Conversely, another group of critics charges that ADR is too available: it is too often imposed on middle and low income clients with "simple" cases or contractual obligations to arbitrate disputes, and it too often offers second-class justice. From this perspective, informal, streamlined structures appear to deprive weaker parties of crucial protections. For example, according to one study, the odds of employers winning in ADR proceedings with employees were five to one. Only repeat players had incentives to investigate the past records and predispositions of ostensibly neutral decision makers, and some of those decision makers had incentives to please sources of future business.[59] So too, mediation between parties with unequal power may reinforce their inequality and encourage negotiation of rights that should be non-negotiable. Cases involving domestic violence pose particular risks.[60]

Although some mediators attempt to mitigate disparities in parties' bargaining capacities, or refuse to ratify settlements that seem clearly unfair, such non-neutral conduct raises its own set of ethical difficulties. Active intervention by ostensibly neutral mediators can compromise their credibility and capacity to achieve solutions. And it can expose participants to manipulation under undisclosed standards and unstructured procedures lacking formal mechanisms of accountability.

A related concern is that informal processes oriented toward private settlements may undervalue society's interest in having

59. Richard C. Reuben, "Lawyer Turns Peacemaker," ABA J., Aug. 1996, at 61; Richard C. Reuben, "The Bias Factor," California Lawyer, Nov. 1999, at 25; See Jeffrey W. Stempel, "Reflections on Judicial ADR and the Multidoor Courthouse at Twenty: Fait Accompli, Failed Overture or Fledgling Adulthood," 11 Ohio State J. in Disp. Resol. 297, 319, 339, 351 (1996).

60. Leigh Goodmark, "Alternative Dispute Resolution and the Potential for Gender Bias," Judges Journal, Spring 2000, at 21; Trina Grillo, "The Mediation Alternative: Process Dangers for Women," 100 Yale L.J. 1545 (1991).

publicly accountable judges interpret and implement publicly acceptable norms. A process geared toward compromise may also provide inadequate deterrence of unlawful conduct. Where ADR decision makers or facilitators need not adhere to formal rules or give reasons for their judgments, the process appears arbitrary in a sense that adjudication does not.[61]

Yet as ADR supporters note, these criticisms often proceed by comparing alternative processes to an idealized image of adjudication. Before denouncing such processes as second-class justice, it is important to inquire whether first class is actually available and for whom. The preferred trial procedure implicit in criticism of ADR is a well-functioning adversary system: each party is assumed to be represented by a competent advocate, making presentations before a competent and disinterested judge. That model is very expensive, for it involves three professionals each with substantial income expectations. Also implicit in a "fair" adversarial procedure is discovery such as that afforded under the Federal Rules of Civil Procedure, which itself is a costly process compared to many ADR hearings. If a jury is also included, there are the additional expenses of assembling and providing for the jury panels. The process is too costly for all but a small percentage of disputes.

What to do about those disputes poses related concerns. Under existing law, wealthy parties can agree to the most expensive forms of ADR or, in ordinary litigation, can spend whatever they consider worthwhile. A vital inquiry, therefore, is whether critics of "second class justice" would want to prohibit wealthier litigants from using their resources for such purposes. A related question is whether there would be any chance of obtaining such a change in the law.

It also bears note that the limited empirical evidence available suggests that in some contexts, parties prefer informal dispute resolution to current alternatives.[62] While parties' satisfaction should not be the sole criteria for evaluation, it is surely relevant.

In evaluating these critiques and defenses of ADR, the safest generalization may be that no single process is necessarily best in all circumstances in accomplishing all dispute resolution objectives. Those objectives include: insuring full disclosure of relevant facts, offering adequate remedies, providing principles and guidance for future cases, encouraging compliance, and fostering confidence and

---

61. Owen M. Fiss, "Against Settlement," 93 Yale L.J. 1073, 1085–87 (1984).

62. Brenner, supra note 46, at A1; Robert J. MacCoun, E. Allan Lind, & Tom R. Tyler, "Alternative Dispute Resolution in Trial and Appellate Courts," in Handbook of Psychology and Law 95, 99–100 (D.K. Kagehiro & W. S. Laufer, eds. 1992).

good relations between the parties. Available research does not establish that either adjudication or ADR is always more effective in realizing any of these objectives.[63] Nor does that research suggest consistent differences between ADR and adjudication in cost, speed, and party satisfaction.[64]

Given that neither ADR nor adjudication is clearly preferable for every context, many experts argue that parties should have a broad range of dispute resolution choices and the information necessary to make them. The public should also have ways to insure that the parties' procedural choices are subject to reasonable constraints based on the societal values at stake. So, for example, many commentators support "multidoor courthouses" that have been established in a growing number of jurisdictions. These court systems allocate different types of cases to "appropriate dispute resolution" processes based on several key criteria: the nature of the controversy; the relationship between the parties; the priorities that the participants attach to various features of the dispute resolution process; and the public interests at issue. Cases involving relatively small monetary damages and the application of settled legal precedents may not justify the expense of full-scale adjudication. In other contexts, the relationship between the parties may argue for ADR procedures that are better able than litigation to address power disparities or to foster long-term working relationships.[65] Some cases, like those involving domestic violence, may be inappropriate for informal dispute resolution.

Support is also increasing for comprehensive ethical rules for ADR practitioners. Not all of these individuals are lawyers and their practices vary considerably concerning issues such as fairness, confidentiality, and conflicts of interest. There are similar variations in the ethical codes drafted by different professional organizations, such as the American Arbitration Association, the Society of Professionals in Dispute Resolution, and the CPR–Georgetown Commission on Ethics and Standards in ADR.[66] Questions remain as to whether all ADR professionals should be held to some uniform standards and, if so, how they should be defined and enforced.

---

63. Marc Galanter & Mia Cahill, "Most Cases Settle: Judicial Promotion and Regulation of Settlements," 46 Stan. L. Rev. 1339, 1388 (1994).

64. Id.; Rhode, supra note 11, at 132–34.

65. Rhode, supra note 11, at 133–34.

66. See CPR—Georgetown Commission on Ethics and Standards in ADR, Proposed Model Rule of Professional Conduct for the Lawyer as Third Party Neutral (Discussion Draft, April1999), and sources cited. See also "Symposium on ADR and the Professional Responsibility of Lawyers," 28 Fordham Urban L.J. 991 (2001).

However, many commentators agree that lawyers should discuss ADR options with their clients and that when lawyers act as third party neutrals, they should be subject to ethical rules analogous to those applicable in other contexts. So, for example, lawyers serving as third party neutrals should exercise independent judgment and disclose all circumstances that might reasonably be perceived to constitute conflicts of interest or to jeopardize their impartiality.[67] The American Bar Association recently amended its Model Rules of Professional Conduct to include a provision governing neutrals. See Model Rule 2.4. Other proposed ethical rules direct lawyers to "discuss confidentiality rules and requirements at the beginning of the proceeding and obtain party consent with respect to any ex parte communication or practice."[68] Whether or not lawyers will become subject to formal ethical rules on such ADR issues, practitioners in this area have an obvious financial and reputational interest in upholding broadly shared norms of fairness and integrity. And the entire legal profession has a stake in addressing legitimate criticism of present dispute resolution procedures.

67. CPR—Georgetown Commission, supra note 66 (Proposed Model Rule 4.5.3).

68. Id., Proposed Model Rule 4.5.2.

Chapter VII

TRANSACTIONAL PRACTICE

A. Introduction

Although the cultural image of the American lawyer is that of a courtroom advocate, in reality, most legal practice occurs in transactional settings. What attorneys do on a day-to-day basis typically involves documentation, counseling, negotiation, and lobbying. Even litigation matters are seldom fully litigated; about 95 percent of all civil and criminal cases settle prior to trial.

The fact that most of lawyers' work occurs outside the structure of court procedure has obvious ethical significance. That point was underscored a half-century ago in a prominent Joint Conference Report on Professional Responsibility by the American Bar Association and the Association of American Law Schools. As the Report noted:

> The most effective realization of the law's aims often takes place in the attorney's office, where litigation is forestalled by anticipating its outcome, where the lawyer's quiet counsel takes place of public force. Contrary to popular belief, the compliance with the law thus brought about is not generally lip-serving and narrow, for by reminding him of its long-run costs the lawyer often deters his client from a course of conduct technically permissible under existing law, though inconsistent with its underlying spirit and purpose.

> Although the lawyer serves the administration of justice indispensably both as advocate and as office counselor, the demands imposed on him by these two roles must be sharply distinguished. The man who has been called into court to answer for his own actions is entitled to a fair hearing. Partisan advocacy plays its essential part in such a hearing, and the lawyer pleading his client's case may properly present it in the most favorable light. A similar resolution of doubts in one direction becomes inappropriate when the lawyer acts as counselor. The reasons that justify and even require partisan advocacy in the trial of a cause do not grant any license to the lawyer to participate as legal adviser in a line of conduct that is immoral, unfair, or of doubtful legality. In saving himself from this unworthy involvement, the lawyer cannot be guided solely by an unreflective inner sense of good faith; he must be at

pains to preserve a sufficient detachment from his client's interests so that he remains capable of a sound and objective appraisal of the propriety of what his client proposes to do.[1]

There is no evidence, nor could there be any systematic data, on the extent to which lawyers in that era provided such "sound and objective appraisal." However, most members of the bar believed in that ideal. Much of the distress within the profession in recent years can be attributed to the recognition that realizing this aspiration today is increasingly difficult. The challenge in attempting to do so is the subject of the materials that follows.

B.　Document Preparation and Retention

Two of lawyers' most critical transactional roles involve documents: creating documents to govern transactions, and crafting policies and practices concerning retention of documents. Documents are of critical importance in a legal relationship because they have formality and particularity far beyond oral communication. Such written materials can create, modify, or negate legal obligations. And a document once created, unlike an oral communication, is permanent proof of its content–unless, of course, the document is destroyed. Hence the phrase "smoking gun."

As Chapter VI notes, most ethical obligations governing lawyers in litigation draw on other law, specifically the law of procedure. That is, ethical rules for litigators seldom go beyond what the law otherwise requires. The same is true of bar standards governing lawyers' transactional work. Ethical rules governing such conduct largely track criminal and civil prohibitions. With respect to preparing documents or providing document-related advice, a lawyer may not "counsel a client to engage, or assist a client, in conduct that the lawyer knows is criminal or fraudulent." Model Rules of Professional Conduct, Rule 1.2(d). See also DR 7–102(A)(7). Nor may a lawyer knowingly "make a false statement of material fact or law to a third person, or fail to disclose a material fact to a third person when disclosure is necessary to avoid assisting a criminal or fraudulent act, unless disclosure is prohibited by [the rule governing client confidences]." Model Rule 4.1. See also DR 7–102. In essence, the rules governing documentation simply incorporate the background law of fraudulent misrepresentation.

With respect to document production and retention, Rule 3.4 of the Model Rules provides that lawyers may not "unlawfully ob-

---

1. Lon L. Fuller & John D. Randall, "Professional Responsibility: Report of the Joint Conference," 44 ABA J. 1159, 1161 (1958).

struct another party's access to evidence or unlawfully alter, destroy or conceal a document or other material having potential evidentiary value." DR 7–109 of the Code of Professional Responsibility similarly prohibits lawyers from suppressing any evidence that they or their clients have a legal obligation to reveal. Both the Code and the Model Rules also prohibit conduct "prejudicial to the administration of justice," which would include unlawful document destruction. Model Rule 8.4 and DR 1–102(A).

These rules, although clear in their intended purpose, can be difficult to interpret in practice. Part of the problem involves indeterminacies in the law of fraud as applied to particular transactions. Whether statements are materially misleading, or whether disclosures are necessary to prevent a third party's misapprehension of a material fact, often may be open to dispute. So too, although many state, local, and federal laws regarding document retention are unambiguous, others leave room for argument about their applicability in a particular setting. Typically, these provisions prohibit destruction or concealment only if the individual believes that an official proceeding is pending or about to be instituted.[2] If a lawyer discovers documents establishing that a client is liable to a third party, but does not know with certainty whether that party will file suit, then it will be arguable whether the documents must be retained. Similar ambiguities may arise concerning the level of factual certainty required before a lawyer "knows" that the client is engaging in fraud.

In resolving these ambiguities, prudent lawyers generally consider pragmatic as well as ethical considerations. In many transactional contexts, one of lawyers' primary functions is to provide assurances that the matter complies with all legal requirements. In some instances, those assurances must explicitly be based on some kind of inquiry or investigation conducted by the lawyer. Such an inquiry is often referred to as one involving "due diligence," that is, one conducted with thoroughness appropriate to the situation. In other circumstances, a third party's reasonable reliance will create similar obligations. Lawyers who do not responsibly perform this gatekeeping role risk being held accountable by government regulators or defrauded parties. Even if lawyers ultimately manage to escape legal liability, the financial, psychological, and reputational costs of their defense are likely to be substantial.

---

2. See e.g., Model Penal Code § 241.7 (1962). Other jurisdictions prohibit destruction or concealment if the material is relevant to pending criminal proceedings or to any ongoing investigation. Thousands of state, federal, and local laws require retention of certain records for specified periods. See Deborah L. Rhode & David Luban, Legal Ethics 281, 285–86 (3d ed. 2001).

So too, the risks to clients of arguably illegal conduct may be greater than they anticipate, and lawyers play an important role in persuasively communicating those risks. If, for example, relevant documents are destroyed when a legal proceeding is clearly foreseeable, the judge and jury may be permitted to draw adverse inferences about their contents. In many cases, those inferences will be more damaging than the contents themselves. Compromising documents can sometimes be explained; the intentional destruction of documents removes that possibility. Moreover, in an age of widespread photocopying and electronic transmission, it can be difficult to destroy all copies of inculpating material. Unsuccessful efforts to do so are likely to be extremely damaging for all concerned, including lawyers.[3] One crucial counseling function is to help clients establish appropriate document retention policies that will ensure conformity with applicable laws while avoiding unnecessary storage.

C. Counseling

Bar ethical rules on counseling again mirror broader civil and criminal prohibitions. A lawyer "shall not counsel a client to engage, or assist a client, in conduct that the lawyer knows is criminal or fraudulent, but a lawyer may discuss the legal consequences of any proposed course of conduct. . . ." Model Rules, Rule 1.2(d). See also DR 7–102(A)(7). If lawyers discover that a client is engaging in criminal or fraudulent conduct, they must avoid any assistance and withdraw from the representation. The Comment adds: "In some cases, withdrawal alone might be insufficient. It may be necessary for the lawyer to give notice of the fact of withdrawal and disaffirm any opinion, document, affirmation or the like." Model Rules, Rule 1.2 Comment, and Rule 1.16(a). In providing legal advice, "a lawyer may refer not only to law but to other considerations such as moral, economic, social, and political factors, that may be relevant to the client's situation." Model Rules, Rule 2.1.

Some evidence suggests that clients are more likely to welcome non-legal advice than lawyers often assume. For example, in one study, corporate executives and corporate counsel were asked how frequently lawyers should limit their opinions to what they think the law is rather than the action that they think the company

---

3. For examples, see Ralph Nader and Wesley J. Smith, No Contest: Corporate Lawyers and the Perversion of Justice in America 141–57 (1996). C. Evan Stewart, "Andersen: Renewing Ethics of Document Shredding," N.Y. Law J., Apr. 15, 2002, at col. 1; Myron Levin, "British American Tobacco Admits Destroying Files: Cancer Victim Wins Damages," L.A. Times, Apr. 12, 2002, at C3.

should or should not take. Clients' answers clustered between "rarely" and "sometimes"; lawyers' answers clustered between "sometimes" and "often."[4]

Other research suggests that nonlegal advice will be most acceptable when it is framed in pragmatic rather than moral terms.[5] Private practitioners rarely report giving advice that expressly invokes "the public interest."[6] Yet concerns about public welfare will often inform even the most pragmatic "bottom line" counseling. By exploring the full costs of ethically dubious conduct, such as adverse publicity, loss of reputation, and risks of litigation, lawyers frequently demonstrate that the "right" course of conduct is also the economically prudent one.[7]

The most difficult dilemmas in counseling arise when that form of persuasion falls short. Such dilemmas require analysis on two levels. First, how does a lawyer, or any decision maker, determine the propriety of particular conduct when competing values are involved? Second, under what, if any, circumstances, should lawyers decline to assist client conduct that they find morally objectionable? Little in abstract ethical philosophy provides concrete guidance concerning these issues. There is, of course, agreement on some general principles: that dishonesty and theft are wrong and that unnecessary harm to third parties should be avoided. But, to borrow the celebrated phrase from Justice Oliver Wendell Holmes, "general principles do not decide concrete cases." In this respect, ethics in professional practice is no different from ethics in ordinary life; in both spheres the "right thing to do" usually depends on circumstances.

Since counseling issues cannot be resolved in the abstract, it is helpful to consider some concrete factual contexts. For example, how should lawyers respond when they believe that a corporate client is selling products, permitting workplace conditions, or releasing industrial pollutants that are not clearly unlawful but that pose excessive safety risks? What should lawyers do if management decides to permit regulatory violations that are unlikely to result in detection or serious sanctions? These problems are most likely to arise in circumstances where legal standards are set too low due to

---

4. Edward A. Dauer, "Attorneys Underestimate Clients' Desire for Business Involvement, Survey Shows," Preventive Law Reporter, Dec. 1988, at 19.

5. Robert Jackall, Moral Mazes: The World of Corporate Managers 108–24 (1988); Rhode & Luban, supra note 2, at 348–59.

6. Robert L. Nelson, "Ideology, Practice, and Professional Autonomy: Social Values and Client Relationships in the Large Law Firm," 37 Stan. L. Rev. 503, 533 (1985).

7. See e.g. Lynn Sharp Paine, "Moral Thinking in Management: An Essential Capability," in Ethics in Practice 59 (Deborah L. Rhode ed., 2000).

lack of information or political leverage, or where enforcement is too infrequent due to inadequate regulatory resources or difficulties in policing compliance.

Such examples come from corporate practice, but similar problems arise in representing individuals. For example, what are a lawyer's responsibilities if a client wants to sell property with problems that the buyer has not discovered? Or what if a client wants to buy property from a needy retired couple at a modest price when the lawyer knows that an imminent zoning change will make the property much more valuable? Should lawyers ever refuse to assist transactions that comply with the letter of the law but that frustrate its objectives?

In a recent speech at a Securities and Exchange Commission Conference, the Commission's chair, Harvey L. Pitt addressed some of these counseling issues. His remarks endorsed a view of lawyers' ethical obligations consistent with the ABA–AALS report quoted earlier. According to Pitt:

> Lawyers are paid, and are professionally obligated, to advocate legitimate views and interests of their clients, with emphasis on the word "legitimate".... [E]xperience teaches it is inappropriate for corporate lawyers to assist clients in finding ways to evade legal requirements, or disserve the public interest, even if those results can be achieved in a manner arguably within the literal letter of the law.[8]

This statement provoked immediate controversy. Critics wondered what "experience" Mr. Pitt was referring to, to what "disserve the public interest" really meant, and how lawyers were supposed to know. If in doubt, who should they ask? "Their rabbi?" "Harvey Pitt"?[9] In critics' view, clients are entitled to information about the letter of the law and to decide for themselves whether to press its limits. If lawyers believe that such conduct would be unwise, they are "free to share that advice." But if the public is ill served when clients comply only with the letter of the law, then critics believe that "the answer is to change the letter, not change the ethical foundations of lawyering."[10]

A serious difficulty, of course, is that changing the law may require information and political leverage that are unlikely to be forthcoming in time to avert serious harm. The question then

---

8. Harvey L. Pitt, Remarks at SEC Speaker Conference (Feb. 22, 2002). See also Harvey L. Pitt, Remarks before the American Bar Association, Aug. 12, 2002.

9. Lawrence J. Fox, "This Idea Is the Pitts," U. Ill. L. Rev (forthcoming 2002).

10. Id.

becomes under what, if any, circumstances do lawyers have the responsibility to make their own assessments of the public interest and to determine an appropriate response.

As discussion in Chapter VIII notes, lawyers representing organizations are obligated to represent the entity, not any of its constituent members. In some instances, where illegal conduct is involved, that obligation may entail seeking reconsideration of managerial decisions by the organization's highest authority. See Model Rule 1.13 the federal Sarbanes-Okley Act of 2002. A central issue is what lawyers should do when the conduct is not clearly illegal or when the highest authority acts in ways that the lawyer believes will compromise public interests.

In considering that issue, the first question is whether lawyers in a particular context can come to a satisfactory determination of what the public interest in fact requires. That in turn will often depend on the clarity of information available and the nature and importance of the values at stake. Consider, for example, how lawyers could assess the appropriate level of safety for client products, working conditions, or industrial pollutants. Modifications that would increase safety are generally available, but at a significant cost. One conventional way to analyze the issue is from a utilitarian standpoint, weighing the full costs and benefits of plausible alternatives. Although clear in principle, this approach is generally indeterminate in practice, given the ambiguities inherent in estimating and valuing benefits and risks. For example, should the safety of an automobile be assessed in terms of a particularly risky feature, or the overall performance of the car compared with its competitors? In some celebrated cases involving automobile gas tanks that exploded in low speed collisions, the subcompact cars at issue had generally good safety records in comparison with other cars in the same price range but performed much worse in the relatively infrequent circumstances of rear end collisions.[11]

A related problem involves quantifying consequences. For example, if particular safety decisions impose some increased risk of fatalities, what price should be placed on human life? Federal agencies operate with widely varying figures ranging from under $100,000 to over $100 million.[12] Jury verdicts also reflect significant variations that partly depend on the age, gender, race, and earning

---

11. Gary T. Schwartz, "The Myth of the Ford Pinto Case," 43 Rutgers L. Rev. 1013, 1032 (1992).

12. Marianne Lavalle, "Placing a Price on Human Life," Nat'l L. J., Oct. 10, 1988, at 26–28 (comparing for example, a decision on space heaters by the Consumer Protection Safety Commission with a pesticide ban by the Food and Drug Administration).

potential of the victim. A very different measure comes from the value that individuals place on their own lives, estimated by the salary premiums that they demand for dangerous working conditions. [13]

Further indeterminacies arise in quantifying other costs that may result from unsafe products, working conditions, or industrial pollutants, such as impaired reputation from high visibility litigation, or diminished quality of life for workers and community residents. By the same token, the long-term price of safety improvements may be equally hard to predict. That price would need to take into account not only the direct costs of modification, but also the indirect costs associated with lower profits and higher prices, such as lost sales, jobs, and stock value. Those outcomes may have further ripple effects that are even harder to assess, such as loss of pension savings and increased risks of plant closings, with all their attendant costs for workers, their families, and their communities.

Another difficulty in applying a cost-benefit analysis involves the distance between those who make the calculation and those whose welfare is at issue. Responsibility for such calculations always rests with someone in authority, typically business managers or public officials. The individuals whose welfare is at stake usually are far lower down in the hierarchy. The difference in views between these groups is often reflected in jury verdicts and in the reaction to those verdicts by corporate decision makers. Those who occupy leadership positions often view jury awards as "irresponsibly high." The discrepancy between public and professional views is also reflected in elected officials' extreme reluctance to address such issues explicitly. These individuals, who hold office by vote of ordinary people but who often take substantial campaign contributions from business leaders, often see little to gain from direct confrontation with cost/safety tradeoffs. The result is a high degree of abstraction, or euphemisms about "adequate" protection.

Given the indeterminacies of cost-benefit calculations, and the perceived callousness that quantification of consequences may imply, American lawmakers are often drawn to three alternatives. One approach is to adopt highly protective standards with little expectation that they will be widely observed or enforced. A familiar example is the 55 mile-per-hour speed limit that purportedly governs highways on which everyone in fact drives at 65 or 70 miles per hour. Other examples are the elaborate written warning requirements that almost no one reads concerning products like household cleansers or power tools. Of course, the trouble with

13. See Rhode & Luban, supra note 2, at 331.

rules that are widely ignored is that full enforcement is impractical and selective enforcement depends on administrative discretion, litigation resources, or both. In form, these regulations provide "equal protection" for everyone; in practice, their impact is uneven, and mediated by lawyers as government officials, corporate counsel, and litigators on behalf of injured parties.

A second approach is to dilute rigorous requirements with highly technical exceptions. The federal income tax law exemplifies this technique, where high nominal rates are offset by all kinds of credits, deferrals, and exemptions. The impact of these standards often depends on gaining assistance from professionals willing to exploit loopholes or the low risk of serious sanctions.

A third regulatory strategy is to impose elaborate procedural requirements in enforcement. These include such requirements as prompt notice, formal complaints, extensive discovery, rights to counsel, trial, appeal, and, more recently, mandatory mediation. Under this approach, the role of lawyers in navigating the process becomes critical. Elaborate procedure is both a part of the regulatory deterrent (from the viewpoint of the regulatory authorities) and a means of avoiding or blunting the impact of the rules (from the viewpoint of the actor being regulated).

All three approaches–demanding requirements but extensive exceptions and elaborate procedures–distinctively require lawyers for their interpretation and application. Their very technicality may diffuse or obliterate the moral foundations of the regulation. A familiar ethics hypothetical makes the point: Is it immoral or anti-social for a truck company to use schedules requiring its drivers to travel above the fifty-five mph speed limit on roads where the average speed is actually sixty-five? What advice should a morally sensitive lawyer give to clients worried about their ability to survive in increasingly competitive transportation markets?

Yet while many situations raising such ethical issues may not yield any single "right" answer, some answers will be better than others–more respectful of the available evidence and more responsive to all the values at issue. Lawyers have assisted client actions that many disinterested decision makers have found difficult to reconcile with accepted ethical principles or any coherent notion of public interests. Commonly cited examples involve the attorneys who were active, sometimes "cheerful abettors" of conduct such as: the distribution of hazardous Dalkon shields; the suppression of information related to tobacco and asbestos health risks; and the financially irresponsible transactions of many savings and loans institutions and corporate giants like Enron.[14] The question that these cases raise is whether lawyers who would find such conduct morally problematic have some obligation to withhold their assistance.

Bar ethical rules recognize lawyers' right to decline representation or to withdraw from cases that they find "repugnant" or "with which [they have] a fundamental disagreement." Model Rule 1.16, Comment; See DR 1–110(c). Whether they have a moral responsibility to do so is a more difficult question on which the profession has long been divided. American legal ethics commentators in the first half of the nineteenth century maintained that lawyers had an obligation to refrain from pursuing unjust causes at least in certain contexts.[15] Some contemporary commentators take a similar position.[16] In making the case for "compliance counseling," Professor Robert Gordon notes:

> Suppose the legal rule is clear, yet the chance of detecting violations low, the penalties small in relation to the gains from noncompliance, or the terrorizing of regulators into settlement by a deluge of paper predictably easy. The mass of lawyers who advise and then assist with noncompliance in such a situation could, in the vigorous pursuit of their clients' interests, effectively nullify the laws. The only justification for their doing so would have to be their confidence that the system was self-equilibrating, so that some countervailing force would operate to offset their efforts. But such confidence is unfounded. . . .
>
> [T]he critic then says: all right, lawyers play legitimate roles in [encouraging legal compliance but they] have no right to intrude their opinions, their influence, their political values. They are neither elected officials nor their agents; lawyers have

14. Robert W. Gordon, "A Collective Failure of Nerve: The Bar's Response to Kaye Scholer," 23 Law & Soc. Inquiry 315, 316 (1998); see Deborah L. Rhode, In the Interests of Justice (2002); Nader & Smith, supra note 3; Bruce A. Green, "Thoughts About Corporate Lawyers After Reading the Cigarette Papers: The Wise Counselor Gives Way to the Hired Gun," 51 DePaul L. Rev. 407 (2001);William H. Simon, "The Kaye Scholer Affair: The Lawyer's Duty of Candor and the Bar's Temptations of Evasion and Apology," 23 Law and Soc. Inquiry 243 (1998); Robert Gordon, "Portrait of a Profession in Paralysis," 54 Stan. L. Rev. 1425 (2002); Deborah L. Rhode & Paul Patton, Lawyers, Ethics, and Enron, Stan.J. L. Bus. & Finance (forthcoming 2003).

15. David Hoffman, Fifty Resolutions in Regard to Professional Deportment in A Course of Legal Study (2d ed. 1836). George Sharswood, Essay on Professional Ethics (1854).

16. David Luban, Lawyers and Justice: An Ethical Study (1988); Rhode, supra note 14; William H. Simon, The Practice of Justice: A Theory of Lawyers' Ethics (1998). For an overview, see Deborah L. Rhode, "The Profession and the Public Interest," 54 Stan. L. Rev. 1499 (2002).

no special authority to go around telling people how they should behave.

The traditional response to this is simple: lawyers do indeed have an official status as licensed fiduciaries for the public interest, charged with encouraging compliance with legal norms. In contexts like counseling, where there is no official third party like a judge to oversee the interaction between the client and the state, the lawyer is not only supposed to predict the empirical consequences of certain behavior, but also to represent the viewpoint of the legal system to the client. Lawyers can't coerce anyone; they can only advise and persuade, sometimes only under the threat of resignation rather than disclosure. Surely the right of the lawyer to encourage compliance with the law's purposes through persuasion is at least as clear as the client's right to demand the lawyer's help in exploiting the law's ambiguities and procedural opportunities and in engaging in strategic behavior designed to evade the law. The other and even better response to the critic is that even conceding that lawyers have no special authority to guide their clients, neither do they have any special immunity from responsibility for the things they help their clients do....[17]

Other commentators believe that such an assumption of power is unwarranted. If lawyers threaten to withdraw from representation when their ethical advice is not taken, "the result is a reversal of the underlying structure of responsibility for the ... conduct. The adviser become the ultimate arbiter and the client a subordinate."[18] And if lawyers do withdraw, there is always the risk that their successors will be worse.

These concerns, while not without force, are not always conclusive. As Chapter VI suggested, unless the lawyer is the last in town, his or her advice may not be peremptory. Rather, it may simply require a client to reassess the conduct at issue or to assume the financial and psychological costs of finding alternative counsel. And as moral philosophers note, the risk of a less ethical replacement may be relevant but not determinative of an individual's own

---

17. Robert W. Gordon, "The Independence of Lawyers," 68 B.U. L. Rev. 1, 72–73 (1988); see also Robert W. Gordon, Why Lawyers Can't Just be Hired Guns, in Ethics in Practice, supra note 7, at 42.

18. Geoffrey C. Hazard, Jr., Ethics in the Practice of Law, 136, 143–45 (1978). For similar views, see Lee A. Casey & David B. Rivkin, Jr., "Devil's Advocate: The Danger of Judging Lawyers by their Clients," Policy Rev., Feb.-March 2002, at 15; Ted Schneyer, "Reforming Law Practice in the Pursuit of Justice: The Perils of Privileging 'Public' Over Professional Values," 70 Fordham L. Rev. 1831 (2002); Monroe H. Freedman, "How Lawyers Act in the Interests of Justice," 70 Fordham. L. Rev. 1717 (2002).

responsibility. For example, we would not exonerate those who assisted Nazi genocide efforts or the 9/11 terrorist attacks on the ground that their successors would have been worse.

Withdrawal from representation is, of course, an unpalatable prospect for all concerned, and it should come as no surprise that lawyers rarely report refusing a matter on ethical grounds.[19] For obvious reasons, lawyers generally choose clients and practice settings that are likely to minimize moral conflicts. Economic and psychological pressures also encourage practitioners to evaluate information and arguments in ways that avoid such conflicts. As social science research makes clear, individuals who are assigned a particular position become more likely to believe in its validity, and those who have a self-interest in a given practice become more likely to interpret and recall facts in a manner that supports their position.[20] Yet by the same token, lawyers who have less personal stake in a particular decision than their clients will be able to evaluate its ethical implications from a more disinterested perspective. And where important values are at issue, lawyers have the right, and many argue the responsibility, to act in accordance with their own convictions.

Underlying some of these issues are broader questions of political morality. The example of the fifty-five mph speed limit is familiar, but the ramifications often are not fully considered by lawmakers. Such a rule makes it primarily a matter of discretion on the part of the police as to who will be stopped and charged. That discretion in turn invites exercise of similar discretion by the prosecution and by the judges in the lower courts. It also can lead indirectly to patterns of discrimination, for example, racial profiling in arrest patterns. Consequences of that kind diminish confidence in the integrity of the law itself, and invite charges of systematic hypocrisy. Thus, some surveys indicate widespread belief in a perverse version of the Golden Rule: "Those with the gold make the rules." Certainly, those with the gold are in the best position to hire lawyers to influence, manipulate, or evade the pervasive rules characteristic of modern government. And that political reality raises the stakes in debates over the lawyer's counseling role.

19. Nelson, supra note 6, at 535–37.

20. See sources cited in Rhode, supra note 2, at n. 45; Thomas Gilovich, How We Know What Isn't So: The Fallibility of Reason in Everyday Life 80 (1991). For discussion of how lawyers' cognitive biases implicate them in unethical conduct, see David Luban, "The Ethics of Wrongful Obedience," in Ethics in Practice, supra note 7, at 95; and Douglas C. Langevoort, "Where Were the Lawyers? A Behavioral Inquiry into Lawyers' Responsibility for Client Fraud," 46 Vand. L. Rev. 75 (1993).

D. Paternalism

Some transactional dilemmas involve issues of paternalism. Here the ethical problem arises not because lawyers' values are inconsistent with clients' interests, but because lawyers believe that clients misperceive their own interests. Where clients appear incapable of rational decision making, or simply are bent on imprudent courses of action, lawyers face a difficult issue. Clearly they can give advice about the wisdom about the client's proposed decision. The hard question is determining the point at which advice becomes unacceptably paternalistic, i.e., inappropriately manipulative or coercive.

At some point, a lawyer may withdraw from a representation if the client proposes a course of conduct that the lawyer regards as foolish (for example, refusing a generous settlement offer). In Model Rule 1.16 as originally drafted, the formulation for withdrawal on this basis was "imprudent;" but the ABA has now adopted the term "fundamental disagreement." The precise formulation is, however, less important than the way it is interpreted in specific circumstances. Relevant facts include not only financial implications but also moral and psychological concerns, including the attitudes of clients (such as the importance of personal vindication), and the attitudes of the lawyer (such as the reluctance to get bogged down in a hopeless cause).

Bar ethical codes also include rules designed to protect clients from decisions that are inherently likely to prove prejudicial or susceptible to improper lawyer influence. So, for example, clients may not prospectively waive rights to sue for malpractice unless they have independent representation, and may not have their lawyer prepare a will that includes a bequest for the lawyer. Model Rule 1.8(h) and (c); DR 6–102(A). As Chapter VIII's discussion of conflicts of interest notes, the point of such rules is not only to protect clients but also to preserve public confidence in the profession.

Another ethical rule, Model Rule 1.14, provides protection and guidance where clients have "diminished capacity." Under its terms:

(a) When a client's capacity to make adequately considered decisions in connection with a representation is diminished, whether because of minority, mental impairment or for some other reason, the lawyer shall, as far as reasonably possible, maintain a normal client-lawyer relationship with the client.

(b) When the lawyer reasonably believes that the client has diminished capacity, is at risk of substantial physical, financial or other harm unless action is taken and cannot adequately act in the client's own interest, the lawyer may take reasonably necessary protective action, including consulting with individuals or entities that have the ability to take action to protect the client and, in appropriate cases, seeking the appointment of a guardian ad litem, conservator, or guardian.

Yet what constitutes a "considered decision" or appropriate "protective action" are matters open to dispute. Since such issues cannot be resolved in the abstract, it is helpful to consider several concrete examples. How should a lawyer handle the following situations?

- In a capital case, a defendant who has been declared competent wants to forego a valid appeal because he believes that he should atone for another crime he committed in an earlier life, and because he believes that he will be reincarnated after his execution.

- An elderly man with incurable cancer wants to rewrite his will and leave his entire estate to a church-of-faith healer who has been supportive but who does not appear to have exercised "undue influence."

- An employee with serious but intermittent mental health difficulties will not accept disability leave or insurance coverage because he believes that it will imply that he is "crazy."

- A sixteen-year-old girl wants to remain in an abusive family situation because she believes that she can handle the abuse by her stepfather, and that, if she discloses it, either her mother won't believe her or it will break up the family and force her into an institution or a foster care situation that would be worse.[21]

The literature on paternalism suggests a number of approaches to these issues. Moral theorist Dennis Thompson proposes a three part test for justifiable interference with an individual's choices: "First, the decision-making capacity of the person who is to be constrained must be *impaired*.... Second, the restriction is as *limited* as possible.... Finally, the restriction prevents serious and

---

21. All of these hypotheticals are based on actual cases. For discussion of Gary Gilmore, who attempted to fire his attorneys after they filed an appeal over his objection. See Norman Mailer, The Executioner's Song 482, 505–06 (1979). See also State v. Berry, 706 N.E.2d 1273 (Ohio 1999) (denying defense attorney's motion to review the competency of a death row inmate who desired abandonment of all appeals).

irreversible *harm.*"[22] Yet each of the highlighted terms–*impaired*
decision, *limited* restriction, and *serious irreversible harm*– is clearly indeterminate across a wide range of situations. Moreover, even
where individuals' decision making capacities are generally unim-
paired, their ability to make a particular choice may be clouded.

Another way to approach these situation-specific incapacities is
what theorists sometimes describe as "hypothetical context."

> [S]ince we are all aware of our irrational propensities, deficien-
> cies in cognitive and emotive capacities, and avoidable and
> unavoidable ignorance it is rational and prudent for us to in
> effect take out "social insurance policies." We may argue for
> and against proposed paternalistic measures in terms of what
> fully rational individuals would accept as forms of protection.[23]

That is, we ask what people *would* consent to if they were fully
rational. Under this approach, hypothetical consent becomes the
touchstone of justifiable paternalism.

The difficulty here, of course, is that we do not know exactly
what "fully rational individuals" would consent to. None of us,
after all, is fully rational under all circumstances.[24] Accordingly,
some theorists propose a third approach, a contextual, ad hoc
paternalism, that attempts to determine whether a particular
choice is consistent with the individuals' core commitments and
concerns. So for example, Professor David Luban argues that
paternalism is justified to protect clients' long term values or
objective interests (such as money or freedom) against momentary
wants or whims. However, paternalism is not justified if choices
that are seemingly contrary to clients' objective interests are rooted
in their deeply held values.[25]

Of course, this approach still requires lawyers to make a
decision that is inevitably influenced by their own values and life
experience. It also entails knowledge about clients' values. Clearly,
lawyers need some criteria for assessing decision-making capacity
apart from the perceived merits of the decision at issue. Otherwise,
the inquiry will become circular: a client who made a seemingly

---

22. Dennis Thompson, "Paternalism
in Modern Law and Public Policy," in
Ethics Teaching in Higher Education
246, 250–51 (Dennis Callahan & Sissela
Bok eds., 1980).

23. Gerald Dworkin, "Paternalism,"
in Morality and the Law 120 (Richard A.
Wasserstrom, ed., 1971).

24. For a critique of hypothetical
consent, see David Luban, "Paternalism
and the Legal Profession," 1981 Wis. L.
Rev. 454, 463–67. For discussion of the
paternalism reflected in bar ethics rules,
see Fred C. Zacharias, "Limits on Client
Autonomy in Legal Ethics Regulation,"
81 Boston U. L. Rev. 198 (2001).

25. Luban, supra note 24, at 367–74.

"irrational" judgment could be deemed incompetent, and an incompetent client could be deemed incapable of rational judgment.[26]

Practitioners who work with clients under some disability have identified a number of criteria for assessing their decision making capabilities and the need for paternalistic intervention. For example, lawyers representing elderly patients should consider factors such as: clients' ability to articulate the reasons behind a decision; the variability in their mental state; their appreciation of the consequences of a particular decision; the substantive fairness of the outcome; and its consistency with their lifetime commitments.[27] Lawyers representing juveniles should similarly take into account issues such as the risks of a "wrong" decision and the minor's age, mental capacity, psychological stability, strength of preferences, and ability to make rational, consistent judgments without undue influence by others.[28]

Certain factors may be more important than others, depending on the context. The ABA Standards of Practice for Lawyers who Represent Children in Abuse and Neglect Cases (1996) recognizes as much. Standard B–4 provides that the attorney generally should "respect the child's expressed preference and follow the child's directions throughout the course of litigation." However, Standard B–4(3) adds:

> If the child's attorney determines that the child's expressed preference would be seriously injurious to the child (as opposed to merely being contrary to the lawyer's opinion of what would be in the child's interest), the lawyer may request appointment of a separate guardian ad litem and continue to represent the child's expressed preference ... The child's attorney shall not reveal the basis of the request for appointment of a guardian ad litem which would compromise the client's position.

26. Rhode & Luban, supra note 2, at 601; Thompson, supra note 22, at 252; Paul R. Tremblay, "On Persuasion and Paternalism: Lawyer Decisionmaking and the Questionably Competent Client," 3 Utah L. Rev. 515, 533–38 (1987).

27. Peter Margulies, "Access, Connection and Voice: A Contextual Approach to Representing Senior Citizens of Questionable Capacity," 62 Fordham L. Rev. 1073, 1084–85 (1994). See also Jan Ellen Rein, "Clients With Destructive and Socially Harmful Choices— What's an Attorney To Do? Within and Beyond the Competency Construct," 62 Fordham L. Rev. 1101, 1108 (1994).

28. Peter Margulies, "The Lawyer as Caregiver: Child Clients' Competence in Context," 64 Fordham L. Rev. 1473, 1487–93 (1996); Willard Gaylin, The "Competence" of Children: No Longer All or None, 21 J. Am. Acad. Child Psychiatry 153 (1982); David R. Katner, "Coming to Praise, Not to Bury, the New ABA Standards of Practice for Lawyers Who Represent Children in Abuse and Neglect Cases," 14 Geo. J. Legal Ethics 103, 113 (2000).

The Comment to this provision notes that one of the "most difficult ethical issues for lawyers representing children occurs when the child is able to express a position ... that could result in serious injury." This is particularly likely when the child desires to "live in a dangerous situation ... rather than risk the unknown world of a foster home or other out-of-home placement." The difficulty will not be resolved by appointment of a guardian ad litem if the child chooses not to disclose the dangerous situation. Under such circumstances, a conscientious counselor might take advantage of the discretion provided under Model Rule 1.14 and pursue other "protective action" reasonably necessary to protect the child as well as any siblings exposed to an abusive environment.

As these examples suggest, effective counseling for clients under a disability may sometimes require therapeutic skills and knowledge about a client that are beyond what a particular lawyer can supply.[29] One of the most important characteristics of conscientious advisors is an understanding of their own limitations and a willingness to seek assistance from others, such as social workers, mental health professionals, family, friends, and coworkers. Such assistance may also be important to protect lawyers' own interests; there is always the risk of later recriminations, sometimes litigation, claiming that the lawyer exercised "undue influence" over the client. Practitioners who represent an individual with diminished capacity have a special obligation to ensure that they have adequate expertise, or that they affiliate with other professionals who do.

E. Negotiation

Few areas are more central in legal practice than negotiation. Bargaining is a mainstay not only in dispute resolution and transactional planning on behalf of clients, but also in lawyers' own workplace relationships. Legal practice requires negotiation not just with opposing counsel, but also with clients, colleagues, supervisors, support staff, and court personnel. Because so much bargaining takes place in settings that lack formal structures of accountability, lawyers' own ethical norms play a critical role.

These norms vary among individuals and across practice settings. The following factors are especially relevant.

- *Relationships between the Participants*

29. See Jean Koh Peters, "The Roles and Content of Best Interests in Client–Directed Lawyering for Children in Child Protective Proceedings," 64 Fordham L. Rev. 1505 (1996); Bruce A. Green and Bernadine Dohrn, "Foreword: Children and the Ethical Practice of Law," 64 Fordham L. Rev. 1281 (1996).

Do the parties have ongoing business or personal relationships, or is the negotiation a one-shot transaction? Do the
lawyers have a continuing relationship? How will particular bargaining tactics affect their reputations and future
dealings?

● *Legal and Social Context*

What are the legal and community norms that govern the
transaction? Do they establish any substantive standards
for fairness? Will the outcome be reviewed by a court or
neutral third party? What are the norms and expectations
of the relevant legal culture?

● *Relative Bargaining Strength*

What are the resources of the parties and their lawyers in
terms of time, money, information, and expertise?

● Personal Characteristics

What are the ethical values, bargaining styles and tolerance for risk of the parties and their lawyers?

To take an obvious example, the level of candor and cooperation in
divorce negotiations will be affected by the likelihood of significant
future dealings between the parties and their lawyers; the need to
comply with specific child support guidelines and obtain judicial
approval of the settlement; the financial stakes involved; the
clients' capacities to subsidize protracted proceedings; the degree of
acrimony and risk averseness among the participants; and the role
orientation of the lawyers (whether they see themselves as "bomb-
ers" or as "problem solvers").

Not only are there substantial differences in negotiation contexts, there are also substantial differences over negotiation principles. As subsequent discussion indicates, surveys of both practitioners and legal ethics experts reveal sharp disagreements on issues
such as disclosure of material information and fairness to other
parties. These disagreements, in turn, help explain why ethical
rules governing negotiation generally do not extend beyond civil
law prohibitions on crime and fraud.

Model Rule 4.1 of the Model Rules of Professional Conduct
provides the primary standard. It prohibits a lawyer from knowingly making a "false statement of material fact or law," and from
knowingly "fail[ing] to disclose a material fact when disclosure is
necessary to avoid assisting a criminal or fraudulent act by a
client" unless disclosure is prohibited by rules governing confidential information. See also DR 7–102 (A)(5). On its face, this Rule

apparently forbids lying to an adversary in a negotiation. However, the Comment to Rule 4.1 adds:

> Whether a particular statement should be regarded as one of fact can depend on the circumstances. Under generally accepted conventions in negotiation, certain types of statements ordinarily are not taken as statements of material fact. Estimates of price or value placed on the subject of a transaction and a party's intentions as to an acceptable settlement of a claim are ordinarily in this category. . . .

An earlier version of this rule proposed by the Commission that drafted the Model Rules would have provided a more demanding standard. It would have added requirements that "in conducting negotiations, a lawyer shall be fair in dealing with other participants" and that a lawyer must disclose a material fact "necessary to correct a manifest misapprehension of fact or law resulting from a previous representation made by the lawyer or known by the lawyer to have been made by the client. . . ."[30] This disclosure requirement paralleled provisions in the Restatement (Second) of Contracts and the Restatement (Second) of Agency, which provide for voiding the transaction or holding agents civilly liable for nondisclosure under similar circumstances.

The proposed Model Rule additions were withdrawn in response to overwhelming opposition from the organized bar. Underlying that opposition were several concerns. Some attorneys appeared reluctant to accept any regulation of their negotiation behavior, at least by bar disciplinary rules.[31] Others objected to the general norms of fairness and disclosure reflected in the proposed draft. In their view, the provisions were set at "too high a level of generality" and failed to acknowledge wide variations in bargaining approaches across geographic locations, substantive fields, and practice settings.[32]

The Model Rules debate revealed not only different conventions concerning candor and disclosure, but also different expectations concerning substantive expertise and technical sophistication among the parties. Many practitioners worried that "[a] rule based on the premise that the legal profession is substantially homoge-

30. ABA Model Rule Of Professional Conduct Rule 4.2, Discussion Draft (January 30, 1980).

31. Geoffrey C. Hazard, Jr., "The Lawyer's Obligation to be Trustworthy When Dealing With Opposing Parties," 33 S.C. L. Rev. 181, 191–96 (1981).

32. James J. White, "Machiavelli at the Bar: Ethical Limitations on Lying in Negotiations," 1980 A.B. Found. Res. J. 926, 927 (1980). See also Hazard, supra note 31, at 192–96. For a subsequent ABA proposal, see ABA Section on Litigation, Ethical Guidelines for Settlement Negotiations (2002).

neous ... would put the technically sophisticated lawyer in a hopeless dilemma when dealing with an unsophisticated opposing counsel."[33] If the sophisticated lawyer exploited his expertise or withheld information that his opponent overlooked, the transaction would be voidable and the lawyer could be subject to discipline. Conversely, if the lawyer supplied the information or tried to equalize the playing field, his client would end up subsidizing both sides of the transaction and adversaries would be allowed to freeload on others' work. According to some law and economics theory, the long term impact of such a rule might prove perverse, because neither side would have adequate incentives to prepare.[34] Sophisticated parties might be reluctant to invest effort on which they could not capitalize; unsophisticated parties might rely on the disclosure obligations of their adversaries rather than spend the effort necessary to duplicate their work.

Supporters of greater honesty and fairness in negotiations respond to such arguments on both practical and ethical grounds. As a practical matter, they invoke research that casts doubt on the efficiency of hard-ball strategies. According to this research, the paradigm case for competitive frameworks involves a "zero-sum" situation in which parties lack a continuing relationship, and are unlikely to detect deception. These circumstances are less typical than is commonly assumed. Most bargaining contexts present mutually advantageous "value-creating" opportunities, as well as zero-sum "value-claiming" opportunities. Misleading or exploitative approaches may preempt the realization of mutually advantageous solutions to joint problems. Classic game theory also verifies what common sense suggests, namely that negotiators who encounter each other repeatedly will penalize aggressive bargainers. Cooperation works better over the long run.[35]

Other commentators argue for cooperation, candor, and fairness on ethical grounds. They claim that individuals' own interests in preserving their honesty, integrity, and fairness deserves a central role in evaluating negotiating behavior. From this perspective, common excuses for deceptive or manipulative tactics are unpersuasive. To rely on rationalizations such as "everyone does it" or "the other side is doing it" presupposes an impoverished

33. Hazard, supra note 31, at 195.

34. Alan Strudler, "Moral Complexity in the Law of Nondisclosure," 45 UCLA L. Rev. 337, 374–75 (1997).

35. See Robert M. Axelrod, The Evolution of Cooperation (1984); Roger Fisher & William Ury, Getting to Yes: Negotiations Agreement Without Giving In (1981). For general arguments favoring cooperative styles, see Carrie Menkel–Meadow, "Toward Another View of Legal Negotiation: The Structure of Problem Solving," 31 UCLA L. Rev. 754 (1984).

view of morality–a view generally rejected in other contexts. Moreover, when lawyers know that their adversary is being deceptive, retaliatory deception is not simply corrective justice; rather, it is an attempt to impose the kind of injury that the lawyers themselves have avoided by discovering the duplicity.

Cutting ethical corners may also involve selective evaluation of the consequences. Consciously or unconsciously, many individuals overvalue the short-term benefits from unethical tactics, and disregard the long-term personal and systemic costs. Deception adversely affects both the parties and the process. When misrepresentation is suspected or revealed, it compromises the lawyer's credibility, and may provoke retaliatory or defensive responses. There is much truth to the adage that it is easy to tell one lie but difficult to tell only one.[36] Deception that remains undetected encourages more deception and ultimately may diminish parties' level of trust, their capacity to reach fair agreements, their ability to exchange credible commitments, and their sense of personal integrity. Honesty and fairness are to some extent collective goods. The more that lawyers seek to become "free riders," the greater the profession's difficulty in maintaining a climate of trust, credibility, and fair dealing.

So too, an unqualified willingness to exploit an opponent's ignorance or mistake carries broader costs. Disparities in talent, resources, and information inevitably skew negotiation results. While it may be unrealistic to expect parties to forego all the advantages that arise from such inequalities, it may be reasonable to expect negotiators to forego some. Particularly where parties lack equal access to relevant facts, it will often be both equitable and efficient to impose reasonable disclosure obligations.

That is, in part, why contract and tort law requires parties to correct material misapprehensions. The prevailing caselaw summarized in Section 161 of the Restatement (Second) of Contracts mandates disclosure when necessary to correct a previous assertion that is erroneous, or when the fact in question concerns a basic assumption of the negotiation and failure to disclose would violate "good faith and ... reasonable standards of fair dealing." The doctrine summarized in Sections 527 and 529 of the Restatement (Second) of Torts, is that an injured party can recover damages caused by materially misleading misrepresentations, including ambiguous statements made with reckless indifference for how they will be interpreted. Partially true statements can be materially

---

36. Sissela Bok, Lying: Moral Choice in Public and Private Life (1978); Reed Elizabeth Loder, "Moral Truth-seeking and the Virtuous Negotiator," 8 Geo. J. Legal Ethics 45 (1994).

misleading if they fail to state qualifying information. Section 551 of the Restatement similarly notes that nondisclosure can result in liability where the undisclosed fact is basic to the transaction and where one party, "because of the relationship [with the other party], the customs of the trade or other objective circumstances, would reasonably expect a disclosure...." Unlike Model Rule 4.1, the Restatement does not expressly distinguish between lies, "generally accepted" puffery, half-truths, and truthful-but-misleading statements. All are tortious frauds if other parties rely on them to their detriment. Some jurisdictions may hold lawyers liable for statements that qualify as fraud under these circumstances. See Restatement (Third) of the Law Governing Lawyers § 98; ABA Section of Litigation, Ethical Guidelines for Settlement Negotiations 4.1.1 (2002).

Professor Donald Langevoort offers an economic justification for this "half-truth doctrine."

> [T]he law of fraud is efficient. It allows the less informed party to forego the costly and duplicative process of factual investigation and information discovery, thereby reducing transaction costs. The law offers a credibility bond for the reliability of factual representations by the informed party. It is not at all hard to extend this same logic to the half-truth.... Language is inherently imprecise; it is not functional to force people to stop and analyze statements to see if there is some subtle limit or ambiguity that must be clarified....[37]

In evaluating these arguments for more or less regulation of negotiating ethics, it is again helpful to consider concrete cases. The following examples reflect common negotiating tactics.

- In a dispute over a hotel's breach of contract to host an organization's conference, the attorney for the defendant hotel makes an initial settlement offer of $50,000. Counsel for the plaintiff organization maintains that his client's officers would never accept such an offer, that damages from the breach are likely to be much higher, and that any jury award would be more substantial. Counsel actually believes that if the case went to trial, his client would receive a substantially smaller sum. Based on that advice, the plaintiff's president had earlier authorized counsel to settle for any amount over $30,000.

   In responding to initial offer, the plaintiff's attorney also represents that it would be impossible for his client to

---

37. Donald C. Langevoort, "Half-Truths: Protecting Mistaken Inferences by Investors and Others," 52 Stan. L. Rev. 87 (1999).

find another suitable hotel under such short notice. When the attorney later contacts his client to report the settlement offer, he learns that another hotel has orally agreed to host the conference. When he then calls the defendant lawyer to accept the settlement, the lawyer opens the conversation by asking, "How are efforts to mitigate the damages coming along?" Plaintiff's counsel responds, "nothing definite yet." The settlement is then finalized at $50,000.[38]

- In negotiations over the property settlement in an uncontested divorce, the husband and wife disagree about the value of certain assets, including real estate and stock in a family corporation. When reviewing the wife's proposed settlement, the husband's lawyer notices a $50,000 calculation error by opposing counsel that understates her alleged interest in jointly owned real estate. The lawyer brings the matter to the attention of his client, who believes that the understated figure is a more accurate reflection of the property's true worth. Accordingly, the lawyer prepares a counteroffer replicating the error in a way that minimizes the likelihood of its discovery. On the mistaken belief that the husband has surrendered his challenge to the value of the real estate, the wife abandons her challenge to the value and ownership of the stock. Both parties ultimately accept a version of the husband's counteroffer and sign a final agreement that recites the disposition of assets without specifying their value.[39]

- In a case involving a bank that inappropriately canceled a loan agreement, the plaintiff-borrowers describe themselves as quite "upbeat." Although they claim that their business was "ruined," they deny experiencing any severe emotional distress. In settlement negotiations, their lawyer nonetheless represents that they have greatly suffered as a result of the canceled agreement. During those discussions, counsel for the bank makes it clear that he thinks the plaintiffs have gone out of business. The plaintiff's lawyer did not make that claim. In fact, the business is continuing, and several important contracts are in the offing. The lawyer finalizes a settlement without correcting her opponent's misimpres-

38. The case is described in Monroe Freedman, "Lying: Is it Ethical?," Legal Times, Dec. 12, 1994, at 20; see also Monroe Freedman, "Acceptable Lies," Legal Times, Feb. 20, 1995, at 24.

39. See Stare v. Tate, 98 Cal.Rptr. 264 (App.1971).

sion.[40]

In a survey of experts on legal ethics, participants considered hypothetical fact situations analogous to those above. With respect to cases like the first example, a majority of experts believed that it was impermissible for a lawyer directly to misrepresent whether a client had authorized settlement for a specific amount. Most of the others indicated that it was permissible but that they would not do it. One expert felt that lying was acceptable because an opponent didn't have a "right to the information."[41] Those who found the conduct unethical noted that experienced negotiators can generally sidestep a direct inquiry about settlement authority with responses such as "Are you able to offer more?," or "I'm authorized to get the best result I can."[42]

The actual case on which the hotel example is based arose during the 1960s, when the Washington, D.C. Mattachine Society planned what it billed as the first national conference to focus on gay and lesbian rights. The Manger Hotel agreed to host the conference with knowledge of its subject. Then, two weeks before the event, after publicity had begun and invitations had been mailed, management in the hotel's chain's home office ordered cancellation of the agreement. Professor Monroe Freedman, the Society's lawyer, later defended his nondisclosure of the client's successful efforts to find a new hotel.

> Was anything definite about mitigation at that point? Is anything ever definite in this life? After all, the Mattachine Society had thought that the deal with the Manger was definite, and it turned out that it wasn't.... The statement about mitigation wasn't a flat-out denial: it was equivocal–an evasion that a careful listener could have picked up on. "What do you mean 'nothing definite'?" he might have said....[43]

According to Freedman, the new offer of a hotel site was confidential information and, as long as he did not make a false statement of material fact, he did not need to disclose it under Model Rule 4.1.

With respect to the bank loan agreement case, about two thirds of the surveyed negotiation experts found the claims about the plaintiff's emotional distress unethical. Of the others, one reasoned

---

40. Larry Lempert, "In Settlement Talks, Does Telling the Truth Have its Limits?," 2 Inside Litigation 1 (1988).

41. See id. at 16.

42. White, supra note 32, at 933 (suggesting evasive responses); Gerald Wetlaufer, "The Ethics of Lying in Ne-

gotiations," 75 Iowa L. Rev. 1219, 1237 (1990) (suggesting that lawyers can challenge the question as inappropriate or justify their preferred figure).

43. Freedman, "Lying: Is It Ethical?," supra note 38, at 20.

that "obviously some [emotional] distress had occurred." If the clients "didn't care at all there wouldn't be a legal matter.... [The lawyer is just] embellishing the concern."[44] Another who agreed that the exaggeration was acceptable drew analogies to bargaining over the sale of a car. To him, the fundamental question was "what are your and my legitimate expectations" as opposing negotiators?[45] Professor Ronald Rotunda invoked the same analogy to arrive at a different conclusion. In his view: "If lawyers want to be like used car salesmen, this is a good place to start."[46]

Those who find "puffing" acceptable generally assume that others will recognize an exaggeration for what it is. But if that were always true, puffing would also be ineffective. The practice continues because sometimes it works and some opponents are deceived. To commentators such as Professor Rotunda and federal judge Alvin Rubin, parties dealing with a lawyer should not need to exercise the same degree of caution as they would if trading at a Far Eastern bazaar.[47]

The divorce case "scrivner's error" example is based on *Stare v. Tate*, 98 Cal.Rptr. 264 (App.1971). There, the court noted:

[t]he mistake might never have come to light had not [the husband] desired to have that exquisite last word. A few days after [the wife] had obtained the divorce he mailed her a copy of the offer which contained the errant computation. On top of the page he wrote with evident satisfaction: "PLEASE NOTE ... MISTAKE IN YOUR FIGURES."

98 Cal.Rptr. at 266.

The wife then filed suit to reform the agreement and the Court granted that motion under § 3399 of the California Code. In terms similar to caselaw in other jurisdictions, the Code provides: "When, through fraud or mutual mistake of the parties, or a mistake of one party, which the other at the time knew or suspected, a written contract does not truly express the intention of the parties, it may be revised on the application of a party aggrieved...."

The court did not consider the lawyers' obligation, but other bar ethics committees have done so. In Informal Opinion 86–1518 (Feb. 9, 1986), the ABA's Standing Committee on Ethics reviewed a situation in which a lawyer discovered that the final draft of a contract prepared by opposing counsel's office erroneously omitted

---

44. See Lempert, supra note 40, at 18 (quoting Charles Craver).

45. Id. (quoting James White).

46. Id. (quoting Ronald Rotunda).

47. Alvin B. Rubin, "A Causerie on Lawyers' Ethics in Negotiations," 35 La. L. Rev. 577, 589 (1975).

a material provision. In the Committee's view, neither the Model Rules nor the Model Code required the lawyer to obtain the client's permission before correcting the mistake. Although the client had a right to know facts necessary for "informed decisions" on the matter, once he had accepted the provision, no further decision remained to be made. One could view this ABA Informal Opinion as a reflection of appropriate "paternalism," or perhaps mutual protectiveness among lawyers, to cover the kind of mistakes that are bound to occur in legal practice.

For negotiators who confront such issues, the ethical difficulties often resemble the prisoner's dilemma in game theory. As Professor Robert Condlin notes:

> When both bargainers cooperate they receive the benefits of joint action and produce an outcome that is favorable for both. When one cooperates and the other competes, the competitor usually exploits the cooperator and does better. When both compete, they waste resources in ego battles, leave money on the table out of exhaustion and polarization, and frequently end up with a mediocre outcome. In any single negotiation, choosing presents a [prisoner's] dilemma because the rational choice for each individual bargainer often leads to a mutually undesirable outcome. There are ways out of this dilemma in repeat bargaining.... But in any single negotiation, where there is no prospect for future dealing, it is usually irrational for individual bargainers to act cooperatively, and that is the bargainer's dilemma.[48]

In repetitive bargaining contexts, the "way out" is a "tit-for-tat" strategy. The most successful negotiators begin by cooperating; retaliate if the opponent engages in noncooperative or unethical practices; return to a cooperative stance if the opposing side ceases objectionable behavior; and clearly convey this intended course of action.[49] Another way that parties can escape the prisoner's dilemma is to hire attorneys who are committed to maintaining a reputation for cooperation, fairness, and candor.[50]

It might also be possible to increase the likelihood of candor and cooperation in negotiations through formal rules or informal reputational sanctions. In one large national survey of practitioners, about 40 percent believed that revising codified rules would be

---

48. Robert J. Condlin, "Bargaining in the Dark: The Normative Incoherence of Lawyer's Dispute Bargaining Role," 51 Md. L. Rev. 1, 12 (1992).

49. See Axelrod, supra note 35; Fisher & Ury, supra note 35.

50. Ronald J. Gilson & Robert H. Mnookin, "Disputing Through Agents: Cooperation and Conflict Between Lawyers in Litigation," 94 Colum. L. Rev. 509 (1994).

an effective way of improving negotiation conduct.[51] Judge Alvin Rubin has proposed such a revision:

> It is inherent in the concept of professionalism that the profession will regulate itself, adhering to an ethos that imposes standards higher than mere law observance. Client avarice and hostility neither control the lawyer's conscience nor measure his ethics. Surely if its practitioners are principled, a profession that dominates the legal process in our law-oriented society would not expect too much if it required its members to adhere to two simple principles when they negotiate as professionals: Negotiate honestly and in good faith; and do not take unfair advantage of another–regardless of his relative expertise or sophistication.[52]

Even in the absence of a codified rule, many lawyers practice under these principles. And in the long run, both they and the profession would benefit if those norms were more widely reinforced in practice. There is real "market value" in a reputation for candor and fair dealing. As one law firm partner told us: "Our firm's reputation for honesty and accuracy in dealings with the government agencies is one of the most valuable assets we have to sell on behalf of clients. There are many times when it would be difficult to prove some fact or other, but where an agency will take our word for it." Another partner reported giving advice along similar lines to a junior attorney: "If misleading text in your financial documents is not corrected immediately, you are not going to be in your firm for long, nor will you be elsewhere in practice in this town." Of course, these comments presupposed that the lawyers would be repeat players, which is what "reputation" is based on. But all lawyers are repeat players in some practice settings. And for most practitioners, reputation is one of their most crucial, and marketable, assets.

F. Lobbying

The importance of lobbying has increased dramatically over the last half century, and so also has the role of lawyer lobbyists. Before the 1950s, only a few corporations or public interest organizations and a few thousand unions and trade associations had offices in the nation's capitol. Today, over 500 corporations, 2000 public interest organizations, and 85,000 unions and trade associations have such

---

51. Stephen Pepe, "Standards of Legal Negotiation," Interim Report for ABA Commission on Evaluation of Professional Standards and ABA House of Delegates (1983).

52. Rubin, supra note 47, at 593.

offices.[53] Groups range in size and importance from the American Bar Association, with some 400,000 members, to the National Frozen Pizza Institute. Lobbying activities have similarly increased at the state and local level.

The number of lawyers assisting these groups has correspondingly escalated. "Governmental relations" work involves a broad variety of activities, such as providing advice about political and legislative developments; preparing testimony for legislative and administrative hearings; drafting statutes, regulations, and comments; negotiating government contracts; maintaining contacts with public officials and governmental bodies; and coordinating legal, political, and public relations strategies at state, local, and national levels.[54] Performing these functions effectively requires an equally wide array of capabilities, including substantive knowledge, technical expertise, personal contacts and credibility, and sound political judgment. Contrary to public image, lawyer lobbying is far less a matter of "glad handing" than of meticulous preparation.[55] Lawyers help to form an essential bridge between public and private interests, and their lobbying efforts often significantly shape government policies.

This degree of influence imposes corresponding obligations. Leaders of the bar have long emphasized that when lawyers are advising on matters of public policy in a nonadversarial context, they have a special responsibility to consider public welfare. As Professor Paul Freund once put it, an attorney in this setting has a "wider scope and obligation to see around a problem unconstrained by what may be too parochial concerns of his clients, and to advise accordingly."[56] Lawyers' own reputational interests often push in similar directions. Many practitioners who specialize in governmental relations have invested a substantial part of their careers either in serving in public office or in establishing good working relations with those who do. Their effectiveness usually depends on maintaining a reputation for candor, fairness, integrity, and reasonableness among those with whom they will have continued dealings.[57] By the same token, government attorneys who move through the

53. Ronald G. Shaiko, "Lobbying in Washington: A Contemporary Perspective," in The Interest Group Connection: Electioneering, Lobbying, and Policymaking in Washington 3, 7–8 (Paul S. Hernson, Ronald G. Shaiko, & Clyde Wilcox eds., 1998)

54. Id., at 9; Mark J. Green, The Other Government: The Unseen Power of Washington Lawyers (1975); Edward O. Laumann, et al., "Washington Lawyers and Others: The Structure of Washington Representation," 37 Stan. L. Rev. 465 (1985).

55. Laumann, et al., supra note 54, at 495.

56. Green, supra note 54, at 12 (quoting Paul Freund).

57. Laumann, et al., supra note 54, at 490–95.

revolving door between public and private practice also have reputational concerns. The result is that governmental work generally is "characterized less by confrontation and conflict than by cooperation and compromise."[58]

Yet some issues involve intense conflict among interest groups, and between those groups and government regulators. In such contexts, the limited research available suggests that lawyer/lobbyists are no less partisan than advocates in other settings.[59] Prominent recent examples include attorneys for the tobacco industry and for failed savings and loan associations.[60] One legendary case history of the obstructionist abilities of Washington lawyers involved a Covington & Burling partner who helped delay FDA efforts to regulate the peanut content of peanut butter. Although the government finally prevailed, its efforts required twelve years and entailed a 24,000 page hearing transcript and close to 75,000 pages of documents.[61] (The industry position was that the agency was being hyper-purist about what consumers expected in peanut butter.) Such examples are a large part of what fuels widespread public distrust of lawyer/lobbyists. Indeed, in one recent election involving a candidate who had worked in that capacity before running for the Colorado Senate, a media strategist reported that he had "never tested anything that tested worse" on public image than "lawyer-lobbyist."[62]

It is perhaps inevitable that lawyers acting in a political context will be tainted by association with unpopular positions taken by their clients. But it is also fair to ask whether the profession as well as society would benefit if private practitioners involved with public policy issues generally accepted greater responsibility to consider the public interest. Many highly successful government relations attorneys do so, and have withdrawn from celebrated cases such as those involving tobacco companies' resistance to warning labels.

Of course, what constitutes the public interest will often be subject to dispute.[63] On some policy matters, it may be possible to find broad consensus, at least among active participants in popular

58. Id., at 490.

59. Id.

60. See Rhode, supra, note 14, at 1510–11; Rhode & Luban, supra note 2, at 202–10; Nader & Smith, supra note 3; Richard Zitrin & Carol Langford, "The Moral Compass of American Lawyers," in Truth, Justice, Power, and Greed (1999); Simon, supra note 14.

61. Green, supra note 54, at 133–39 (describing efforts of Thomas Austern).

62. Mike Soraghan, "Strickland Changes Tack on 'Lawyer Lobbyist' Label," Denver Post, Sep. 4, 2001, at A10 (quoting Bob Klein).

63. See Rhode, supra note 14, at 1512–15.

debate. However, on many contemporary issues involving financial, safety, and environmental regulation, there is no such agreement. Lawyer/lobbyists often take comfort from this fact and steer their work toward causes with which they are personally sympathetic. As a consequence, lobbyists are often speaking from the heart when they assert that their views reflect the public interest.

Other ethical issues that arise in somewhat distinctive form for lawyer/lobbyists involve conflicts of interest. In order to prevent both the fact and appearance of impropriety, various federal, state, and local laws require detailed disclosure of lobbying activity; they also restrict the gifts, meals, and entertainment that lobbyists can provide to government officials.[64]

Related laws regulate the revolving door between public office and private practice. One underlying concern is that government lawyers who wish to maximize their future employment options might avoid taking positions that could alienate potential clients or employers. A further concern is that when former government lawyers become lobbyists, they will inappropriately capitalize on their prior experience by gaining preferential access and exploiting confidential information.

To address such concerns, federal, state, and local legislation regulates the activities of former public officials. For example, the Ethics in Government Act, 18 U.S.C. § 207, permanently prohibits former executive branch employees (including lawyers) from representing any person on matters in which they participated "personally and substantially" while in office. The Act also provides for a two year "cooling off" period by prohibiting a former executive branch employee from making any communication to, or appearance before, a federal agency or court with the intent to influence a matter actually pending within a year preceding the employee's termination of employment. The Model Rules of Professional Conduct, Rule 1.11 and the Code of Professional Responsibility, DR 9–101(B), similarly bar former government lawyers from representing private clients on matters in which the lawyer had participated personally and substantially while in government. However, the Model Rules permit other lawyers in the same firm to provide such representation, provided that the former government lawyer is screened. These rules attempt to balance the need to prevent improper influence of public officials with the need to preserve the

---

64. See Wright H. Andrews Jr., et al., New Federal Lobbying Disclosure, Gift, and Political Fund Raising Law and Rules: What You Need to Know to do Business in Washington in 1996 (1996); Shaiko, supra note 53, at 13–15.

attractiveness of government employment for talented professionals who might later desire careers in the private sector.[65]

Another common issue involving conflicts of interest for lawyer/lobbyists arises in representation of trade associations. Here, the primary question is whether lawyers or firms who represent the association may undertake work adverse to one of its members. In essence, reported decisions and bar ethical opinions generally conclude that the lawyer or firm may accept such work as long as they are not deemed to represent the individual member as well as the association.[66] That is a factual question, which depends both on the member's reasonable expectations and on the likelihood that the lawyer acquired confidential information about the member during the course of representation.[67]

A final ethical issue that has recently gained increased attention involves the scope of confidentiality protections for lawyers' lobbying activities. In a widely publicized decision, a federal district judge for the Southern District of New York held that neither the attorney-client privilege nor the work product doctrine protected documents and testimony relating to a presidential pardon request.[68] The case involved the fugitive American business executive Mark Rich, who obtained a pardon from President Clinton during his last days in office. According to the district court, Rich's lawyers were "acting principally as lobbyists and not primarily as lawyers."[69] The lead attorney who secured the pardon had been hired for his political not legal skills and his team was "being used principally to put legal trappings on what was essentially a lobbying and political effort."[70] Communications and materials connected with this effort were therefore not protected from government subpoena.

The court's analysis in the Rich case presents obvious difficulties for lawyer/lobbyists, who are often hired to pursue both legal and political strategies. One likely result is that more firms will construct strong "Chinese Walls" between litigation and lobbying.[71] Another possibility is that clients will be less disposed to hire

65. For an overview, see Rhode & Luban, supra note 2, at 507–17; Geoffrey C. Hazard, Jr., et al., The Law and Ethics of Lawyering 684–704 (1999).

66. D.C. Ethics Op. 305 (2001); Ernest T. Lindberg, "Representation of Trade Association," Wash. Lawyer, Feb. 2002, at 10; Westinghouse Electric Corp. v. Kerr–McGee Corp., 580 F.2d 1311 (7th Cir.1978).

67. See sources cited in note 64.

68. In re Grand Jury Subpoenas dated March 9, 2001, 179 F.Supp.2d 270 (S.D.N.Y.2001).

69. Id., at 289.

70. Id., at 290.

71. Louis Jacobson, "Were They Lawyers or Lobbyists?," Nat. L J., Jan. 12, 2002, at 109.

lawyers for multifaceted governmental relations work, or to be less candid with those they do hire.[72] A countervailing benefit, however, is that prosecutors and the press will face fewer obstacles in discovering illegal conduct and in providing a credible deterrent for lawyers' involvement in such conduct. However, in this as in other contexts, the best deterrent will be lawyers' own internalized standards, reinforced by the profession's workplace norms and practices.

72. Id.

Chapter VIII

CONFLICTS OF INTEREST

A. Introduction

Basic to the client-lawyer relationship is the duty of loyalty. Conflicts of interest arise when lawyers have other professional or personal relationships that could compromise that loyalty.

Conflicts of interest are an integral and increasingly contested feature of American legal practice. A rapid growth in the size of private firms and their organizational clients, together with the expansion of branch offices and corporate subsidiaries, has increased the possibility of actual, attenuated, or inadvertent conflicts. More client engagements of law firms involve short-term specific matters, rather than long-term retainers, so the typical "portfolio" of law firm clients is in constant turnover. Similarly, a growing specialization in legal practice within and among firms has generated greater potential for simultaneous or successive representation of competing interests. The more technically complex the matter, the greater the premium placed on prior expertise and the greater the likelihood that the client will seek an attorney who has had some previous involvement with the general subject-matter. So too, an increase in lateral mobility among lawyers has led to an increase in circumstances that permit vicarious disqualification of colleagues.

Firms that enjoy geographic, substantive or "social network" monopolies are most likely to encounter demands for assistance from parties that have, or might have, incompatible concerns.[1] A recent survey by Susan Shapiro of the American Bar Foundation found that large firms estimate that they turn away anywhere from a third to a half of all potential cases because of conflicts of interest; small firms estimate that they decline five to ten percent of prospective business for that reason.[2]

As conflicts problems have grown more pervasive, so also have conflicts disputes, both within and across firms. Internally, particularly in large firms, the issue of which business to accept has become increasingly divisive. In a firm's external relationships, the conflicts issue now generates frequent dispute, primarily because of

---

1. Susan P. Shapiro, "Tangled Loyalties: Conflict of Interest in Legal Practice" (forthcoming 2002), (excerpted in Researching Law, American Bar Foundation Newsletter, Winter 2002, at 1).

2. Id.

the remedy typically pursued–disqualification. Other ethical rules usually are enforced through bar disciplinary actions or malpractice proceedings after the fact, but violations of conflicts rules can result in disqualification of the offending attorney before or during representation. If a court finds that a lawyer has misused confidential information, it may also prohibit the lawyer from turning over work products to successor counsel. Such disqualification remedies are a powerful strategic weapon for increasing an opponent's expense and delay. So too, when clients suffer substantial costs from disqualification or inadequate representation due to conflicts of interest, they are increasingly likely to sue for malpractice. These remedies help explain why conflicts doctrine has been so extensively litigated.

Conflicts of interest can arise in a wide variety of circumstances but generally take one of the following forms:

- Multiple representation: representing more than one client in the same matter where their interests diverge;

- Successive representation: representing a current client against a former client in a related matter;

- "Personal" conflicts: representing clients in a context where their interests conflict with the attorney's own financial, professional, or other interests (including those of close family members);

- Positional conflicts: representing a client whose legal position could adversely affect another client in a factually unrelated matter;

- Vicarious conflicts: representing clients in a matter where another member of the lawyer's organization has one of the preceding non-personal conflicts

B.   Representing Multiple Interests

The term "lawyer for the situation" was coined by Louis Brandeis in the 1916 Senate hearings on his proposed confirmation as a Justice of the United States Supreme Court. Brandeis' appointment had aroused considerable opposition partly on the unstated grounds that he was liberal and Jewish, and partly on the stated grounds that he had represented parties with conflicting interests. Critics objected to his representation of a family business after a dispute arose among family members, his oversight of a business transaction for several different parties, and his mediation of differences between owners and creditors of a business in order to keep it afloat. Although the clients had given their consent, dispute centered on whether Brandeis could adequately represent the conflicting interests involved and whether he had provided sufficient information to the parties concerning the risks of joint representation. While acknowledging that his disclosures may not always have been sufficient, Brandeis defended his practice of acting as "lawyer for the situation." Eventually, the ethical accusations subsided in the face of concessions by other reputable lawyers that they had engaged in similar conduct.[3]

Brandeis' view of the lawyer's role has inspired continuing debate. Critics have objected that lawyers are not retained by a "situation," and that they and their clients may have very different views as to what a given context requires.[4] The interests of multiple clients are seldom, if ever, totally congruent, and if subsequent disputes arise, an advocate for "everyone" may look like an advocate for no one.

The key concept in bar ethical rules on multiple representation is "adversity" of interests. That concept refers both to the likelihood that a conflict will develop, and to the probable intensity of any that does. The issue is not only whether parties have divergent interests or inclinations, but also how far they are likely to pursue their differences.[5] That, in turn, often depends on legal advice, which sometimes threatens to make the conflict inquiry circular. The parties are asking the lawyer whether problems are likely to develop, while the lawyer should be asking the same question.

As a general matter, multiple representation carries both benefits and costs. For parties, it avoids the expense and possible acrimony involved in having separate counsel. For lawyers, serving all the parties may result in additional fees and less delay and divisiveness. The risk, however, is that if a conflict develops, parties can end up with additional costs and delays. They will need to hire separate counsel, who typically will have to duplicate or even contest prior legal work. Under such circumstances, attorneys often become scapegoats for problems not necessarily of their making. In contexts of multiple representation, lawyers are expected both to *be* fair and to *seem* fair to everyone. They are also expected to foresee the likelihood of conflict at the outset. This is an inherently

---

3. Geoffrey C. Hazard, Jr., Ethics in the Practice of Law 58–62 (1978); David Luban, "The Noblesse Oblige Tradition in the Practice of Law," 41 Vand. L. Rev. 717 (1988).

4. John P. Frank, "The Legal Ethics of Louis D. Brandeis," 17 Stan. L. Rev.

683, 702 (1965); John S. Dzienkowski, "Lawyers as Intermediaries: The Representation of Multiple Clients in the Modern Legal Profession," 1992 U. Ill. L. Rev. 741, 784 (1992).

5. Hazard, supra note 3, at 69.

difficult task, since it will depend not only on the objective facts of a transaction but also on the subjective attitudes of parties, all of which can change over time.[6]

Analysis here begins with a distinction between conflicts arising in concurrent or simultaneous representation and conflicts arising in successive representation. The primary ethical rules governing conflicts in simultaneous representation are Model Rule 1.7 and DR 5–105. The rules governing conflicts in successive representation are Model Rule 1.9 and, under the Code, an improvisation from Canon 9, which deals with the "appearance of impropriety."

In contexts involving simultaneous representation, Model Rule 1.7 prohibits representation that will be directly adverse to another client or that will be "materially limited" by obligations to another client. The first of these restrictions prohibits a lawyer or law firm from representing opposing parties in litigation and in similar contentious proceedings. This restriction on directly adverse representation cannot be waived; clients cannot consent to such simultaneous representation because of the likely adverse effects on their own interests and on the system of justice. The second restriction, which applies both to litigation relationships and to transactional matters, prohibits a lawyer from representing a client when doing so would be "materially limited" by responsibilities to another client. This restriction can be waived; clients who have full information can consent to such simultaneous representation if the lawyer reasonably believes that he will be able to provide competent and diligent assistance to each affected party. The Code provision, DR 5–105, is cast in somewhat different terms, but as applied it has essentially the same meaning. It provides that lawyers must decline representation if their professional judgment on behalf of another client will be "adversely affected," or if it is not "obvious" that they can "adequately represent the interests of each."

As the Restatement (Third) of the Law Governing Lawyers notes, another reason to prohibit joint representation of adverse parties in litigation involves the need to protect "the integrity of a proceeding."[7] A lawyer who attempted to present both sides of a dispute might fail to provide the forceful advocacy necessary for informed decisionmaking. Both the fact and appearance of justice would be at risk, and reported cases recognize as much.

6. Id. at 70–73.

7. Restatement (Third) of the Law Governing Lawyers, § 201 (1991) . See also Fred C. Zacharias, "Waiving Conflicts of Interest," 108 Yale L. J. 407, 413–415 (1998).

California is the only state with a significantly different ethical rule. It permits any joint representation where clients give informed consent. California Rule 3–310(B). However, California courts have declined to permit joint representation of clients with an actual (as opposed to potential) conflict during litigation, on the ground that any purported consent would be "neither intelligent nor informed."[8]

In assessing whether clients are in a position to give informed consent, courts and commentators stress several factors:

- the nature of client interests and services to be provided;
- the timing, extent, and intelligibility of lawyers' disclosures concerning issues such as loyalty, confidentiality and the attorney-client privilege;
- clients' capacity to assess the nature of their interests and the consequences of joint representation; and
- clients' ability to exercise uncoerced choice.

So, for example, in matters involving large stakes, unstable circumstances, and adversarial or coercive relationships, joint representation is far less likely to be appropriate than in matters involving smaller stakes, routine services, and cooperative, ongoing relationships. A factor of obvious importance, frequently noted in reported decisions, is whether the client was independently represented in considering and agreeing to a waiver. The most common situation of this kind is where an independent law firm seeks a waiver from a corporate client that is advised by its in-house law department. Conflict waivers obtained on this basis are, quite properly, difficult to invalidate.

The middle ground among these extremes is where most problems arise. Particularly when dealing with unsophisticated parties, prudent lawyers make sure to provide a realistic appraisal of the advantages as well as costs of separate counsel. Many individuals who are involved in coordinated projects are understandably inclined to take an optimistic view of their ventures and to discount the likelihood of later conflicts. Lawyers, who have their own interests in maximizing fees and minimizing transaction costs, may be similarly inclined. But as the Restatement (Third) of the Law Governing Lawyers notes, informed consent requires that the client have "reasonably adequate information about the material risks [involved]."[9] And all participants will be well served if the attorney attempts to be as candid as possible in projecting those risks.

---

8. Klemm v. Superior Court, 142 Cal.Rptr. 509, 512 (App.1977).

9. Restatement of the Law Governing Lawyers, supra note 7, at § 202.

Clients can waive future as well as current conflicts of interest. However, as the ABA Ethics Committee emphasized in Formal Opinion 93–372 (Apr. 16, 1993), such a waiver must describe the conflict with sufficient clarity so that the client's consent is truly informed. A prospective waiver that does not identify either the potential opposing party or at least the class of potentially conflicting clients and interests would be unlikely to survive scrutiny. Id.

Joint representation of multiple plaintiffs or defendants in litigation poses special concerns. The chief advantages to litigants from representation by the same lawyer are readily apparent. First, and most obviously, the clients save money. By pooling their resources, parties often obtain the services of an expert attorney who would otherwise be unaffordable. In some civil and white-collar criminal contexts, an employer may be willing to subsidize a unified defense but reluctant to pay for separate counsel for all employees as well as the organization, unless required to do so by an indemnification agreement. From the standpoint of both individuals and their employer, joint representation can facilitate mutually advantageous "stonewalling," the tactic of using the same attorney to establish a "common front" by several litigants or targets of investigations.

However, each of these advantages of multiple representation carries corresponding disadvantages. Most obviously, the lawyer might pass up opportunities to assist one client at the expense of another. Where a common front strategy is being subsidized by an employer (or by an organized crime conspiracy), counsel might refrain from negotiating a settlement or plea agreement that would be advantageous for one client in exchange for cooperation that would adversely affect another.

Stonewalling can be a risky proposition even when the attorney attempts in good faith to advance the individual interests of multiple clients. If a common front does not work, hindsight may show that one of the clients would have been better off with a separate deal. Professor Kenneth Mann's study of white collar criminal defense describes this fact-pattern: "[E]ach client holds inculpatory evidence against the other, and the government has just enough evidence to consider asking for an indictment against each, but not enough to dismiss the option of granting immunity to one client in order to get determinative evidence against the other." Mann concludes that "it is difficult for an attorney to act without compromising one of the client's interests. If he advises neither to make a deal because he believes that he may be able to win the case for both, he is sacrificing certain success for one of them. And he clearly cannot advise one to make a deal against the other's interest."[10]

This fact-pattern reflects the well-known "prisoner's dilemma" in game theory discussed in Chapter VII. If both clients stonewall, each may stand a better chance of escaping indictment than if both try to make a deal where the prosecutor will immunize only one of them. But, from another point of view, each fares better trying for an immunity deal regardless of what the other one does. If his codefendant refuses to cooperate, the client who makes the deal obtains immunity while the stonewalling partner goes to jail. Conversely, if his codefendant strikes a bargain, the client's refusal to cooperate is a path to likely conviction. The prisoner's dilemma makes it rational for each client to seek an immunity deal, even though both can foresee that the other will do the same, and that they would both be better off stonewalling. As two game theorists put it: "True, players will find themselves completely frustrated; nonetheless they have no real alternative."[11]

Lawyers advising clients under such circumstances confront a similar dilemma. Those who propose a common front strategy are asking the clients to trust each other, even though each client should know that the other has a strong incentive to deal with the prosecution. But is it prudent to counsel a client to trust someone who has such a powerful reason to violate that trust? Moreover, each client knows that the other knows about that reason. Each, therefore, has grounds to suspect that the other will undertake a "preemptive" deal. As a practical matter, the lawyer's role in such contexts may sometimes be to try to convince each client that the other is trustworthy. By breaking the spiral of mutual suspicion, the lawyer may be able to prevent bargains that are less desirable than a united strategy. But this requires advising clients to follow a course that carries significant risks.

There are similar risks, although perhaps less obvious ones, in civil litigation. For example, codefendants have common interests in opposing the plaintiff's claims but each may also have incentives to settle and to offer evidence shifting liability to the other. However, in criminal cases, the risks involved in multiple representation are of special concern because of the constitutional interests at issue. Supreme Court decisions have established standards for determining when conflicts of interest jeopardize a defendant's Sixth Amendment right to effective assistance of counsel. In Hollo-

10. Kenneth Mann, Defending White Collar Crime: A Portrait of Attorneys at Work 170 (1985).

11. Duncan Luce & Howard Raiffa, Games and Decisions 101 (1957).

way v. Arkansas, 435 U.S. 475 (1978), the Court held that a conviction will be reversed when counsel is forced to represent codefendants over a timely objection unless the trial court finds that no conflict of interest existed. In Cuyler v. Sullivan, 446 U.S. 335 (1980), the Court declined to extend this reversal rule to circumstances in which no objection is made. In such cases, the conviction will be overturned only if the defendant can demonstrate that a conflict of interest adversely affected the lawyer's performance. And in Mickens v. Taylor, __ U.S. __, 122 S.Ct. 1237 (2002), the Court adhered to that rule even in a capital murder case where the trial judge knew that defense counsel apparently had a conflict arising from his prior representation of the victim.

By the same token, the Supreme Court has sustained a trial court's grant of a prosecution motion to disqualify counsel over a defendant's objection. Wheat v. United States, 486 U.S. 153 (1988). The government's concern is that a defendant might, in a subsequent proceeding, assert the defense lawyer's conflict of interest in order to establish ineffective assistance of counsel. Of course, allowing the government to assert a conflict when the defendant has waived any such objection opens the possibility that the government's true motive is to remove a particularly effective adversary. However, the Court expressed confidence that trial judges can take that possibility into account when ruling on joint representation. Id. The underlying concept is that a conflict is, in effect, "unwaivable" if it is of "such a serious nature that no rational defendant would knowingly and intelligently desire that attorney's representation."[12]

The problems created by multiple representation in criminal cases, including the effects of successful stonewall defenses on the administration of justice, have led some countries' legal systems to require separate counsel.[13] Supporters of this approach point out that the tactical advantages of multiple representation could be accomplished with fewer risks through joint defense agreements among separately represented parties. Such agreements permit defendants to share confidential information without waiving the attorney-client privilege.[14] However, separate representation under these agreements still imposes the financial costs of duplicative

12. United States v. Schwarz, 283 F.3d 76, 95 (2d Cir.2002). See also United States v. Fulton, 5 F.3d 605 (2d Cir. 1993).

13. Deborah L. Rhode & David Luban, Legal Ethics 465 (3d ed. 2001) (discussing West Germany's prohibition on joint representation).

14. See Amy Foote, Note, "Joint Defense Agreements in Criminal Prosecutions: Tactical and Ethical Implications," 12 Geo. J. Legal Ethics 377 (1999).

work, which individual defendants and state-subsidized indigent defense systems are sometimes reluctant to assume. In any event, as long as joint representation is a viable option, defense counsel have a special responsibility to ensure that clients are fully aware of the risks before accepting such arrangements.

In civil litigation, only in unusual circumstances will an unsuccessful litigant be able to nullify a judgment on the ground that the lawyer had an improper conflict of interest and had improperly obtained a conflict waiver. A case suggesting that possibility is Amchem Products, Inc. v. Windsor, 521 U.S. 591 (1997), which set aside a class action certification on the basis of class counsel's conflict of interest. A more common remedy if clients can establish an improper conflict that impaired their representation is a malpractice judgment against the lawyer.

C. Positional Conflicts of Interest

A "positional" conflict of interest arises when a lawyer for one client adopts a position that might have a negative impact on another client who is not directly involved in the matter. A familiar example is the assertion of a novel theory for protection of borrowers that is advanced by a lawyer who also represents commercial lenders, such as banks. A positional conflict arises when the theory, if accepted by the courts, could be disadvantageous to banks in the future.

Neither the Code nor the Model Rules categorically forbid positional conflicts of interest. Yet both codes include prohibitions that would encompass such conflicts in certain situations. First, if a positional conflict would compromise the lawyer's "independent professional judgment" on behalf of either client, it is impermissible under Model Rule 2.1 and DR 5–105 of the Code. If the representation would be directly adverse to another client, it would be impermissible under Model Rule 1.7(a)(1). If a positional conflict risks the misuse of a client's confidences, it is impermissible under both Canon 4 of the Code and Model Rule 1.6.

With respect to influences on lawyers' judgment and performance, the Comment to Model Rule 1.7(b) states:

> Ordinarily a lawyer may take inconsistent legal positions in different tribunals at different times on behalf of different clients. The mere fact that advocating a legal position on behalf of one client might create precedent adverse to the interests of a client represented by the lawyer in an unrelated matter does not create a conflict of interest. A conflict of interest exists,

however, if there is a significant risk that a lawyer's action on behalf of one client will materially limit the lawyer's effectiveness in representing another client in a different case; for example, when a decision favoring one client will create a precedent likely to seriously weaken the position taken on behalf of the other client. Factors relevant in determining whether the clients need to be advised of the risk include: where the cases are pending, whether the issue is substantive or procedural, the temporal relationship between the matters, the significance of the issue to the immediate and long-term interests of the clients involved and the clients' reasonable expectations in retaining the lawyer. If there is significant risk of material limitation, then absent informed consent of the affected clients, the lawyer must refuse one of the representations or withdraw from one or both matters.[15]

Under that framework, the important questions are what constitutes a limitation on effectiveness and who should decide.

Significant positional conflicts clearly run the risk of antagonizing clients. Causing distress to a client (such as a bank in the example above) does not, and should not, amount to a violation of the ethics codes (although, of course, it might lead the client to employ other counsel). In practice, lawyers and firms frequently find themselves taking positions that run counter to the concerns of some client or other. Free expression of legal argument, with its corresponding policy implications, gives life to the ideal of professional independence in the practice of law. It is that ideal that makes possible truly disinterested counsel. [16]

Protecting the independence of lawyers is also important to ensuring their participation in law reform efforts. Much of the work of bar associations involves such efforts. Of course, law reform activity may permit axe-grinding on behalf of clients, but it can also provide opportunities for more or less disinterested participation by well-informed professionals, who advocate views that their clients would disapprove. The bar has long supported such involvement. Ethical Consideration 8–1 of the ABA Code emphasizes that lawyers "should participate in proposing and supporting legislation and programs to improve the system, without regard to the general interests or desires of clients or former clients," And EC 7–17 similarly insists that a lawyer "may take positions on public issues

15. The Restatement of The Law Governing Lawyers, § 128, Cmt. f, takes the same position.

16. See for example, Elihu Root, quoted in Martin Mayer, The Lawyers 6

(1967); and Norman W. Spaulding, "The Prophet and the Bureaucrat: Positional Conflicts in Service Pro Bono Publico," 50 Stan. L. Rev. 1395 (1998).

and espouse legal reforms he favors without regard to the individual views of any client."

A variation of positional (or personal) conflicts involves what are often termed "ideological" conflicts. One such conflict arises when a lawyer's position in a particular matter antagonizes another client even though no directly adverse interests are implicated. These conflicts help explain why specialists in certain substantive areas typically represent only "one side of the street"; personal injury plaintiffs' lawyers generally do not take insurance defense cases, and union lawyers do not represent management. Another type of ideological conflict involves political affiliations. Some lawyers are conspicuous conservatives, while others are moderates or left liberals, and many clients are either attracted or repelled by such affiliations.

Ideological conflicts also can constrain lawyers' pro bono work. Model Rule 6.4 states that "A lawyer may serve . . . an organization involved in reform of the law . . . notwithstanding that the reform may affect the interests of a client." Nonetheless, many firms reportedly are "careful not to step on the toes of their clients' important interests" or to offend their values.[17] Yet lawyers' willingness to take unpopular cases can also be a source of enormous pride, both for them and for the profession. Bar associations often confer their highest awards on lawyers who have risked alienating other clients or potential sources of business. Part of what distinguishes law as a profession is the willingness of its members to put principles above profit in accepting pro bono cases.

D. Successive Representation

Cases involving conflicts between a current and former client pose somewhat different concerns than cases involving conflicts among current clients. To current clients, lawyers owe obligations of loyalty and confidentiality. To former clients, the obligations of loyalty are far more circumscribed. Protecting former clients in perpetuity according to the same standard applicable to current clients would virtually destroy independent law practice: A lawyer who once served a client could never undertake a matter adverse to that client, or one that would involve a "positional" conflict with

---

17. Abe Krash, "Professional Responsibility to Clients and the Public Interest: Is There a Conflict?" 55 Chi. B. Rec. 31, 45 (1974). See Esther F. Lardent, "Positional Conflicts in the Pro Bono Context: Ethical Considerations and Market Forces," 67 Fordham L. Rev. 2279 (1999); Spaulding, supra note 16; John S. Dzienkowski, "Positional Conflicts of Interest," 71 Tex. L. Rev. 457 (1993).

the client. As attorneys' careers progressed and their number of past clients increased, the ability to accept new cases would proportionately decrease. In effect, counsel would become forever identified with particular clients.

However, although lawyers should be able to accept matters that are adverse to former clients, some obligations to those clients persist after representation is over. Lawyers may not use the confidences of former clients against them and may not directly attack work done for those clients. With respect to loyalty, the Restatement (Third) of the Law Governing Lawyers § 132, Comment b explains: "[A]t the time the lawyer represented the former client, the lawyer should have no incentive to lay the basis for subsequent representation against that client, such as by drafting provisions in a contract that could later be construed against the former client."

With respect to the protections involving confidentiality, courts and ethical codes have focused on whether there is a substantial relationship between a current and earlier representation. Under Model Rule 1.9, "[a] lawyer who has formerly represented a client in a matter shall not thereafter represent another person in the same or a substantially related matter in which that person's interests are materially adverse to the interests of the former client unless the former client gives informed consent, confirmed in writing." Matters are considered substantially related if there is a "substantial risk that confidential factual information as would normally have been obtained in the prior representation would materially advance the client's position in the subsequent matter." Restatement 132, Comment. When the previous and new matters are "substantially related," a presumption arises that relevant confidences were imparted to the lawyer and that a conflict of interest exists. The rationale for that presumption is that former clients should not have to prove that confidences actually passed, which might require revealing the very matters that were intended to remain secret.[18]

However, under the Model Rules, the presumption of disabling confidences does not apply if representation was provided by a firm that the lawyer has left and the lawyer had no personal involvement with the prior matter. Model Rule 1.9(b) provides that where an attorney's former firm represented a client in the same or substantially related matter, the attorney may not accept a new

---

18. See T.C. Theatre Corp. v. Warner Bros. Pictures, 113 F.Supp. 265, 268 (S.D.N.Y.1953); Analytica Inc. v. NPD Research Inc., 708 F.2d 1263, 1266 (7th Cir.1983).

representation only if the interests of the current client are adverse and if the attorney personally acquired confidential information material to the matter. Similarly, in cases where the representation involves matters that are not substantially related, Model Rule 1.9(c) requires simply that the attorney not use confidential information to the disadvantage of the former client. In addition, under Model Rule 1.10(b), lawyers remaining in a firm that a lawyer has left are not barred from taking matters adverse to the departing lawyer's client if none of the remaining lawyers were personally involved in the prior matter.

Somewhat more permissive rules apply to former government lawyers. The Code and Model Rules reflect the approach taken by most courts and bar ethics committees and codified in the Federal Ethics in Government Act.[19] Model Rule 1.11(a) provides that a lawyer who has formerly served as a public officer or employee of a government agency may not use confidential information to the disadvantage of the government and may not "represent a client in connection with a matter in which the lawyer participated personally and substantially as a public officer or employee, unless the appropriate government agency gives its informed consent, confirmed in writing, to the representation." Under Model Rule 1.11(b), when a government lawyer is disqualified from representation:

> no lawyer in a firm with which that lawyer is associated may knowingly undertake or continue representation in such a matter unless:
>
> > (1) the disqualified lawyer is timely screened from any participation in the matter and is apportioned no part of the fee therefrom; and
> >
> > (2) written notice is promptly given to the appropriate government agency to enable it to ascertain compliance with the provisions of this rule.

See also DR 9–101(B).

The permissibility of screening for government lawyers reflects the fact that many of these lawyers do not plan on remaining permanently in public service. The American political system contemplates party-affiliated governmental leadership, including party-affiliated lawyers, who will leave office if their party loses. After such a loss, the lawyers then typically return to the private sector, and often hope for a later return to public service. This pattern is commonly described as a "revolving door." Private sector employ-

---

19. 18 U.S.C. §§ 201–219. See ABA Formal Op. 342 (1976).

ment for lawyers includes reentry into law firms. If conflict of interest rules for former public officials were too stringent, the revolving door would stop revolving, and the ability of government to recruit talented lawyers (especially at the relatively low salary levels now prevailing) would be seriously compromised.

Undue restrictions on career mobility would also deprive the public sector of fresh perspectives, and would deprive the private sector of lawyers with valuable government experience. Yet concerns for both the fact and appearance of integrity among former public officials make some regulation necessary. Screening has been the strategy of choice. Accordingly, as noted below, a screen around a former government lawyer prevents imputation of the lawyer's conflicts to others in the new practice situation. However, validation of the screening mechanism in this context has raised a fundamental question about conflicts rules more generally. If such a mechanism works for former government employees, why wouldn't it work for other lawyers as well?

E. Vicarious Disqualification and Screening Strategies

The bar's traditional position on conflicts of interest has been that the disqualification of one lawyer in a law firm or other legal organization is imputed to all its other members. Model Rule 1.10, DR 5—105(b). The only exceptions are for government lawyers and for conflicts that are "based on a personal interest of the prohibited lawyer and ... [that do] not present a significant risk of materially limiting the representation of the client by the remaining lawyers in the firm." Model Rule 1.10(a); DR 9–101(B) . The theory underlying vicarious disqualification is that colleagues share revenue, reputation and future prospects, as well as opportunities for exchange of confidences that are not readily detected. Professor Charles Wolfram summarizes the conventional objection to screening: "In the end there is little but the self-serving assurance of the screening-lawyer foxes that they will carefully guard the screened-lawyer chickens."[20] One of the few efforts to test that proposition found that virtually all surveyed lawyers believed that an opponent's screen could be breached without detection.[21]

Yet strict vicarious disqualification rules have come to seem more and more problematic in an era of increasing size among law firms and increasing lateral mobility among their members. Partic-

---

20. Charles Wolfram, Modern Legal Ethics 402 (1986).

21. Lee A. Pizzimenti, "Screen Verite: Do Rules About Ethical Screens Reflect the Truth About Real–Life Law Firm Practice?," 52 U. Miami L. Rev. 305, 331–32 (1997).

ularly in large firms, which have hundreds of lawyers spread over multiple branch offices, a presumption of shared confidences appears anachronistic, and may unduly restrict clients' access to qualified counsel. The approach developed in accounting firms of "insulation walls" to segregate employees with conflicts of interest has accordingly gained support in the legal profession as well. A small but growing number of states have provided that screening is an effective antidote for at least some vicarious conflicts.[22] The ABA Ethics Commission 2000 recommended that screening be permitted, with notice to any affected clients, when a disqualified lawyer makes a lateral move to a new firm, as long as any confidential information is not likely to be significant in the future representation. Although the ABA House of Delegates rejected that proposal, it is likely to remain a subject of ongoing debate and possible adoption by states.

As matters now stand, firms take a variety of approaches in identifying conflicts of interest. Susan Shapiro's study found four primary strategies. A few lawyers, the "ostriches" of the group, do not specifically address the issue and hope for the best. A small minority, the "elephants," trust that they will never forget a matter that they have undertaken, and rely simply on the memories of lawyers and staff. This is seldom fully effective because recollections fade and institutional history disappears when lawyers retire or move to another firm. A third group of firms, the "squirrels," hold on to as much paper as possible, and pore over their records when a new case is proposed. In some firms, lawyers or staff simply consult a client list to ensure that the adverse party in a potential new matter is not already a client. In others, lawyers scrutinize mailing lists and time, billing, or accounting records. A fourth group, "cybersquirrels," have developed electronic databases to manage conflicts of interest. These systems vary in sophistication, but are often highly complex and labor intensive. Experience has demonstrated that even the most sophisticated computer conflict checks require monitoring by legal staff. Some large firms employ as many as ten specialists whose sole responsibility is revising the database and conducting computerized conflicts searches, which are then reviewed by lawyers.[23] The limited empirical evidence available suggests that the procedures in many firms leave much to be desired in terms of the quality of information collected about conflicts, the frequency with which the information

22. Christopher S. Dunnigan, "The Art Formerly Known as the Chinese Wall: Screening in Law Firms: Why, When, Where, and How," 11 Geo. J. Legal Ethics 291 (1998).

23. Shapiro, supra note 1, at 9.

is updated, the notice provided to parties about screening, and the procedures for maintaining screens.[24]

The frequency of conflicts problems has led to a growing reliance on "contract screening." This term describes arrangements under which the client waives defined conflicts, present and sometimes future, and the law firm agrees to screen the lawyers serving adverse interests. It is likely that contract screening will become standard practice as firms grow larger and encounter new engagements under greater time pressure. Indeed, some law firms, whose services are regarded as unique or nearly so, now insist on broad conflicts waivers as a matter of course.

The cumulative effect of these trends is that in a large firm there can be a dozen or more "screens" in effect within a single office at any time. In states that have the most permissive rules on screening, the systems tend to be subject to greater regulation and supervision than in states that allow them only for former government employees, for lawyers with "personal" conflicts, or for lawyers who implement them voluntarily (often as a condition of a client's waiver).[25] Ironically enough, a liberal rule on screening thus appears to offer clients more protection than most jurisdictions' restrictive frameworks.

In today's competitive climate, law firms must also continually consider whether taking a particular new matter will foreclose more valuable future business. Decisions about which clients to select often become highly divisive. Powerful partners who feel that they have been too often "conflicted out" of desirable business can take their talents elsewhere, and their threats to do so are an ongoing source of friction in many practice contexts.

If current trends continue, the bar will face increasing challenges in developing cost-effective strategies concerning conflicts of interest. Already many firms face a daunting task in managing their data bases and preventing turf battles. Tens of thousands of otherwise billable hours are devoted to screening and infighting over new business.[26] Although much of the cost is inherent in an increasingly complex and competitive legal environment, efforts to minimize conflicts over conflicts is an important priority for the profession.

----

24. Pizzimenti, supra note 21, at 321–24.

25. Id.

26. Shapiro, supra note 1, at 9–11.

F. Representing Organizations

In addition to conflicts of interest between past and present clients, conflicts can also arise within a client organization. In general, bar ethical rules and legal doctrine instruct lawyers to represent the interests of the "entity" rather than any of its particular constituents. Model Rule 1.13 Comment 1. However, such instructions may be of limited assistance when the issue is what those interests are, and who should decide.

In a substantial fraction of law practice, and probably most transactional matters, lawyers represent organizations, and the particular individuals with whom the lawyers interact are not technically "clients." Whether officers, directors, employees, or other agents, they are agents of or trustees for the organizational client. The organization is the beneficiary of lawyers' duties of loyalty and confidentiality, and is the holder of the company's legal rights and attorney-client privilege. Lawyers owe allegiance to the entity and reasonable care in fulfilling the representation. Where they fall short, they are subject to discharge and malpractice claims by the entity. These consequences follow from the law of corporations, partnerships, and agency. As a consequence, all interchanges between the client and the lawyer for an organization involve "role" on each side. The organization's leaders act in the role of agents for the legal entity, while lawyers act in the role of counsel to the entity.

However, the corporation speaks and acts through its individual constituents. In visible and physical terms, these individuals embody the organization, but in law they do not. This distinction is the source of special conflicts problems in corporate practice. In addition to circumstances where lawyers represent two corporations with competing interests, lawyers representing a single corporation encounter problems in determining who "personifies" the corporation, i.e., who can speak and act on its behalf.

In corporate representation, these later conflicts of interest assume multiple forms. Common examples involve determining management compensation; defending the corporation and its officers in shareholder derivative actions; representing both the entity and its employees in litigation; and investigating or litigating possible misconduct by employees that might also be imputed to the organization.

Model Rule 1.13 codifies the legal relationships involved. Rule 1.13(a) states the premise that the client is the organization and not its "constituents," such as officers, directors, and employees. This is basic corporation law: the entity is a separate legal construct, with an independent capacity to engage counsel. Model Rule

1.13(b) and (c) then address the implications of this premise. In general terms, if the lawyer confronts conduct by officers or employees that violates their duties to the corporation or that will likely subject the corporation to significant liability, the lawyer must pursue the organization's "best interests." Basically, the lawyer is obliged to admonish, object, and, if necessary, take the matter to higher authority within the organization.

The key question in this regard is not: who is the client. Rather, the central intertwined issues are: (1) what does the lawyer know about what is happening; (2) how legally serious is the situation; and (3) what are the professional and personal stakes of the corporate officials and the lawyers in the matter. On one hand, if the lawyer learns about an imminent blunder, is motivated to correct it, and has top management support, the matter is likely to be remedied. On the other hand, if the lawyer has some information indicating a possibly serious legal violation, but knows or suspects that top management will not support appropriate responses, then the lawyer may be tempted to avoid and, if necessary, later deny knowledge of the problem. In many cases, the wrong will surface only much later, perhaps never, and both the lawyer and responsible corporate officials may have passed from the scene.

Under these circumstances, in-house counsel face greater difficulties than other lawyers. In-house counsel usually know much more about the corporate workings, including attitudes of top management, and usually have a general responsibility to take care of all the company's legal problems rather than specific ad hoc assignments. In-house counsel are also professionally more vulnerable because they have only one client who is providing their salary and benefits, and who can fire them without cause. In short, in-house counsel have maximum information, maximum responsibility, and minimum job security.

Model Rule 1.13 recognizes that the interests of corporate counsel and corporate "constituents" can diverge. This rule gives directions to the lawyer when the organization's interests may be adverse to those of constituents: "the lawyer should advise any constituent ... of the conflict or potential conflict of interest.... Care must be taken to assure that the individual understands that, when there is such adversity of interest, the lawyer for the organization cannot provide legal representation for that individual, and that discussions between the lawyer for the organization and the individual may not be privileged." As a practical matter, however, the more explicit the lawyer's warning, the less likely individuals are to cooperate with an inquiry or investigation that may expose compromising information but that may also be essential for an appropriate organizational response. In recognition of this obvious tradeoff, the Comment to Model Rule 1.13 obliquely provides: "[w]hether such a warning should be given by the lawyer for the organization to any constituent individual may turn on the facts of each case."

A related issue, whether a lawyer can jointly represent the organization and any of its constituents, will also depend on the facts of a particular case. The general considerations are those set forth above in the discussion of multiple representation and those in Model Rule 1.8(h) on third-party payments of legal fees. This Rule prohibits a lawyer from accepting compensation from another party unless: the client gives informed consent; there is no interference with lawyer's independent judgement or relationship with client; and confidential information is not disclosed.

Joint representation under these circumstances has the obvious advantages of minimizing expenses and coordinating a unified defense with a consistent version of events.[27] The obvious disadvantage with such arrangements is that the interests of the organization and the officer or employee may ultimately diverge. If both are vindicated, joint representation has been a benefit. But if they are not, the organization may want to repudiate the conduct of the employee and may seek indemnification on the theory that the employee was solely responsible. Differences can then arise as to whether employees were acting within the scope of their employment or under directions from a supervisor, or whether particular actions were within the scope of an insurance policy. Typically, the risks will be greater for individuals than for the organization, given the frequent pressures they face to consent to joint representation, and the biases created by the attorney's own employment relationship. Such concerns impose a special responsibility on corporate counsel to ensure that consent to joint representation is not only fully informed, but is also reasonable under the circumstances. If a conflict is likely, lawyers should not wait to withdraw from the representation until it surfaces, because by then the individual's interests may already be irreparably injured. And if lawyers have acquired compromising confidential information, they may be forced to withdraw from representing both the organization and the individual, an outcome especially problematic for in-house attorneys.[28]

---

27. Nancy J. Moore, "Conflicts of Interest for In House Counsel: Issues Emerging From the Expanding Role of the Attorney–Employee," 39 S. Tex. L. Rev. 497, 508 (1998).

28. Id., at 508–09; Nancy J. Moore, "Ethical Issues in Third–Party Payment: Beyond the Insurance Defense Paradigm," 16 Rev. of Litigation 585 (1997).

Shareholder derivative suits can pose related issues. The Comment to Model Rule 1.13 views joint representation of the organization and its management and officers as presumptively valid:

> Most derivative actions are a normal incident of an organization's affairs, to be defended by the organization's lawyer, like any other suit. However, if the claim involves serious charges of wrongdoing by those in control of the organization, a conflict may arise between the lawyer's duty to the organization and the lawyer's relationship with the board.

By contrast, the Restatement (Third) of the Law Governing Lawyers § 219 follows recent case law and finds joint representation presumptively invalid. Unless the shareholders' claims clearly lack merit on their face, separate representation is generally thought advisable.[29] Because in-house counsel are closely identified with management, a standard practice is for the corporation to create an independent committee of outside directors not named as defendants to review the merits of the claim and, where appropriate, to select outside legal counsel for the organization.

G.   Representing The Government

Related issues arise in identifying "the client" of the government lawyer. Theoretically, the client could be the public, the government as a whole, the branch of government in which the lawyer is employed, the agency in which the lawyer works, or the officials responsible for the lawyer's actions. Courts, commentators, and bar ethical codes have taken different views, although they all maintain that lawyers in public office owe special responsibilities to the public.[30] The difficulty lies in determining what constitutes the public's interest and what it requires when members of the government disagree.

That difficulty arises in a wide variety of factual settings. In some instances, lawyers in one agency are responsible for repre-

29. Geoffrey C. Hazard, Jr., Susan P. Koniak, & Roger C. Cramton, The Law and Ethics of Lawyering 729–30 (3rd ed. 1999).

30. See Gray Panthers v. Schweiker, 716 F.2d 23, 33 (D.C.Cir.1983); Freeport–McMoRan Oil & Gas Co. v. FERC, 962 F.2d 45, 47 (D.C.Cir.1992); Model Rule of Professional Conduct 1.13; Model Code of Professional Responsibility EC 7–13 (1969); Steven K. Berenson, "Public Lawyers, Private Values: Can, Should, and Will Government Lawyers Serve the Public Interest?" 41 B. C. L. Rev. 789 (2000); Jack B. Weinstein & Gay A. Crosthwait, "Some Reflections on Conflicts Between Government Attorneys and Clients," 1 Touro L. Rev. 1 (1985); William Josephson & Russell Pearce, "To Whom Does the Government Lawyer Owe the Duty of Loyalty When Clients Are in Conflict?" 29 How. L. J. 539 (1986).

senting another agency's position but find that position inconsistent with applicable laws, policies, or societal concerns. In other contexts, higher authorities within the lawyers' own agency or the central administration may direct them to act in ways that they find similarly problematic. For example, a change in administration during the pendency of litigation may result in directives for a government lawyer to "switch sides," although the lawyer believes that the new position is unsupported by the law or facts. At another level, an unwillingness by the legislative or executive branch to provide adequate funding for government institutions, such as prisons or mental health facilities, may place attorneys in the position of defending conditions that they believe violate constitutional standards or individual rights. Another common dilemma arises when lawyers learn confidential information that they believe should be shared with other legislative, executive, or judicial decision makers or with the general public.

Very little case law is available to help identify the "client" in such circumstances.[31] Commentators and bar ethics codes have taken three primary approaches. One position is that the client is normally the government agency that employs the lawyer. This "agency approach" is reflected in Rule 1.13 of the Federal Bar Association's Model Rules of Professional Conduct for Federal Lawyers. However, the Rule includes the caveat that a government lawyer may have "authority to question such conduct more extensively than ... a lawyer for a private organization in similar circumstances." The Restatement (Third) of the Law Governing Lawyers reflects a variation of the agency approach. The Comment to § 156 suggests that in most cases, the client of the government lawyer is the agency involved in the underlying dispute, but that the lawyer's responsibility may vary depending on the circumstances.

The primary advantage of the agency approach is clarity in application. In essence, this approach models the relationship between lawyers and clients in private practice. So too, some commentators have argued that an agency framework fosters political accountability. By limiting the government lawyer's discretion to make independent judgements of the public's interest, this approach vests decision-making authority with elected officials who are more directly responsible to the public.[32]

---

31. For a summary, see Hazard, Koniak, & Cramton, supra note 29, at 787.

32. See, e.g., Catherine J. Lanctot, "The Duty of Zealous Advocacy and the Ethics of the Federal Government Lawyer: The Three Hardest Questions," 64 S. Cal. L. Rev. 951, 1012–17 (1991); Jonathan R. Macey & Geoffrey P. Miller, "Reflections on Professional Responsi-

Yet in some contexts, an agency framework reflects an unrealistic assumption of political accountability and an impoverished conception of the government lawyer's social responsibilities. After all, most government decisions are made by middle level bureaucrats who are not in any direct sense subject to majoritarian control. Even senior agency officials have attenuated democratic accountability. High-ranking federal officials can owe their appointments to a single election where no candidate has even received a majority of the popular vote.[33] More fundamentally, the agency-as-client framework may unduly restrict the lawyer's obligation as a government employee to ensure that government policy is appropriately carried out. Where, for example, higher level officials are directing a lawyer to act in ways that defy applicable law, regulations, or well-established legal principles, some effort to challenge that decision is consistent with democratic values.

To that end, a second approach identifies the client of the government lawyer as the government as a whole. The Model Rules take that view. The Comment to Rule 1.13 notes:

> Defining precisely the identity of the client and prescribing the resulting obligations of such lawyers may be more difficult in the government context and is a matter beyond the scope of these Rules.... Although in some circumstances the client may be a specific agency, it may also be a branch of government, such as the executive branch, or the government as a whole. For example, if the action or failure to act involves the head of a bureau, either the department of which the bureau is a part or the relevant branch of government may be the client for purposes of this Rule. Moreover, in a matter involving the conduct of government officials, a government lawyer may have authority under applicable law to question such conduct more extensively than that of a lawyer for a private organization in similar circumstances....

This approach, however, raises as many questions as it answers. Indeed, the Rule itself recognizes as much, by placing beyond its scope the question of what concrete actions lawyers should take in the face of wrongful conduct.

---

bility in a Regulatory State," 63 Geo. Wash. L. Rev. 1105, 1116 (1995); Geoffrey P. Miller, "Government Lawyers' Ethics in a System of Checks and Balances," 54 U. Chi. L. Rev. 1293, 1294–95 (1987); Michael Stokes Paulsen, "Hell, Handbaskets, and Government Lawyers: The Duty of Loyalty and Its Limits," 61

Law & Contemp. Probs., 83, 85–86 (1998).

33. Note, "Rethinking the Professional Responsibilities of Federal Agency Lawyers," 115 Harv. L. Rev. 1170, 1175 (2002). See also Berenson, supra note 30, at 823.

A final approach, which views the public as the client, is plausible in principle but even more indeterminate in practice. Some efforts have been made to specify the implications of this approach in particular contexts. For example, Model Rule 3.8 and the ABA Standards Relating to the Administration of Criminal Justice: The Prosecution Function, elaborate the prosecutor's obligation to "seek justice," not simply convictions.[34] That obligation includes:

- filing only charges supported by probable cause;
- making timely disclosure of exculpatory or mitigating evidence; and
- ensuring that the accused has a reasonable opportunity to obtain counsel.

Efforts to define the government lawyer's obligations in civil contexts have been more limited and less specific. For example, EC 7–14 of the Code states:

A government lawyer in a civil action or administrative proceeding has the responsibility to seek justice and to develop a full and fair record, and he should not use his position or the economic power of the government to harass parties or to bring about unjust settlements or results.

Yet what constitutes an "unjust" settlement is often open to dispute. Agency lawyers have taken different views on such questions as whether the government should disclose adverse material facts, assert a statute of limitations, or fail to inform opposing counsel of impending procedural defects in order to defeat an otherwise meritorious claim.[35] Lawyers in the United States Solicitor General's office have long agreed that it is sometimes appropriate for the government to "confess error" and to ask the Supreme Court to vacate a lower judgment in the government's favor. But Solicitor General lawyers have disagreed about which particular cases warrant such a request.[36]

In addressing the government lawyers's responsibility to seek justice, Federal District Judge Jack Weinstein gives an example from his experience as counsel for a New York county. The case involved a condemnation proceeding in which government negotiators had worked out a property valuation settlement with an

34. The phrase comes from Berger v. United States, 295 U.S. 78, 88 (1935).

35. Bruce A. Green, "Must Government Lawyers 'Seek Justice' in Civil Litigation?," 9 Widener J. Public Law 235 (2000).

36. David A. Strauss, "The Solicitor General and the Interests of the United States," 61 Law & Contemp. Probs. 165, 169 (1998).

elderly couple who were unrepresented by counsel. The offer was about a third of what county appraisers had estimated the property to be worth, the couple was unaware of its value, and Weinstein believed that it was inappropriate for a public servant to exploit the landowner's ignorance.[37] On similar reasoning, a state bar ethic committee concluded that it was appropriate for a municipal lawyer to inform an unrepresented civil opponent that he faced risks of self-incrimination and might profit from advice of counsel.[38]

Greater difficulties arise when a government lawyer is not in a position to make the final decision on a contested matter. One possibility is withdrawal, or in cases of fundamental importance, resignation. Another option, in cases of exceptional importance, is a public statement registering disagreement with the position taken. A celebrated example involves Lawrence Wallace, a career government attorney serving as Acting Solicitor General, when he was defending the Internal Revenue Service's denial of a tax exemption to a university practicing racial discrimination. While the case was pending, there was a change of administration and its new leaders instructed the office to reverse its position and to support the university. Wallace filed a brief that complied with the instruction but included a statement that it did not reflect the views of the Acting Solicitor General.[39]

To the extent that such cases suggest generalizable principles, they imply some obligation on the part of attorneys to preserve governmental legitimacy by promoting compliance with applicable laws and ensuring fairness in substantive and procedural decisions. When a proposed governmental action appears inconsistent with these principles, attorneys have, at minimum, a responsibility to seek internal review and reconsideration. If such internal efforts are unsuccessful, lawyers should consider the need for disclosure of information to others, such as the legislature, the courts, or the public. These bodies may or may not secure reversal of the decision in the case at issue, but they may be able to alter future policy.

In contexts involving illegal activities by government officials, disclosure of relevant information may be mandatory or protected under federal and state law.[40] For example, federal employees are

---

37. Jack B. Weinstein, "Some Ethical and Political Problems of a Government Attorney," 18 Me. L. Rev. 156, 169 (1966).

38. N.Y. State Bar Association, Committee on Professional Ethics, Op. 728 (2000).

39. Philip B. Heymann & Lance Liebman, The Social Responsibilities of Lawyers: Case Studies, 139, 181 (1988).

40. See Hazard, Koniak, & Cramton, supra note 29, at 807–11; Roger C. Cramton, "The Lawyer as Whistleblower: Confidentiality and the Government required to inform the Attorney General of possible criminal violations by federal officers. The Whistleblower Protection Act of 1989 also prohibits a federal agency from taking an adverse personnel action against an employee who discloses information that reveals a violation of law, rule or regulation; gross mismanagement; gross waste of funds; an abuse of authority; or a specific and substantial danger to public health and safety.[41] Whistleblowing is seldom a costless enterprise for government employees, but it can also result in enormous public benefits and the personal satisfaction that comes from acting from moral commitment.[42]

H. Class Action Representation

A final form of intra-group conflicts of interest arise in class action lawsuits. The interests of class members seldom fully coincide, the ideological and financial interests of lawyers and clients may diverge dramatically, and class members may be unaware of the conflicts or even that they are part of a lawsuit. With the rise of class actions as a distinctive feature of American legal processes, conflicts have emerged in a wide variety of settings, such as consumer suits, mass tort claims, employment discrimination cases, and public interest litigation. Although the structural features of these class actions somewhat differ, they also present certain common concerns.

The basic framework for these cases is Rule 23 of the Federal Rules of Civil Procedure and its state law analogues. Under Rule 23, class actions are appropriate if:

> (1) the class is so numerous that joinder of all members is impracticable, (2) there are questions of law or fact common to the class, (3) the claims or defenses of the representative parties are typical of the claims or defenses of the class, and (4) the representative parties will fairly and adequately protect the interests of the class.

Under the rules of civil procedure, bar ethical codes, and relevant caselaw, attorneys, as well as the named class representatives must "fairly and adequately protect the interests of the class." However, judicial and bar ethics decisions have provided little guidance about lawyers' concrete responsibilities. Among the unanswered questions are whether "interests" means anything other than preferences,

Lawyer," 5 Geo. J. Legal Ethics 291 (1991).

41. 28 U. S. C. § 535; 5 U.S. C. § 3202(b).

42. Myron Glazer and Penina M. Glazer, The Whistleblowers: Exposing Corruption in Government and Industry (1989).

and what steps counsel must take to identify and address conflicts within a class.

The most serious threshold issue will be whether the proceeding is certified, that is, declared by the trial judge to be a proper class suit. After certification, almost all class suits are settled. Indeed, many class proceedings are certified only when there has been agreement on settlement terms between counsel for the class and the opposition. There is almost always some conflict between the interest of class counsel (notably, the size of the fee) and the interest of the class.

Other common disputes center around the distribution of monetary awards within the class and the tradeoffs between injunctive and financial remedies. In public interest litigation, the remedial conflicts can be more complicated. School desegregation cases have repeatedly demonstrated these difficulties. For example, dispute has centered on the relative importance of integration, financial resources, curricular improvements, and minority control in remedying educational inequalities. Even constituencies that support school integration in principle have disputed its value in particular settings where long bus rides or white flight are likely results. So too, parents challenging the adequacy of bilingual or special education programs have differed over whether mainstreaming or upgrading separate classes represents the better solution. Suits involving mental health treatment have involved conflict over whether to demand improvement in residential facilities or creation of community care alternatives. In employment discrimination cases, controversy can arise on the tradeoffs between back-pay awards and prospective relief, the formulas for computing damages, and the means chosen to restructure hiring, promotion, and transfer systems.[43]

Like other litigants, class members may also differ in their willingness to compromise or to assume the risks of protracted proceedings. Given the uncertainty of outcome and indeterminacy of relief in many class actions, risk-averse plaintiffs may be prepared to make substantial concessions. Other class members may prefer to fight, "if not to the death, at least until the Supreme Court denies certiorari."[44] The conflicts are compounded where the settlement provides generously only for the named plaintiffs, or favors current over future class members.

---

43. For examples see Nancy Morawetz, "Bargaining, Class Representation, and Fairness," 54 Ohio St. L. J. 1, 37–38 (1993); Deborah L. Rhode, "Class Conflicts in Class Actions," 34 Stan. L. Rev. 1183, 1185–91 (1982).

44. Rhode, supra note 43, at 1191.

Although courts have the ultimate responsibility for ensuring substantive and procedural fairness in class action litigation, they often place corresponding obligations on lawyers. As one federal court of appeals put it, "class action counsel possess, in a very real sense, fiduciary obligations to those not before the court."[45] Principal among those duties is the responsibility to inform the trial judge of conflicting interests that may call for separate representation or other corrective measures.

This responsibility is straightforward in principle but difficult to enforce in practice. Although many attorneys make considerable efforts to identify and accommodate differences within a class, many also face significant pressures to present a united front. Most obviously, lawyers want to avoid laying foundations for opponents to challenge certification of the class. If such efforts prove successful, lawyers may lose a substantial investment that they cannot recover from the clients. At a minimum, controversy over certification results in expense and delay that divert resources from trial preparation. Certification disputes may also trigger involvement of additional lawyers, who will seek to share the limelight, the control over litigation decisions, and the resources available for attorneys' fees.

Exposing conflicts can also frustrate objectives that attorneys believe will serve the best interests of the class. A common example involves institutional reform proposals that offer generous settlement terms for current class members but little protection or precedential value for future members or victims.[46] Such proposals may also pose conflicts between clients and lawyers' own interests that are difficult to prevent or address. These concerns make judicial oversight crucial, however difficult to institutionalize in practice.

I.   Lawyer/Client Conflicts of Interest

Fiduciary law and bar ethical rules prohibit lawyers from representation that will be "materially limited" by their own personal interests unless they reasonably believe that they will be able to provide "competent and diligent" assistance and the client gives informed consent. Model Rule 1.7. See also DR 5–101. Both the

45. Greenfield v. Villager Indus., Inc., 483 F.2d 824, 832 (3d Cir.1973). See generally Rhode, supra note 43, at 1204–05.

46. For recent cases in which the Supreme Court was critical of class ac-

tion attorneys who failed adequately to represent the interests of future class members, see Amchem Products, Inc. v. Windsor, 521 U.S. 591 (1997), and Ortiz v. Fibreboard Corp., 527 U.S. 815 (1999).

Model Rules and Code also regulate specific conduct likely to pose conflicts, such as lawyer-client business transactions, gifts, financial assistance, and sexual relationships. Model Rule 1.8; DR 5–104. Underlying these regulations are certain principles designed to prevent exploitation of client ignorance, vulnerability, or lack of bargaining power. So, for example, lawyers may not enter into business transactions with clients unless the terms are fair, reasonable, and fully disclosed, and the client gives informed written consent after being advised to seek independent legal advice. Model Rule 1.7. See also DR 5–104. Some conduct is so fraught with the potential for abuse that it is categorically prohibited, such as preparation of wills with testamentary gifts to the preparers, prospective limitations on malpractice liability to clients who lack independent counsel, or sexual relationships with clients that do not predate the legal representation. Model Rule 1.8(c), (h) and (j).

The primary objective of such rules is protection of clients, but some restrictions on conflicts of interest also seek to protect the public and to preserve confidence in the profession. For example, the prohibition on "maintenance"–i.e., financial assistance to clients for personal expenses–is partly designed to prevent "encourag[ing] clients to pursue lawsuits that might not otherwise be brought." Model Rule 1.8 Comment. The Rule also seeks to prevent lawyers from competing for clients though monetary inducements and from having such a stake in the outcome that it might compromise their ethical obligations. Id.

Whether all of these provisions in fact serve the public, however, is open to debate. The prohibition on maintenance has been subject to particular criticism. According to some courts and commentators, a categorical restriction on loans to needy clients prevents suits that *should* be brought; it forces litigants with meritorious claims to accept inadequate settlements instead of holding out for an appropriate judgment.[47] Such concerns underlie the more permissive approach of The Restatement of the Law Governing Lawyers. Section 48 allows a lawyer to make a loan on "fair terms" if it is necessary "to enable the client to withstand delay in litigation that might unjustly induce the client to settle or dismiss a case because of financial hardship rather than on the merits; and if the lawyer does not promise or offer the loan before being retained."

---

47. See Rhode & Luban, supra note 13, at 694–95; Fred C. Zacharias, "Limits on Client Autonomy in Legal Ethics Regulation," 81 Boston U. L. Rev. 198, 236–37 (2001).

Other potential lawyer/client conflicts are regulated less by ethical rules and legal doctrine than by organizational policies and malpractice insurance requirements. For example, neither the Model Rules nor the Code prohibits lawyers from sitting on the board of directors of a client, although the Comment to Model Rule 1.7 cautions against such a dual role under circumstances where it would "compromise the lawyer's independence of professional judgment." Many ethics experts believe that the risks of such circumstances are always present.[48] Accordingly, some law firms have policies against lawyers serving on client boards and some legal malpractice insurance policies exclude coverage for lawyers in that role. By contrast, other firms are willing to assume some risk of conflicts in exchange for the advantages that come with lawyers' board service, such as enhanced prestige, credibility, and personal relationships with corporate decision makers.[49]

Similar differences in organizational policy have emerged concerning lawyers' investment in clients. During the boom in internet and other high-technology companies in the late 1990s, many prominent law firms pioneered fee arrangements in which cash-strapped entrepreneurs compensated lawyers with shares or investments in their start-up companies. This practice has a long history. For example, taking a "piece of the action" instead of a cash fee has been common in real estate development. It has always been somewhat controversial within the bar, both because it threatens to compromise lawyers' independent judgment and because lawyers sometimes receive large payouts that seem grossly disproportionate to the services rendered.

In response to such concerns, ABA Formal Opinion 00–418 (2000) concluded that compensation in the form of client shares does not violate either the Model Rules or the Code if the terms were reasonable under circumstances ascertainable at the time of the transaction. To minimize disputes over what was reasonable, some experts and bar ethics committees advise lawyers to retain an investment professional who can estimate the value of the interests at issue. To minimize the risk that lawyers' professional judgment will be skewed by a desire to protect their investment, some firms

48. See Wolfram, supra note 20, at 739; Craig C. Albert, "The Lawyer–Director: An Oxymoron?," 9 Geo. J. Legal Ethics 413, 426 (1996).

49. For an overview of the debate, see SEC Staff Report on Corporate Accountability F2G–F31 (1980); Dean Starkman, "Lawyers Debate Ethics of Role in Boardrooms," Wall St. J., Aug. 5,

1996, at B1. Samuel C. Stretton, "Lawyers Serving as Corporate Directors May Have a Conflict If They Represent the Company," 25 Pa. L. Wky. 244 (2002); Susanna M. Kim, "Dual Identities and Dueling Obligations: Preserving Independence in Corporate Representation," 68 Tenn. L. Rev. 179 (2001).

have created common fund arrangements. In these firms, securities from any client go into a single fund in which firm members may invest. The result of these arrangements is to dilute the impact that legal advice to a particular client might have on a lawyer's personal investments. Whether such arrangements are sufficient protections against conflicts of interest is likely to remain an issue of ongoing debate in the bar.[50]

These investment arrangements are, however, not the only, or even the primary, sources of lawyer-client conflicts concerning legal fees. As discussion in Chapter X indicates, almost all forms of payment pose some risk that lawyers' financial interests will depart from those of their clients. An hourly fee arrangement creates incentives to expand work to fit the budget available.[51] By contrast, a contingent fee agreement can create the opposite incentive. In these cases, clients are not paying for the attorneys' time so their interest centers solely on the result attained. Attorneys, by contrast, need also to consider the efforts necessary to achieve a good result and the competing claims on their resources.

The potential for attorney-client conflicts is compounded when a proposed settlement includes a provision for legal fees that is extremely generous or totally inadequate. These difficulties are also common when the litigation is governed by a fee-shifting rule, which provides attorneys' fees to a prevailing plaintiff. A dilemma then arises if the opposing party offers a generous settlement to the client but a paltry fee–or none at all–for counsel. Decisions of the Supreme Court permit the opposing party either to condition settlement on a waiver of attorney's fees or to avoid statutory fee awards by settling without a judgment on the merits.[52] The opposite problem arises with settlements that make lawyers the major beneficiaries; they receive millions for minimal work while class members recover only nominal damages or largely worthless coupons for the defendant's products.[53] Plaintiffs' attorneys generally

50. For an overview see Brian J. Redding, "Investing In or Doing Business With Clients: Some Thoughts on Lawyer Liability and Legal Ethics Issues," Professional Lawyer 113 (Fall 2000); Debra Baker, "Who Wants to Be a Millionaire?," ABA J., Feb. 2000, at 36; Edward H. Cohen, "Lawyers Investing in Their Clients: The Rules of Professional Responsibility," 14 Insights 2 (2000); Gwyneth E. McAlpine, "Getting a Piece of the Action: Should Lawyers Be Allowed to Invest In Their Clients' Stock," 47 UCLA L. Rev. 549 (1999).

51. Deborah L. Rhode, In the Interests of Justice: Reforming the Legal Profession 61 (2000).

52. Evans v. Jeff D., 475 U.S. 717 (1986); Buckhannon Bd. and Care Home, Inc. v. West Virginia Dept. of Health & Human Resources, 532 U.S. 598 (2001).

53. See examples cited in Rhode & Luban, supra note 13, at 553–54; Rhode, supra note 51, at 176; Susan P. Koniak & George M. Cohen, "In Hell There Will Be Lawyers Without Clients or Law," in argue that such cases serve a valuable function in deterring misconduct where the individual injuries are too small to justify litigation. However, commentators often question whether the amount of fees is proportionate to the results achieved or to the effort expended. In theory, judicial oversight of class action settlements and contingent fees is designed to prevent such abuses. In practice, however, trial courts are often reluctant to disturb agreements that clear their dockets and impose no risk of appeal.[54]

Nonfinancial conflicts of interest are even harder for courts, clients, and bar disciplinary authorities to address. Lawyers often have career concerns that compete with fiduciary obligations. For example, they may be interested in attracting publicity, expanding their organizational turf, or gaining trial experience.[55] Lawyers also have long-term interests in maintaining good relationships with opposing counsel, potential clients, and other participants in the legal system such as judges, police, insurance adjusters, and agency officials. These interests may sometimes conflict with a particular client's objectives. So too, in contexts involving public interest or governmental litigation, attorneys may have ideological commitments that diverge from those of the class or agency that they represent. In commenting on such conflicts, Professor Derrick Bell has observed that concerns of principle, "though rarer than greed" are harder to control.[56] Where formal mechanisms of accountability are lacking, lawyers have a special responsibility to ensure that their own views on the merits do not supplant those of parties who will have to live with the results.

Ethics in Practice 177–204 (Deborah L. Rhode, ed. 2000).

54. See sources cited in note 53, and Judith Resnik, Dennis Curtis, & Deborah R. Hensler, "Individuals Within the Aggregate: Relations, Representation, and Fees," 71 N.Y. U. L. Rev. 296 (1996).

55. See Berenson, supra note 30, at 808–11. Macey & Miller, supra note 32, at 1117–19; Michael Selmi, "Public vs. Private Enforcement of Civil Rights: The Case of Housing and Employment," 45 UCLA L. Rev. 1401 (1998).

56. Derrick A. Bell, "Serving Two Masters: Integration Ideals and Client Interests in School Desegregation Litigation," 85 Yale L. J. 470, 504 (1976). For other examples, see Rhode, supra note 43.

Chapter IX

ACCESS TO JUSTICE

A. The Nature of the Problem

It is widely perceived that America has too much law and too little justice–too much litigation for those who can afford it and too little access to legal remedies for those who cannot. A majority of Americans believe that the nation has too many lawyers and that they file too many lawsuits.[1] A majority also agree that wealth matters in the kind of justice people receive.[2] There is, however, considerably less agreement about what, if anything, should be done about those problems. Part of the difficulty is that many individuals are poorly informed or deeply ambivalent about access to justice. They underestimate the true costs of legal process, overestimate the extent of litigiousness among the "haves," and are reluctant to subsidize adequate services for the "have nots."

Litigiousness

Most complaints about litigiousness rest on three assumptions: that the nation has an excessive number of lawyers, that they file too many lawsuits, and that legal proceedings cost too much. The factual basis for each of these claims deserves closer exploration.

Since the Colonial era, Americans have complained about the number of lawyers, and early settlers made some efforts to exclude them entirely or at least to limit their role.[3] During the late eighteenth century, there were mob uprisings against the "cursed hungry Caterpillars" preying on the Commonwealth.[4] The contemporary tort reform movement often builds on similar sentiments, acerbically expressed in antilawyer humor.[5] Such criticisms typical-

1. See sources cited in Deborah L. Rhode, In the Interests of Justice: Reforming the Legal Profession 117 (2000); Deborah L. Rhode, "Too Much Law, Too Little Justice: Too Much Rhetoric, Too Little Reform," 11 Geo J. L. Ethics 989 (1998); ABA Section of Litigation, Public Perceptions of Lawyers Consumer Research Findings 7 (2002).

2. Marc Galanter, "Farther Along," 33 Law & Soc'y Rev. 1113 (1999); ABA, Perceptions of the U.S. Justice System 5 (1999) (finding that only a third of surveyed Americans believe that the justice

system tries to treat wealthy and poor alike).

3. See Lawrence M. Friedman, A History of American Law 45–46 (1985); Terence C. Halliday, "Six Score Years and Ten: Demographic Transitions in the American Legal Profession, 1850–1980," 20 Law & Soc'y Rev. 53 (1986).

4. Friedman, supra note 3, at 96.

5. See Rhode, In the Interests of Justice, supra note 1, at 119; Pamela Sherrid, "Lawyers on Trial," U.S. News & World Report, Dec. 17, 2001; Marc Galanter, "Predators and Parasites: Law-

ly presuppose, but rarely defend, some evaluative standard by which America's legal profession looks too big. The implicit assumption is that this nation has a disproportionate number of lawyers compared to other societies.

Many critics, however, have key facts wrong. For example, although some politicians have asserted that America has seventy percent of the world's lawyers, informed estimates put the figure somewhere between a quarter and a third, which is roughly the United States' share of the world's combined Gross National Product.[6] Cross-cultural comparisons also can be misleading since they fail to reveal the number of practitioners in other countries who are not licensed members of the bar but who receive legal training and perform tasks that in this country are largely reserved for lawyers. In Germany, for example, in-house corporate counsel do not belong to the bar and are not counted as members of the legal profession, but provide the same services as American lawyers. In Japan, the number of individuals who are certified to act as courtroom advocates represents only a small fraction of those who receive legal education in universities and who give legal advice and prepare legal documents. The reason for Japan's disparity between licensed professionals and law-trained specialists is that pass rates on bar exams are kept at artificially low levels, under five percent.[7]

Claims about America's oversupply of lawsuits are equally in need of qualification. Experts generally agree that current litigation rates in the United States are not exceptionally high, either in comparison with rates in prior historical eras or with those in many other Western industrial nations not known for contentiousness. Higher per capita rates of litigation occurred in some American communities in the colonial era and in the nineteenth and early twentieth centuries.[8] Contemporary rates of United States court filings are in the same range as Canada, Australia, New Zealand, England, Denmark, and Israel.[9] In any event, court filings are not necessarily a barometer of cultural combativeness. Over ninety-eight percent of American litigation occurs in the state courts,

yer–Bashing and Civil Justice," 28 Ga. L. Rev. 633 (1994).

6. Marc Galanter, "News from Nowhere: The Debased Debate on Civil Justice," 71 Denv. U. L. Rev. 77, 80 (1993); Marc Galanter, "Pick a Number, Any Number," Legal Times, Feb. 17, 1992, at 26.

7. Junjiro Tsubota, "Myth and Truth on Non–Litigiousness in Japan," 30 U. of Chi. L. School Record 8 (1984).

8. See Marc S. Galanter, "Reading the Landscape of Disputes: What We Know and Don't Know (and Think We Know) About Our Allegedly Contentious and Litigious Society," 31 UCLA L. Rev. 4, 55–58 (1983).

9. Marc Galanter, "The Life and Times of the Big Six; or, the Federal Courts Since the Good Old Days," 1988 Wis. L. Rev. 921, 942–45 (1988).

where uncontested matters such as divorces and probate account for a large proportion of the caseload.[10]

The other most frequently cited evidence for America's undue litigiousness relies on anecdotal examples of seemingly avaricious lawyers who bring frivolous claims. Yet what constitutes frivolity is in the eye of the beholder, and media portraits can be misleading. A textbook illustration involves a multimillion dollar verdict against the McDonalds fast-food chain. The conventional description of the case was that summarized by the national Chamber of Commerce: "Is it fair to get a couple of million dollars from a restaurant just because you spilled hot coffee on yourself?"[11] On closer examination, however, that description is highly misleading. The plaintiff, a 79 year-old woman, suffered acutely painful third-degree burns from 180–degree coffee. Only after McDonalds refused to reimburse her eight days of hospital expenses did she bring suit. At trial, jurors learned of 700 other burn cases involving McDonalds' coffee during the preceding decade, and warnings by medical experts that the beverage temperatures were causing serious injuries. The jury's verdict of $2.3 million included punitive damages reflecting two days of coffee sales revenues, and the judge reduced the judgment to $640,000. To avoid an appeal, the plaintiff then settled the case for a smaller amount. McDonalds put up warning signs and other fast-food chains adopted similar measures. While evaluations of this final result may vary, it was not the patently "ridiculous" travesty that media critics described.[12]

So too, other cases where the individual losses are small can serve as a useful deterrent to corporate negligence or misconduct. And for cases that are truly without merit, an appropriate response is the kind of sanctions that Chapter VI proposed, not a categorical indictment of lawyers and lawsuits. A more productive debate over litigiousness requires deeper analysis of fundamental questions. How much are we prepared to pay for legal remedies? How does access to the legal system compare with other demands on our social resources? What are the alternatives to litigation? Are law and lawyers handling public needs in the most cost-effective manner? Would tighter limitations on expensive discovery processes be desirable, or should losers pay their opponents' attorneys' fees?

On most of these issues, the public is divided, but concerns about the price of legal process are widely shared. Over four-fifths

10. National Center for State Courts, "Examining the Work of State Courts, 10, 13 (2001).

11. See Rhode, In the Interests of Justice, supra note 1, at 122.

12. Id. See also Ralph Nader & Wesly J. Smith, No Contest 267–72 (1996).

of surveyed Americans believe that litigation takes too long and costs too much; about three-quarters believe that it is damaging the country's economy.[13] Yet here again, the factual basis for the latter assumptions is weaker than commonly supposed. Although we lack reliable assessments of the total costs of civil liability, the best available calculations for the tort system do not reveal a substantial adverse effect on economic productivity. For example, Brookings Institution research estimates that tort liability could represent no more than two percent of the total price of United States goods and services, an amount "highly unlikely" to have a substantial impact on American competitiveness. Other estimates similarly suggest that businesses' total liability for all legal claims, including torts, is about 25 cents for every 100 dollars in revenue.[14]

So too, many Americans, including some prominent critics of the legal profession, seriously underestimate the need for legal assistance and the factors that make it inherently expensive to provide. To function effectively, this nation's adversary system generally requires parties to have competent lawyers with sufficient resources to present their case before a neutral judge. Such a process requires multiple professionals, office facilities, communication systems, and a supporting cast of clerks, reporters, bailiffs, administrative staff, and so forth. Transactional practice, as distinct from litigation, generally requires fewer professionals, but other services and facilities are still necessary. A lawyer's office work, if done properly, can usually prevent or ameliorate legal problems, but it too can be expensive to provide. Many legal matters require a significant investment of time, either by an attorney or by someone with substantially equivalent skills.

Those skills generally command a substantial market price. Lawyers have abilities that are highly valued, both within and outside the legal system. Practitioners are not only literate and knowledgeable about the law, they also tend to be astute problem solvers and financial planners. These skills enable many lawyers to move into other well-paid occupations if legal work is insufficiently rewarded. This "lawyer labor market" is the basic cost component in the legal process. It is not driven simply by what lawyers would like to charge. Rather, it reflects their alternative employment opportunities. Many attorneys have a broad range of options:

13. Randall Samborn, "Anti–Lawyer Attitude Up," Nat. L. J. Aug. 9, 1993, at 20; Marc Galanter, "The Regulatory Function of the Civil Jury," in Verdict: Assessing the Civil Jury System 61 (Robert E. Litan ed., 1993).

14. Robert E. Litan, "The Liability Explosion and American Trade Performance: Myths and Realities," in Tort Law and the Public Interest: Competition, Innovation, and Consumer Welfare 127–28 (Peter H. Schuck ed., 1991); Nader & Smith, supra note 12, at 279.

finance, real estate, insurance, sales, corporate management, public administration, lobbying, and so forth, all of which may provide compensation in the same target range as law. About a quarter of all law school graduates eventually end up in these alternative markets.[15] Such is the price structure of access to legal services, and protecting individual rights bound to come at considerable cost.

Litigation, which generally entails legal expenses for at least two parties and the adjudicative process, necessarily increases the cost. The price of legal services is, of course, lower if the parties dispense with lawyers, but so often is the "quality" according to widely shared conceptions of justice. And if one side is represented but not the other, the outcome may be skewed accordingly.

Before concluding that litigation is unduly expensive, it is necessary to consider the benefits as well as the costs. To take a commonly cited example, the expenses attributable to product liability lawsuits have significantly increased the price of a football helmet. But they have also significantly reduced the frequency of serious head injuries.[16] Whether such precautions are worth the price involves complex contextual judgments. As Professor Lawrence Friedman points out, the benefits of legal claims are "often quite intangible and immeasurable: expanded opportunities for women and minorities, expansion of civil liberties, fair procedures within institutions, limits on government. Who would deny that these are significant gains?"[17] Americans also turn to law for concerns that other countries address through direct government regulation, and for needs that they meet through centralized administrative measures such as guaranteed health benefits. As long as this nation relies so heavily on legal entitlements, litigation is likely to remain at substantial levels, and to impose substantial expenses.

The real issue, then, is not whether the current system "costs too much" in some abstract sense. Rather, the critical question is "compared to what." Is the current process the most cost-effective means of protecting legal rights? For example, a wide array of research suggests that the current tort system undercompensates victims and overcompensates intermediaries, including lawyers. Almost all major studies indicate that a large proportion of victims fail to recover adequate compensation, and that legal expenses

15. Joe G. Baker, "Employment Pattern of Law School Graduates," The Law School Admission Council Research Report 00–01 1 (2001).

16. Compare John Stossel, "Protect Us From Legal Vultures," Wall St. J., Jan. 2, 1996, at A8 with Rhode, In the

Interests of Justice, supra note 1, at 127–28.

17. Lawrence M. Friedman, "Litigation and Society," 15 Ann. Rev. Soc. 17, 26–27 (1989).

consume a grossly disproportionate share of payouts by defendants. For example, a survey of 30,000 New York hospital records found that only about twelve percent of patients who sustained injuries from negligent medical care even filed malpractice claims.[18] Full recoveries have been rarer still, and transaction costs have been extremely high. Of the amounts paid by insurance companies in surveyed tort cases, victims have received only about thirty-seven to forty-one percent; in asbestos cases, it has cost about $2.71 to place $1.00 in the hands of a plaintiff.[19]

Despite such expense, Americans still seem to favor governance by legal proceedings over governance by administrative authorities. This society's preferred system, if it is to be effective, requires a relatively costly procedural structure. Such a structure results in substantial inequalities in opportunities to use it, and individuals of modest means with moderate injuries will often be priced out of the system entirely. Without the prospect of a substantial recovery, it will make no economic sense to pay for litigation. Nor will competent attorneys generally be willing to pursue such cases on a contingent fee. The result is that for most Americans, the greatest problem is not too much litigation, but too little.

Legal Needs

Bar association and government surveys generally reveal substantial levels of unmet legal need. They estimate that about four-fifths of the civil needs of the poor, and two- to three-fifths of the needs of middle-income individuals, are not addressed.[20] It is likely that these surveys understate the extent of the problem, since they typically rely on individuals' own perceptions of their needs, and individuals are not always aware of matters that would justify legal remedies. For example, parties may not know that they are entitled to certain benefits, that their consumer loans fail to meet legal requirements, or that their apartments violate housing code standards. Most legal needs surveys also exclude collective public interest concerns such as environmental risks, or racial discrimination in school financing or political redistricting plans.

18. Kenneth Jost, "Still Warring over Medical Malpractice," ABA J., May 1993, at 68; Richard L. Abel, "The Real Tort Crisis–Too Few Claims," 48 Ohio St. L.J. 443 (1987); Paul C. Weiler, "The Case for No–Fault Medical Liability," 52 Md. L. Rev. 908, 912–13 (1993).

19. James S. Kakalik et al., Costs of Asbestos Litigation vi, viii (1983); James S. Kakalik & Nicholas M. Pace, Costs and Compensation Paid in Tort Litigation xiii (Rand Institute for Civil Justice, 1986).

20. See sources cited in Deborah L. Rhode, "Access to Justice," 69 Fordham L. Rev. 1785 (2001); ABA, Public Perceptions, supra note 1, at 26.

Moreover, counting problems does not of itself provide an adequate profile of unmet needs because such an approach makes no distinctions between urgent concerns and minor grievances; between matters that require extensive assistance and those that demand only minimal help; or between problems that call for attorney expertise and those that could be addressed through less expensive means, such as aid from lay specialists and self-help materials. The best solution to law-related needs is not always more law, lawyers, and legal proceedings. Professor Marc Galanter puts the relevant question, presumably rhetorically: "is the utopia of access to justice a condition in which all disputes are fully adjudicated?"[21] After all, access to the justice system does not guarantee justice in a substantive sense. As Chapter VI notes, the "haves" are still likely to come out ahead, given other advantages apart from lawyers, such as the resources to take risks, tolerate delay, structure transactions to preempt potential claims, and lobby for the reversal of unfavorable legal decisions.[22]

Americans like to believe that "social justice" (i.e. fairer distribution of societal resources) can be realized through "civil justice" (i.e., access to courts).[23] But as a political matter, it is a very dubious proposition. Distributive justice can be achieved only in part through a legal system, and only through very substantial public subsidies of legal assistance. Indeed, much of the political opposition to subsidized legal services is based on objections to using litigation as a redistributive strategy–as a means of allocating resources such as housing, education, and health care. Many Americans believe that these distributive issues should be resolved through democratic political processes, and not through counter-majoritarian judicial proceedings. As discussion below notes, this view has severely constrained the kinds of legal aid that publicly-funded programs can supply.

The problem of unmet need is further compounded by considering the quality of assistance necessary to ensure that access to the legal system is truly meaningful. "Equal justice under law" is a common slogan on courthouse doors, but it is not what guides the nation's funding priorities. Except in a few limited contexts, parties with civil legal needs are not entitled to any legal assistance, let alone equal assistance. In Lassiter v. Department of Social Services,

---

21. Marc Galanter, "Justice in Many Rooms," in Access to Justice and the Welfare State 147, 150–151 (Mauro Cappelletti ed. 1981).

22. Marc Galanter, Farther Along, 33 Law & Soc'y Rev. 1113, 1114 (1999); Marc Galanter, "Why the Haves Come

Out Ahead: Speculations on the Limits of Legal Change," 9 Law & Soc'y Rev. 95 (1974).

23. Geoffrey C. Hazard, Jr., "Social Justice Through Civil Justice," 36 U. Chi. L. Rev. 699 (1969).

452 U.S. 18 (1981), the Supreme Court held that the Constitution required provision of counsel in civil cases only where the proceedings would otherwise prove fundamentally unfair, a standard that is almost never met in practice.[24]

Even in the criminal law system, where indigent defendants have a constitutional right to effective assistance of counsel, few experts believe that the right is anywhere close to being realized in practice. Public defender caseloads and reimbursement rates for court-appointed counsel are set at grossly unrealistic levels, which make adequate investigation and trial preparation for most defendants a statistical impossibility. Caseloads can range as high as 3500 misdemeanors and 900 felonies per lawyer per year, and $1000 limits for counsel fees in felony matters are common.[25] Despite the poor quality of representation that inevitably results, trial judges have declined to find ineffective assistance of counsel in all but a tiny fraction of cases; one study found that 99 percent of such claims were unsuccessful.[26] Convictions, even in death penalty cases, have been sustained where attorneys were asleep, drunk, on drugs, suffering from severe mental illness, or parking their car during key parts of the prosecution's case.[27] Some lawyers have spent less time preparing for a felony trial than the average American spends showering before work.[28] Yet challenges to inadequate statutory fees for private attorneys and excessive assignments for public defenders have rarely been successful.[29] Indeed,

24. See Rhode, supra note 20, at 1798. In Payne v. Superior Court, 553 P.2d 565 (Cal.1976), the California Supreme Court held that a prisoner seeking to defend a civil action should be entitled to counsel if a continuance was not feasible, if his property interests would be affected, and if an attorney would be helpful. Accord Yarbrough v. Superior Court, 702 P.2d 583 (Cal.1985).

25. Rhode, supra note 20, at 1788–89; Martin Lasden, "For a Fistful of Dollars," Cal. L. Rev. Nov. 2001, at 28; Mike McConville & Chester Mirsky, "Guilty Plea Courts: A Social Disciplinary Model of Criminal Justice," 42 Soc. Probs. 216 (1995).

26. Victor E. Flango & Patricia McKenna, "Federal Habeas Corpus Review of State Court Convictions," 31 Cal. W. L. Rev. 237, 259–60 (1995).

27. Stephen B. Bright, Statement Before the Senate Committee on the Judiciary on the Innocence Protection Act of 2001, Federal News Service, June 27, 2001; David Cole, No Equal Justice: Race and Class in the American Criminal Justice System 87 (1999); Bruce A. Green, "Lethal Fiction: The Meaning of 'Counsel' in the Sixth Amendment," 78 Iowa L. Rev. 433, 499–501 (1993); James S. Liebman, "The Overproduction of Death," 100 Colum. L. Rev. 2030, 2104–06 (2000); Stephen B. Bright, "Sleeping on the Job," Nat'l L.J., Dec. 4, 2000, at A26. But see Burdine v. Johnson, 262 F.3d 336 (5th Cir.2001)(en banc), cert. den. 122 S.Ct. 2347 (2002)(overturning conviction where defense attorney slept).

28. Bright, "Sleeping on the Job," supra note 27, at A26.

29. See FTC v. Superior Court Trial Lawyers Ass'n, 493 U.S. 411, 435–36 (1990) (finding that boycott of court-appointed cases by private defense attorneys seeking higher compensation constituted an antitrust violation); cf. Frances A. McMorris, "Giuliani's Hard Line judges, who face crushing caseloads of their own, often have been reluctant to encourage effective advocacy that would result in more time-consuming trials and pretrial proceedings.[30]

B. An Overview of Possible Responses

Law, of course, is not the only context in which basic needs remain unmet and the "have nots" are at a significant disadvantage. Yet the gap between the aspiration and the operation of our legal system is of special concern. Access to justice is critical to sustain the legitimacy of legal and democratic processes.[31] As the Supreme Court has recognized, the right to "sue and defend" is a right "conservative of all other rights, and lies at the foundation of orderly government."[32] For most individuals, in most contexts, that right of access will not be meaningful without some legal assistance.

Yet providing sufficient assistance poses both practical and theoretical difficulties. As a practical matter, how could any right to civil legal aid be kept within economically manageable limits? If parties who could not realistically afford counsel were guaranteed representation, what would deter them from pursuing minor or dubious claims and inflicting unwarranted costs on opponents? And what would convince politicians and the public to allocate the funds necessary for assistance? The ultimate legal cost of representation could be quite substantial since it would include the price not only of legal aid but also of opposing parties' legal fees and any remedies that legal proceedings could secure. If the poor could assert all their entitlements under common law and government programs, the financial implications would be dramatic. In the current political climate, the prospects for such a reform agenda are unpromising, to say the least.

However, it by no means follows that we have done all that is feasible to address unmet needs and to reduce inequalities in legal representation. Many less wealthy nations do a better job than the United States along these dimensions, and promising reform proposals for the American system are readily available.

Breaks Strike at New York City Legal Services," Wall St. J., Oct. 6, 1994, at B11.

30. See James L. Kelley, Lawyers Crossing Lines: Nine Stories 171–72 (2001); McConville & Mirsky, supra note 25; Sara Rimer & Raymond Bonner, "Texas Lawyer's Death Row Record a Concern," N.Y. Times, June 11, 2000, at A1; sources cited in Rhode, In the Interest of Justice, supra note 1, at 62–63, 227–28, n. 32.

31. David Luban, Lawyers and Justice: An Ethical Study, 263–64 (1988).

32. Chambers v. Baltimore & Ohio R.R., 207 U.S. 142, 148 (1907).

There are three principal ways of increasing access to justice: strategies that reduce the need for legal intervention and assistance; strategies that minimize the cost of legal procedures and services; and strategies that increase opportunities for subsidized legal representation.

The first strategy involves simplification or modification of legal rules and processes. Plain-English statutes, no-fault insurance schemes, standardized forms for simple wills and uncontested divorces, and automatic wage garnishment for obligations such as child support payments are examples of efforts to minimize individuals' need for legal assistance. A second approach is to reduce the cost of such assistance through greater reliance on paralegals, hotlines, routine form-processing services, computer programs, online aid, courthouse services for pro se litigants, and alternative dispute resolution procedures that do not require lawyers. A third approach is to expand access to lawyers through publicly subsidized legal aid programs and pro bono contributions by the private bar.

C. Procedural Simplification and Nonlawyer Services

In "poor peoples' courts" that handle housing, bankruptcy, small claims, and family matters, parties without lawyers are less the exception than the rule. Cases in which at least one side is unrepresented are far more common than those in which both have counsel.[33] In some of these courts, over four fifths of the proceedings involve pro se litigants.[34] Yet the systems in which these parties operate have been designed by and for lawyers. A challenge for societies committed to access to justice is to make those systems effective for those who cannot afford counsel. Excluding lawyers entirely is not the answer. America's legal process is founded on the premise that all individuals have a right to be heard, and that this right may be exercised by counsel trained to speak on their behalf. The only way to retain this guarantee while also addressing the inequalities that it produces is to reduce the advantages that professional assistance confers.

To that end, a growing number of jurisdictions have developed pro se assistance programs involving procedural simplification,

---

33. Russell Engler, "And Justice For All–Including the Unrepresented Poor: Revisiting the Roles of the Judges, Mediators, and Clerks," 67 Fordham L. Rev. 1987 (1999); Jona Goldschmidt, "How Are Courts Handling Pro Se Litigants?," 82 Judicature 13, 14 (1998).

34. Engler, supra note 33, at 2047; Goldschmidt, supra note 33, at 13; Jona Goldschmidt et. al, Meeting the Challenge of Pro Se Litigation: A Report and Guidebook for Judges and Court Managers (1998); Robert B. Yegge, "Divorce Litigants Without Lawyers," 28 Fam. L. Q. 407 (1994).

standardized forms, educational publications, on-line materials, self-help centers with interactive kiosks for information and document preparation, and free in-person advice from volunteer lawyers or court personnel.[35] Yet a majority of surveyed court systems still have no formal pro se services.[36] Many of the services that are available are unusable by those who need help most: uneducated litigants with limited computer competence and English language skills.[37] All too often, these litigants are expected to navigate procedures of bewildering complexity, and to complete forms with archaic legal jargon.[38] Court clerks and mediators are instructed not to give legal advice, since that, technically, would constitute a violation of statutes prohibiting "unauthorized practice of law" and could be seen as undermining procedural neutrality.[39]

These statutory prohibitions have also blocked out-of-court efforts to make legal services more accessible. Every state imposes criminal penalties for engaging in the unauthorized "practice of law" by individuals who are not licensed members of the bar. What falls within this prohibition varies across jurisdictions, but the dominant approach is to ban any personalized legal advice.[40] In general, lay practitioners may type documents, but may not answer even the simplest law-related questions or correct obvious errors. Internet providers may supply information and generic documents,

---

35. ELawyering Task Force, http://www.elawyering.org; Jennifer Dee, "Dot-Com, Esq: Legal Guidance, Lawyer Optional," N.Y. Times, Feb. 22, 2001, at G1; ABA Standing Committee on the Delivery of Legal Services, Responding to the Needs of the Self–Represented Divorce Litigant 12–13 (1994); Family Law Section Committee on the Probate and Family Court, Massachusetts Bar Association, Changing the Culture of the Probate and Family Court 29 (1997); Goldschmidt, supra note 33, at 29–34; Engler, supra note 33, at 2049; Dianne Molvig, Growing Solutions to Unmet Legal Needs, 69 Wis. Law. 10 (Aug., 1996).

36. Goldschmidt, supra note 33, at 20.

37. Lillian C. Henry & Gillian N. Bush, "California's Family Law Facilitator and Arizona's Self–Service Center: Success and Limitations of Two Systems Designed to Meet the Challenges of Legal Services," 34 (1999) (unpublished paper, Stanford Law School).

38. Engler, supra note 33; Joel Kurtzberg & Jamie Henikoff, "Freeing the Parties from the Law: Designing an Interest and Rights Focused Model of Landlord/Tenant Mediation," 1997 J. Disp. Resolution 53, 70 (1997); Erica L. Fox, "Alone in the Hallway: Challenges to Effective Self–Representation in Negotiation," 1 Harvard Neg. L. Rev. 85, 92 (1996); Yegge, supra note 34, at 410.

39. Engler, supra note 33, at 2056, 2060, 2064; John M. Greacen, "No Legal Advice from Court Personnel: What does That Mean?," 34 Judges' J. 10 (Winter 1995); Kurtzberg & Henikoff, supra note 38, at 90; Maryland Opinion, Attorney General 95–056 (Dec. 19, 1995); Judith S. Kaye & Jonathan Lippman, Breaking New Ground, 2 (1997).

40. See Rhode, supra, note 1, at 136; Deborah L Rhode, "The Delivery of Legal Services by Non-lawyers," 4 Geo. J. Legal Ethics 209, 210–11 (1990).

but not specific advice.[41] Bar ethical rules also prohibit lawyers from assisting the unauthorized practice of law. Model Rule 5.5; DR 3–101(1).

These ethical and statutory prohibitions have been subject to increasing criticism. During the last decade, courts and legislatures in over half the states have considered proposals involving nonlawyer specialists. Such proposals are in part a response to simplification of certain legal processes, and the increasing availability of computer software, standardized forms, and alternative dispute resolution proceedings that facilitate alternatives to lawyers. The push for nonlawyer assistance also comes from research surveying their performance here and abroad, which finds that lay specialists are generally at least as qualified as lawyers to provide assistance on routine matters where legal needs are greatest.[42] That is not entirely surprising since law schools do not usually teach, and bar exams do not test, the specialized information involved in dealing with divorces, landlord-tenant disputes, bankruptcy, immigration, welfare, and similar claims.

Accordingly, most scholars and bar association commissions that have systematically studied the issue believe that unauthorized practice rules should be reconsidered, and some experts have recommended alternative forms of regulation.[43] For example, states could develop licensing systems for nonlawyers and Internet services and enforce more narrowly drawn prohibitions against unethical or unqualified providers. Lay practitioners and services could also be required to carry malpractice insurance, contribute to compensation funds for defrauded clients, and observe the same ethical obligations as lawyers concerning confidentiality, competence, and conflicts of interest. Responsibility for enforcement of

---

41. Debra Baker, "Is This Woman a Threat to Lawyers," ABA J., June, 1999, at 54; Fifteenth Judicial District Unified Bar Association v. Glasgow, 1999 WL 1128847 (Tenn.App.1999); ABA, Consumer's Guide to Legal Help on the Internet; Self–Help, available at http://www.abanet.org/legalservices/publicdiv.html; Model Rules of Professional Conduct, Rule 5.5, Cmt. (2002).

42. See sources cited in Rhode, Interests of Justice, supra note 1, at 136–38; Herbert Kritzer, Legal Advocacy: Lawyers and Nonlawyers at Work 193–203 (1998); Judith Citron, The Citizens Advice Bureau: For the Community, By the Community (1989); In re Unauthorized Practice of Law Rules Proposed by

South Carolina Bar, 422 S.E.2d 123, 124–25 (S.C.1992); Yegge, supra note 34, at 408. In the one reported survey of consumer satisfaction, nonlawyers rated higher than lawyers. Rhode, supra note 40, at 23–31.

43. See sources cited in Rhode, In the Interests of Justice, supra note 1, at 136–38; Kritzer, supra note 42; Deborah L. Rhode, "Professionalism in Perspective: Alternative Approaches to Nonlawyer Practice," 22 N.Y.U. Rev. of L. & Soc. Change 701, 705 (1996); ABA Commission on Nonlawyer Practice, Nonlawyer Activity in Law–Related Situations: A Report with Recommendations (1995), California Commission on Legal Technicians Report (July, 1990).

such regulatory systems should rest with local prosecutors and consumer protection authorities rather than with the organized bar, which has an obvious economic stake in restricting nonlawyer competitors.

Another approach would be to create a position like lawyer assistant to a court or agency. This assistant would not be a judge, but would be available to consult with pro se litigants and to make comments to the tribunal concerning facts and law. Many judges and mediators now try to perform something like this function, but are constrained by the need to maintain neutrality. In domestic relations and juvenile courts, an equivalent consulting function is often performed by court staff having legal training or experience. The bar could provide further support and clarification for this role, much as it has recently done for arbitrators and mediators.[44]

D. Subsidized Legal Services

The first American legal aid society was founded in 1876 as part of an organization to assist German immigrants. Within the next several decades, legal services programs were established in various urban areas through private charity and municipal subsidies. In 1919, Reginald Heber Smith published a landmark study, Justice and the Poor, which reported a total of only about 40 organizations throughout the country, with woefully inadequate resources. The ABA subsequently appointed Smith to head its Standing Committee on Legal Aid, which began providing modest support to local offices. However, as late as 1963, there were only some 250 legal services offices with a combined annual budget of approximately four million dollars.[45] Many bar associations initially opposed expansion of legal services organizations out of concern that they would compete for clients with private practitioners and pave the way to greater state and federal control of the profession (the legal analogue to "socialized medicine"). According to one ABA president, "the entry of the government into the field of providing legal services is too dangerous to be permitted ... in our free America."[46]

44. See Model Rules of Professional Conduct, Rule 2.4 (2000).

45. Bryant G. Garth, Neighborhood Law Firms for the Poor: A Comparative Study of Recent Developments in Legal Aid and in the Legal Profession 19–20 (1980). For accounts of the earlier development of legal aid programs, see Ronald Pipkin, "Legal Aid and Elitism in the American Legal Profession," in Before the Law: An Introduction to the Legal Process 185 (John J. Bonsignore et al., eds. 2d ed. 1979).

46. Jerold S. Auerbach, Unequal Justice: Lawyers and Social Change in Modern America 236 (1976) (quoting Harold J. Gallagher); Alan W. Houseman, Political Lessons: Legal Services

The War on Poverty brought a massive influx of federal aid, widespread bar association support, and a new reformist ethos to civil legal aid programs. The consequences were quickly apparent, as poverty law offices achieved significant victories in consumer, welfare, housing, health, and related legal areas. However, these victories also resulted in political backlash, which translated into curtailment of funds and restrictions on the kinds of cases and activities that lawyers could pursue.[47] To provide somewhat greater political insulation for poverty law offices, in 1974, Congress established the Legal Services Corporation, with board members appointed by the President and confirmed by the Senate. Although the Corporation has supervisory authority over legal services programs, Congress has the power to curtail their efforts by cutting the budget for legal assistance and by preventing federally-subsidized programs from pursuing controversial activities. At current funding levels, legal aid programs can serve less than a fifth of their target population; their combined annual budget works out to less than $10 for every person officially classified as poor.[48] Prohibited activities include lobbying, community organizing, class action lawsuits, and cases involving prisoners, undocumented aliens, abortion, homosexual rights, school desegregation, and housing for accused drug dealers.[49] Although the Supreme Court has struck down one restriction on welfare reform litigation as unconstitutional viewpoint discrimination, lower courts have consistently upheld the other limitations as permissible conditions on federal funding.[50]

Despite strong support from the organized bar, efforts to expand the budgets and activities of legal service providers have encountered substantial resistance. Criticism of these programs comes from all points on the ideological spectrum. Critics from the right have often denounced poverty lawyers as ideological vigilantes who have attempted to mastermind social change without any "public direction or public accountability."[51] Other commentators

for the Poor–A Commentary, 83 Geo. L. J. 1669, 1678 (1995).

47. See Legal Services Corporation Act, 42 U.S.C. § 2996 et seq. (1974). Legal services' annual funding under the Reagan Administration was cut from $321 million to $241 million. Richard L. Abel, "Law Without Politics: Legal Aid Under Advanced Capitalism," 32 U.C.L.A. L. Rev. 474, 532 (1985).

48. See Rhode, supra note 20, at 1785.

49. See U.S.C. § 2996 et. seq.

50. Legal Services Corporation v. Velazquez, 531 U.S. 533 (2001); Legal Aid Society of Hawaii v. Legal Services Corporation, 145 F.3d 1017 (9th Cir.1998).

51. Spiro Agnew, "What's Wrong With the Legal Services Program," 58 ABA J. 930, 931 (1972). See also Steve Largent, "It's a Good Idea Gone Bad," USA Today, May 25, 1995, at A12; sources quoted in Rhode, supra note 20, at 1794; Patrick J. Kiger, An Unsolved Mystery: Why are Rogue Politicians Trying to Kill a Program that Helps their Neediest Constituents? 2 (2000).

have questioned the effectiveness of legal services in redistributing income and power. In their view, the costs of legal proceedings will be passed on to other low-income individuals in the form of higher prices.[52] Alternatively, recognition of formal rights may have little concrete effect, given the post-judgment relations of the parties, the difficulties of enforcement, and the possibility of legislative reversal. Some critics also question whether providing legal services is a more cost-effective means of transferring goods and services to the poor than subsidizing those goods directly, for example, through housing grants, community redevelopment programs, or broader coverage of medical needs.[53]

Critics from the left raise other concerns. One is that publicly subsidized legal assistance may sometimes work against fundamental change by channeling disputes into individualized grievances that exact small scale remedies but do not challenge systemic problems or basic power relations. Because congressional restrictions prevent lobbying, class actions, and community organizing, it is difficult for legal aid lawyers to address the structural causes of poverty-related needs. Another concern is that federally-funded programs, in order to appease legislative critics and avoid further budgetary cutbacks, have been forced to focus on maximizing the number of individuals assisted in noncontroversial matters. The result is to compromise the quality of representation provided and to leave the most politically vulnerable causes with no legal protections.[54] A final concern is that some poverty lawyers are insufficiently sensitive to the needs of the racial, ethnic, and economically subordinate communities they serve, and have failed to empower clients, individually or collectively, to address their own problems.[55]

By contrast, defenders of civil legal aid view it as a vital means of securing basic rights, challenging government and corporate misconduct, and empowering low-income constituencies. For many impoverished clients, legal services may be the only way to meet fundamental needs in areas involving health, housing, welfare, education, family law, or related matters. Also, since courts, unlike legislatures, are open as of right, they are often the most accessible, if not always the most effective, forums in which to seek redress.[56]

52. Hazard, supra note 23, at 737.

53. Richard Posner, Economic Analysis of the Law 511–15 (5th ed. 1998).

54. Rhode, supra note 20, at 1796.

55. Paul E. Lee and Mary M. Lee, "Reflections from the Bottom of the Well: Racial Bias in the Provision of Legal Services to the Poor," 27 Clearinghouse Rev. 311 (1993); Marc Feldman, "Political Lessons: Legal Services for the Poor," 83 Geo. L.J. 1529, 1537–41, 1552–56 (1995).

56. For analysis and criticism of arguments against subsidized legal services, see Luban, Lawyers and Justice, supra note 31, at 293–391.

To withhold legal services in the hopes of channeling frustrations into more fundamental change seems to many commentators strategically dubious and morally objectionable. So also, to assume that cash transfers for the poor would be more effective than direct provision of services ignores the political obstacles to achieving such transfers and the importance of meeting nonquantifiable or collective needs. Providing every poor person the cash equivalent of legal aid subsidies–currently about ten dollars per year–would scarcely do much to protect basic needs. By contrast, legal services programs can at least deter or redress some serious injustices and help some clients develop the capacity to help themselves.

To that end, most poverty law experts advocate targeting resources to widely shared problems and collaborative, community-based responses.[57] By focusing on educational projects, self-help programs, and representation of local organizations, legal services offices can aid low-income clients not only in resolving individual problems, but also in challenging certain underlying causes of subordination.

Given the chronic underfunding of legal aid programs, many experts also advocate additional sources of financial support. Proposals include increases in court filing fees and taxes on law-related revenues. Related possibilities include more public interest programs and greater pro bono contributions from the private bar, along the lines discussed below.

E. Public Interest Law and "Cause Lawyering"

Although the terms "public interest law" and "cause lawyering" are relatively recent, the concepts have their roots in earlier civil liberties and civil rights initiatives. The growth of an organized civil liberties movement began during World War I, when a small group of pacifists founded an organization that evolved into the American Civil Liberties Union. Its activities eventually broadened to include not only free speech and association but also equal rights and reproductive choice. So too, America's first major civil rights organization, the National Association for the Advancement of Colored People, emerged in the early twentieth century. In the late 1930s, the NAACP Legal Defense Fund spun off as a separate

---

57. Gerald López, Rebellious Lawyering: One Chicano's Vision of Progressive Law Practice (1992); Paul R. Tremblay, "Toward A Community–Based Ethic for Legal Services Practice," 37 UCLA L. Rev. 1101 (1990); Alan W. Houseman, "Political Lessons: Legal Services for the Poor–A Commentary," 83 Geo. L. J. 1669, 1697 (1995); Matthew Diller, "Lawyering for Poor Communities in the Twenty–First Century," 25 Fordham Urb. L. J. 673, 678 (1998).

organization. Since its founding, the Fund has orchestrated a systematic legal campaign against racial segregation and subordination.[58] Other organizations joined these efforts and served as models for many contemporary public interest organizations.

During the late 1960s and early 1970s, a rise in political activism, together with a large increase in foundation funding, gave birth to new forms of cause lawyering. Judicial and legislative initiatives further encouraged this development. Test-case litigation became a more effective strategy as courts began liberalizing doctrines regarding ripeness, standing, and sovereign immunity, and as Congress began authorizing fee awards to "prevailing parties" in various civil rights, consumer, environmental, and analogous cases.[59]

Public interest legal organizations, as defined by the Council for Public Interest Law, are tax-exempt non-profit groups that employ at least one attorney and devote at least thirty percent of their total resources to the legal representation of previously unrepresented interests on matters of public policy.[60] By the 1990s, some 200 centers with some 1,000 lawyers met that definition. In addition, a substantial number of private firms that did not qualify for tax-exempt status devoted a major portion of their work to public interest representation. Conservative legal foundations also formed to broaden the groups represented. Organizations like the Washington Legal Foundation and the Rocky Mountain Legal Foundation have achieved significant litigation victories on issues such as affirmative action, small-business regulation, and publicly-funded legal services for the poor.[61] Although these foundations have generally operated with tax-exempt status, some industry-sponsored associations fall outside the National Council's definition of a public interest organization because they take positions that are already well-represented by their corporate funders.

The Council's definition raises long-standing questions about the role and meaning of "public interest" organizations. The conventional justification for public interest law rests on the failure of current political and market structures to take adequate account of the concerns of unorganized or subordinate groups. Where transac-

---

58. See Richard Kluger, Simple Justice: The History of Brown v Board of Education and Black America's Struggle for Equality (1976); Mark V. Tushnet, The NAACP's Legal Strategy Against Segregated Education, 1925–1950 (1987).

59. By the close of the 1980s, some 150 statutes authorized fee awards. Nan

Aron, Liberty and Justice for All: Public Interest Law in the 1980's and Beyond 55–56 (1989).

60. Id.

61. Roger K. Newman, "Public Interest Firms Crop Up on the Right," Nat'l. L. J., Aug. 26, 1996, at A1.

tion costs in organizing are high, and parties have limited resources or individual stakes in representation, the rationale for public interest advocacy is greatest. Yet this rationale leaves key definitional issues unresolved. Clearly "underrepresentation" and non-profit status do not of themselves qualify a legal position as being "in the public interest." For example, few individuals would apply the public-interest label to an organization of adults who sought to eliminate prohibitions on sexual relations with children. Yet, if the concept of public interest presupposes some widely shared values or socially defensible criteria, how should these be determined? In a world of limited legal resources, who should decide which interests should be heard and how loudly?

Public interest lawyering raises a broad range of concerns analogous to those involving subsidized legal services. Critics from the right complain that the public interest movement vests too much influence in non-majoritarian institutions, while critics from the left complain that such influence is too limited to produce lasting social change. Conservative objections build on a long tradition of challenges to judicial activism. Litigation that avowedly aims at restructuring institutions or redistributing resources has drawn criticism on the ground that courts lack the competence or accountability for such a role. According to critics, such cases invite rule by an "imperial judiciary" that does not have the necessary training, institutional familiarity, and enforcement mechanisms.[62]

These arguments have prompted responses on several levels. Defenders of public interest advocacy note that it is not inconsistent with democratic principles for the public to delegate certain functions to non-majoritarian processes. Such a delegation is particularly appropriate to protect the needs of "discrete and insular minorities," or diffuse majorities that lack resources to organize in a political system unavoidably shaped by well-financed interests.[63] Courts can play a critical role in enforcing constitutional principles that other branches of government fail to vindicate.

Moreover, public interest work often focuses on lobbying or on legal strategies designed to further, not subvert, legislative intent. Examples include suits seeking compliance with environmental, occupational safety, and consumer regulation. In many contexts, public interest organizations increase accountability in governmental policy making by providing review that is otherwise absent.

---

62. Gerald N. Rosenberg, The Hollow Hope: Can Courts Bring About Social Change? (1991); Donald L. Horowitz, The Courts and Social Policy (1977).

63. United States v. Carolene Products Co., 304 U.S. 144, 152 (1938); Luban, supra note 31, at 358–70.

Elected representatives may lack the time, information, and technical expertise to monitor implementation of statutory mandates. Where courts face similar limitations, they can rely on special masters or broker settlements that take full account of the interests at issue.

While critics from the right worry that public interest lawyering has too much influence, critics from the left worry that it has too little. From their perspective, activist attorneys have overly relied on litigation and formal rights and have diverted efforts from the political organizing necessary to make rights meaningful. According to Professor Gary Bellow:

> [T]he problem of unjust laws is almost invariably a problem of distribution of political and economic power; the rules merely reflect a series of choices made in response to these distributions. If a major goal ... is to redistribute power, it is debatable whether the judicial process is a very effective means toward that end.... There is generally not much doctrinal judicial basis for adequately dealing with such problems, and lawyers find themselves developing cases whose outcomes are peripheral to the basic issues that these problems raise. Secondly, "rule" change, without a political base to support it, just doesn't produce any substantial result because rules are not self-executing: they require an enforcement mechanism.[64]

Too often, public interest lawyers lack resources to monitor compliance with test-case decrees, and some defendants–particularly governmental institutions (such as prisons, schools, or mental hospitals)–lack funds for adequately implementing judicial remedies. Decisions that lack public support are also vulnerable to statutory reversal or administrative agency resistance. Critics claim that public interest lawyers place undue reliance on litigation because their credibility and professional reputations depend on such visible achievements, and because their backgrounds often ill-equip them for other roles such as grass roots organizing. In too many cases, attorneys do not empower clients to challenge their subordination but instead only alleviate its symptoms.[65]

In responding to such concerns, public interest lawyers have emphasized that litigation is not their sole focus. Much law reform activity serves multiple purposes and can be used for "leverage to enable the group to ... increase the potency of its tactics, and for

---

64. Quoted in Comment, "The New Public Interest Lawyers," 79 Yale L. J. 1069, 1077 (1970).

65. López, supra note 57; Steve Bachmann, "Lawyers, Law, and Social Change," 13 N.Y.U. Rev. of Law and Soc. Change, 1, 3 (1985).

publicity, fund raising, mobilizing outside resources, consciousness raising and legitimacy."[66] During the 1980s and 1990s, the increasing conservatism of federal courts, and together with stricter notice and standing requirements, prompted liberal public interest groups to rely less on litigation and more on lobbying, education, organizing, counseling, and related programs. For many organizations, litigation has functioned most often as a threat that confers bargaining leverage in out-of-court settings. For other groups, test cases can serve as a catalyst for political action and organizing efforts. Such litigation can be of enormous importance despite frequent noncompliance. And even when public interest groups "lose" in court, they may win outside in the wider struggle for public support, community empowerment, and policy reforms.

A final set of concerns raised by public interest law involves issues of accountability and conflicts of interest. As Chapter VIII noted, the more unorganized the clients, the fewer the constraints on counsel. In critics' view, lawyers who lack accountability are no more likely to speak for the public than the government officials whose actions are often at issue: "[h]ow are [these attorneys] to succeed where government has failed? Better experts? Bigger hearts?"[67] In what sense can these lawyers claim to be more representative of the public than elected or executive officials?

In response to such criticisms, public interest lawyers note that they are not without some forms of accountability. Their influence depends on credibility with various constituencies: clients, funders, courts, policy makers, commentators, peers, and community organizations. Those constituencies may be more representative than the large donors who influence elected officials. In the long run, the effectiveness of any public interest organization depends on its accountability—its ability to express widely shared values, vindicate critical principles, and justify a need for its continued advocacy.

F. Pro Bono Representation

The "learned professions," including law and medicine, distinguish themselves from business occupations by emphasizing their

66. Joel F. Handler, Social Movements and the Legal System: A Theory of Law Reform and Social Change 210 (1978). See Carrie Menkel–Meadow, "The Causes Of Cause Lawyering: Toward an Understanding of the Motivation and Commitment of Social Justice Lawyers," in Cause Lawyering (Austin Sarat & Stuart Scheingold eds., 1998).

67. Kenney Hegland, "Beyond Enthusiasm and Commitment," 13 Ariz. L. Rev. 805, 813 (1971). See Jeremy Rabkin, "Public Interest Law: Is It Law in the 'Public Interest'?," 8 Harv. J. L. & Pub. Pol. 341, 342–43 (1985).

collective commitment to public service. The bar in this country has a long-standing tradition of service *pro bono publico,*–legal services "for the public good," provided at no cost or at a reduced fee. This concept encompasses a wide range of activities, including law reform efforts, participation in bar associations and civic organizations, and individual or group representation. Clients who receive such assistance also span a broad range including: poor people, nonprofit organizations, ideological or political causes, and friends, relatives, or employees of the lawyer.

Although the bar has long supported pro bono in principle, its commitment in practice has been less resolute. Model Rule 6.1 states that a lawyer "should aspire to render at least (50) hours of pro bono publico legal services per year" and should provide a "substantial majority" of such services to "persons of limited means" or to organizations that are designed primarily to assist such individuals. The Comment to this Rule makes clear that it "is not intended to be enforced through disciplinary process." Ethical Consideration 2–25 of the Code of Professional Responsibility maintains that "[t]he rendition of free legal services to those unable to pay reasonable fees continues to be an obligation of each lawyer." However, the Code's disciplinary rules make no reference to such an obligation.

Over the past two decades, many bar associations and state courts have rejected mandatory pro bono proposals, but a few jurisdictions have imposed limited requirements. The Florida and Maryland Supreme Courts require members of the bar to report their contributions to a voluntary program.[68] El Paso, Texas obligates attorneys to take on two civil cases (usually divorces) annually, which averages about fifteen hours of work a year.[69] New Jersey appoints unpaid counsel in some criminal matters, and other jurisdictions require pro bono assistance by attorneys who wish to be considered for appointments in paying cases. Although the Supreme Court has never issued a full opinion on the constitutionality of requiring uncompensated service, it has suggested in dicta and in a summary dismissal of an appeal that such requirements are permissible.[70]

---

68. The Florida program, developed by the state bar, states an expectation that every Florida attorney will perform at least 20 hours annually of direct pro bono legal services to the poor or make a $350 cash contribution. Each lawyer must report whether the expectation was met, but failure to do so will not result in any disciplinary sanctions. Talbot D'Alemberte, "Tributaries of Justice: The Search for Full Access," Florida Bar J., April, 1999, at 12.

69. Report on the El Paso Pro Bono Project 7 (prepared by Professor W. Frank Newton, Baylor University School of Law).

70. Sparks v. Parker, 368 So.2d 528 (Ala.1979), appeal dismissed, 444 U.S.

Full information about lawyers' pro bono contributions is unavailable. Only one state mandates reporting of contribution levels, and many lawyers take liberties with the definition of "pro bono" to include any uncompensated or undercompensated work, even if performed with the expectation of payment.[71] However, recent surveys indicate that most lawyers provide no significant pro bono assistance. Reported involvement ranges from a high of forty-seven percent in New York to fifteen to eighteen percent in Texas, Minnesota, Michigan and Florida. Contributions by volunteers ranged from an average of forty-two hours per year in New York to a median of twenty hours in Texas.[72] Fewer than ten percent of practitioners accept referrals from federally-funded legal aid offices or bar-sponsored poverty-related programs.[73] Most lawyers are not more charitable with their money than their time. Reported financial contributions range from an average of $82 per year in New York to $32 per year in Florida. In short, the best available research finds that the American legal profession averages less than half an hour of work per week and under half a dollar per day in support of pro bono legal services.[74]

The record for the profession's most affluent members is not significantly better. Only a third of the nation's large law firms have committed themselves to meet the ABA's Pro Bono Challenge, which requires contributions equivalent to three to five percent of gross revenues.[75] And only eighteen of the nation's one hundred most financially successful firms meet the ABA's standard of fifty hours per year of pro bono service.[76] The approximately 50,000 lawyers at these firms averaged eight minutes per day on pro bono activities.[77] Although recent salary wars have pushed compensation

803 (1979); Powell v. Alabama, 287 U.S. 45, 73 (1932).

71. See Carroll Seron, The Business of Practicing Law: The Work Lives of Solo and Small–Firm Attorneys 129–33 (1996); see also sources cited in Rhode, supra note 20, at 1809; Deborah L. Rhode, "Cultures of Commitment: Pro Bono for Lawyers and Law Students," 67 Fordham L. Rev. 2415, 2423 (1999).

72. For the Texas program, see Tex. State Bar, "Civil Legal Services to the Poor in Texas," Report to the Supreme Court of Texas, at 200 (2000). For New York's program, see N.Y. State Unified Court System, Report on the Pro Bono Activities of the New York State Bar, available at http://www.courts.state.ny.us/probono/pbrpt.htm.

73. LSC Statistics: Private Attorney Involvement, All Programs, available at http://www.lsc.gov/pressr/pr_pai.htm.

74. Rhode, supra note 20, at 1810; N.Y. State Unified Court System, supra note 72; D'Alemberte, supra note 68; Access to the Legal System (July 1999).

75. Interview with Esther Lardent, President, Pro Bono Institute (2000).

76. Aric Press, "Eight Minutes," Am. Law., July 2000, at 13.

77. Press, supra note 76, at 13; Press Release, Judicial Council of California, Chief Justice Urges More Lawyers to Donate Time to Pro Bono Efforts, Sept. 16, 2000, available at http://www.courtinfo.ca.gov/press/newsreleases/NR52–00.htm.

levels to new heights, this affluence has eroded, rather than expanded, support for pro bono programs. Over the past decade, the average revenues of the most successful firms increased by over fifty percent, while the average pro bono hours declined by a third.[78]

Efforts to increase the profession's public service commitments through mandatory obligations have met with both moral and practical objections.[79] As a matter of principle, many lawyers insist that compulsory charity is a contradiction in terms. From their perspective, requiring service would undermine its moral significance and infringe lawyers' own rights. To some practitioners, such an obligation seems tantamount to "involuntary servitude."[80] If access to justice is a societal value, then society as a whole should bear its cost. The poor have fundamental needs for food and medical care, but we do not require grocers or physicians to donate their help in meeting those needs. Why should lawyers' responsibilities be greater?[81]

Supporters of pro bono obligations offer several answers. Lawyers have special privileges that entail special obligations. America's highly legalized culture makes legal assistance "essential to virtually all projects of social import[ance]."[82] Attorneys in this nation have a much more extensive and exclusive right to provide legal assistance than attorneys in other countries, and a greater monopoly than other professions in providing essential services.[83] The American bar has long guarded those prerogatives and severely

78. Kate Ackley & Bryan Rund, "Pro Bono: Casualty of Salary Wars?," Legal Times, Apr. 10, 2000, at 1; Mark Hansen, "Trickle-away Economics? Cost of High First–Year Salaries May Be Borne By Pro Bono Recipients," 86 ABA J. 20 (Jul. 2000); Roger Parloff, "Too Rich To Give," Am. Law., Apr. 2000, at 15; Greg Winter, "Legal Firms Cutting Back on Free Services for Poor," N.Y. Times, Aug. 17, 2000, at A1.

79. See generally Marvin E. Frankel, "Proposal: A National Legal Service," 45 S.C. L. Rev. 887 (1994); Largent, supra note 51, at A12; Jonathan R. Macey, "Mandatory Pro Bono: Comfort for the Poor or Welfare for the Rich?," 77 Cornell L. Rev. 1115, 1117 (1992).

80. For further discussion, see lawyers quoted in Deborah L. Rhode, "Ethical Perspectives on Legal Practice," 37 Stan. L. Rev. 589, 610 (1985); Tigran W. Eldred & Thomas Schoenherr, "The Lawyer's Duty of Public Service: More

Than Charity?," 96 W. Va. L. Rev. 367, 391 n. 97 (1993–94); and Michael J. Mazzone, "Mandatory Pro Bono: Slavery in Disguise," Tex. Law., Oct. 22, 1990, at 22.

81. See Committee to Improve the Availability of Legal Services, "Final Report to the Chief Judge of the State of New York" (1990), reprinted in 19 Hofstra L. Rev. 755, 782 (1991); Debra Baker, "Mandating Good Works: Colorado Proposal Requiring Pro Bono Draws Fire From Most Lawyers," 85 ABA J. 22 (March 1999); Frankel, supra note 79, at 890.

82. Harry T. Edwards, "A Lawyer's Duty to Serve the Public Good," 65 N.Y.U. L. Rev. 1148, 1156 (1990).

83. Andrew Boon & Jennifer Levin, The Ethics and Conduct of Lawyers in England and Wales 55–59, 402 (1999); see also Christine Parker, Just Lawyers: Regulation and Access to Justice 1–9 (1999).

restricted lay competition. Under these circumstances, supporters of pro bono work believe that it is not unreasonable to expect lawyers to provide some charitable assistance in return for their privileged status. Requiring the equivalent of an hour per week of uncompensated assistance scarcely seems the functional equivalent of slavery.

Yet many lawyers who support pro bono in principle believe that mandatory obligations would be unworkable in practice. Defining what would qualify as pro bono and monitoring compliance pose significant challenges. If the primary objective is, as the ABA's Model Rules suggest, to assist persons of limited means, then requiring contributions of lawyers with no interest or expertise in poverty law scarcely seems a cost-effective way of providing services. But to supporters of pro bono requirements, the question again is, "Compared to what?" For many low-income groups, some assistance would be better than none, which is their current alternative. Experience with bar-supported voluntary programs suggests that concerns of cost-effectiveness can be addressed by two strategies: offering a diverse range of opportunities for participation, coupled with educational programs and support structures; and allowing lawyers unwilling or unable to provide direct service the option of substituting cash assistance to legal aid providers. Even if full compliance with pro bono requirements could not be assured, these measures would at least support attorneys who would like to participate in such public service but who work in organizations that have discouraged participation.

However the debate over mandatory pro bono is resolved, the bar has strong reasons to encourage greater voluntary involvement. For many lawyers, such involvement provides crucial opportunities to develop new skills, obtain valuable trial experience, and enhance their contacts and reputations in the community. Such opportunities, in the context of causes to which attorneys are committed, are also a way of connecting many practitioners to the concerns that sent them to law school in the first instance. That is a connection that too many attorneys find lacking in their current practice. Indeed, bar surveys consistently report that lawyers' greatest source of dissatisfaction with their careers is the lack of contribution to the social good.[84] Pro bono work not only provides such opportunities, it also gives participants a better understanding of how the justice system functions, or fails to function, for the have-

84. ABA Young Lawyers Division Survey: Career Satisfaction 11 (2000).

nots.[85] Such exposure may build support for reform, and make increased access to justice a greater professional priority.

85. Steven Lubet & Cathryn Steward, "A 'Public Assets' Theory of Lawyers' Pro Bono Obligations," 145 U. Pa. L. Rev. 1245, 1299 (1997); Rhode, supra note 71, at 2420.

Chapter X

REGULATING THE MARKET
FOR LEGAL SERVICES

The standard justification for regulating how lawyers promote, structure, and price their services rests on imperfections in the market for legal assistance. These imperfections include what economists variously describe as information barriers, free riders, and externalities.

An initial difficulty arises from many consumers' inability to make informed assessments about the services they receive, either before or after purchase. Most individual (as opposed to organizational) clients are one-shot purchasers; many will not consult an attorney more than once or twice in a lifetime, and of those who do, a majority will select different lawyers each time. This lack of experience, coupled with the expense and difficulties of comparative shopping for professional services, makes it hard for consumers to identify cost-effective practices. In the absence of external regulation, some clients may suffer significant losses from incompetent or unethical practitioners. When consumers cannot accurately differentiate among the services available, lawyers may lack adequate incentives to provide quality representation and a "market for lemons" may develop.

An additional difficulty involves "free riders"–i.e., those who gain benefits without contributing to collective goods. For example, the bar collectively has an interest in securing the public's trust, and in having lawyers conduct themselves as fiduciaries in such a way as to maintain that trust. However, without effective regulatory structures, individual attorneys may have inadequate economic incentives to avoid cheating; they can benefit as free riders from the bar's general reputation without adhering to basic ethical mandates themselves.

A final category of problems calling for regulatory responses involves external costs to society and third parties from conduct that may be advantageous to particular clients and their lawyers. For example, the public generally has an interest in promoting just and expeditious resolution of disputes and discouraging non-meritorious claims, but in some circumstances, a litigant's or attorney's economic interests may be to the contrary.

167

Although commentators on the legal profession generally agree that these problems call for regulation, there is considerable dispute about the forms it should take, and how much control the profession should exercise over the governance process. The following materials explore these issues.

A. Advertising

Although many lawyers view advertising of legal services as a recent and regrettable development, it is restrictions on advertising that are recent. Practitioners in ancient Greece and Rome were not hesitant to hawk their services. Nor was there any such reluctance among some of this country's most distinguished nineteenth century attorneys, including Abraham Lincoln and David Hoffman, the author of one of the first legal ethics treatises.

However, as the materials in Chapter II indicate, bar leaders at the turn of the twentieth century became increasingly concerned about commercial practices. The ABA's 1908 Cannons of Ethics declared that it was "unprofessional to solicit professional employment" through advertisements. Even indirect promotional methods, such as comments to newspapers, were deemed inappropriate. "Self-laudation" of any form was thought to "offend the traditions and lower the tone of our profession." Canon 2.1. By and large, that remained the bar's position until the 1970s. Legal ethics committees spent more time on refining and enforcing restrictions on advertising and solicitation than on any other subject.[1] Impermissible practices included distributing calendars, embossed matchbooks, or Christmas cards with a lawyer's name and profession; displaying office signs with ostentatiously large lettering; cooperating with a magazine profile of "blue chip firms"; wearing jewelry with the state bar insignia; and using boldface type in telephone books.[2]

The seemingly trivial preoccupations of some ethics opinions should not, however, obscure the serious concerns at issue. To

1. James Willard Hurst, The Growth of American Law: The Law Makers 331 (1950); Philip Shuchman, Ethics and Legal Ethics: The Propriety of the Canons as a Group Moral Code, 37 Geo. Wash. L. Rev. 244, 255–56 (1968).

2. Geoffrey C. Hazard, Jr., Susan P. Koniak, & Roger Cramton, The Law and Ethics of Lawyering 1014 (1999) (discussing magazine profile and calendars); In re Maltby, 202 P.2d 902 (Ariz.1949) (matchbooks); ABA Comm. on Prof. Ethics, Formal Op. 309 (1963) (Christmas cards); In re Duffy, 242 N.Y.S.2d 665 (App.Div.1963) (neon sign); Henry S. Drinker, Legal Ethics 289, app. A., at 289 (1953) (size of sign); Belli v. State Bar, 519 P.2d 575 (Cal.1974) (Scotch); ABA Comm. on Prof. Ethics, Informal Op. C–747 (1964) (state bar jewelry); ABA Comm. on Prof'l. Ethics, Formal Op. 184 (1951) (phone book); but see ABA Comm. On Prof'l. Ethics, Informal Op. 1222 (1972) (jewelry with ABA insignia permissible).

leaders of the organized bar, the prohibitions on advertising and solicitation expressed deeply felt understandings about law as a profession rather than a business. From their perspective, allowing overt self-promotion would erode professionalism, invite deception, and diminish lawyers' public image and reputation.

By the late 1960s and early 1970s, broad prohibitions on advertising came under increasing challenge. The growing diversity of the profession, the rise of a consumer movement, the emergence of legal clinics, and the heightened concerns about unmet legal needs fueled criticism of the bar's anti-competitive policies. Many lawyers viewed these policies as anachronistic; they seemed premised on the model of a small-town legal practice in which professional reputation was a matter of common knowledge and information about the cost and quality of services was readily accessible. In addition, critics objected to the elitist biases underpinning bar policy. Lawyers representing wealthy individuals and corporations had various opportunities for genteel self-promotion; their firms not only subsidized social events and memberships in private clubs, they also purchased listings in bar-approved law directories available to major businesses. By contrast, attorneys representing poor and middle income individuals had fewer chances to publicize their services, and their potential clients were less likely to have other channels of information.

These concerns set the stage for legal challenges that eventually reached the Supreme Court. The first of these suits, Bates v. State Bar of Arizona, 433 U.S. 350 (1977), involved a somewhat colorless advertisement for a legal clinic offering "legal services at very reasonable fees." The ad also listed charges for certain routine services such as uncontested divorces, adoptions, and simple personal bankruptcies. The Supreme Court held that lawyer advertising could not be subjected to blanket suppression, and that the advertisement at issue fell within First Amendment protections.

In a subsequent decision, In re R.M.J., 455 U.S. 191 (1982), the Court again struck down content restrictions on non-misleading advertising claims. Drawing on general commercial speech doctrine as set forth in Central Hudson Gas & Electric Corp. v. Public Service Comm., 447 U.S. 557 (1980), the Court summarized its approach as follows:

> Truthful advertising related to lawful activities is entitled to the protections of the First Amendment. But when the particular content or method of the advertising suggests that it is inherently misleading or when experience has proved that in fact such advertising is subject to abuse, the States may impose

appropriate restrictions. Misleading advertising may be prohibited entirely. But the States may not place an absolute prohibition on certain types of potentially misleading information, e.g., a listing of areas of practice, if the information also may be presented in a way that is not deceptive.... Although the potential for deception and confusion is particularly strong in the context of advertising professional services, restrictions upon such advertising may be no broader than reasonably necessary to prevent the deception.

Even when a communication is not misleading, the State retains some authority to regulate. But the State must assert a substantial interest and the interference with speech must be in proportion to the interest served. Restrictions must be narrowly drawn, and the State lawfully may regulate only to the extent regulation furthers the State's substantial interest. In re R.M.J., 455 U.S. at 203.

Subsequent cases held that states could not prohibit nondeceptive graphic illustrations or descriptions of ongoing litigation, Zauderer v. Office of Disciplinary Counsel, 471 U.S. 626 (1985); mailings targeted to a specific recipient rather than members of the general public, Shapero v. Kentucky Bar Ass'n, 486 U.S. 466 (1988); or accurate identification of an attorney as a certified trial specialist, Peel v. Attorney Registration and Disciplinary Comm'n, 496 U.S. 91 (1990). All of these decisions provoked strong dissent within the Court and dissension within the bar. Surveys following the *Bates* opinion have generally found that most lawyers oppose mass media advertising.[3] By contrast, most consumers find such advertising acceptable.[4] The challenge of reconciling public and professional concerns is reflected in continuing revisions to bar ethical rules.

The Model Rules on advertising provide:

Rule 7.1: Communications Concerning a Lawyer's Services

---

3. Archer W. Honeycutt & Elizabeth A. Wibker, "Consumers' Perceptions of Selected Issues Relating to Advertising by Lawyers," 7 J. of Prof. Services Marketing 119, 120 (1991) (finding that almost ninety percent of surveyed ABA members believe that advertising harms the profession's image). See Mary Hladky, "High Court Case to Test Limits on Lawyer Ads," Legal Times, Jan. 9, 1995, at 1.

4. William E. Hornsby, Jr., "Ad Rules Infinitum: The Need for Alternatives to State–Based Ethics Governing Legal Services Marketing," 36 U. Rich. L. Rev. 49, 87–88 (2002); Milo Geyelin, "Debate Intensifies over State Regulations That Restrict TV Advertising by Lawyers," Wall St. J., Aug. 31, 1992, at B1, B4; Diane B. MacDonald & Mary Anne Raymond, "Attorney Advertising: Do Attorneys Know Their Clients?," 7 J. of Prof. Services Marketing 99 (1991). See generally ABA Commission on Advertising, Lawyer Advertising at the Crossroads: Professional Policy Considerations (1995).

A lawyer shall not make a false or misleading communication about the lawyer or the lawyer's services. A communication is false or misleading if it contains a material misrepresentation of fact or law, or omits a fact necessary to make the statement considered as a whole not materially misleading.

Comment

[2] ... A truthful statement is misleading if it omits a fact necessary to make the lawyer's communication considered as a whole not materially misleading. A truthful statement is also misleading if there is a substantial likelihood that it will lead a reasonable person to formulate a specific conclusion about the lawyer or the lawyer's services for which there is no reasonable factual foundation.

Rule 7.2: Advertising

(a) Subject to the requirements of Rules 7.1 and 7.3, a lawyer may advertise services through ... written, recorded or electronic communication, including public media.

Comment

[3] ... Questions of effectiveness and taste in advertising are matters of speculation and subjective judgment. Some jurisdictions have had extensive prohibitions against television advertising, against advertising going beyond specified facts about a lawyer, or against "undignified" advertising. Television is now one of the most powerful media for getting information to the public, particularly persons of low and moderate income; prohibiting television advertising, therefore, would impede the flow of information about legal services to many sectors of the public. Limiting the information that may be advertised has a similar effect and assumes that the bar can accurately forecast the kind of information that the public would regard as relevant.

These rules incorporate significant revisions made in 2002, in response to recommendations by the Ethics 2000 Commission. The revisions generally reflect a more permissive approach to advertising than the prior standards, and the extent to which states will follow suit remains unclear. Even before the Ethics Commission changes, about four-fifths of the states had provisions that differed from the Model Rules, and most were more conservative than the ABA's draft.[5]

---

5. Louise L. Hill, "Change Is in the Air: Lawyer Advertising and the Inter- net," 36 U. Rich. L. Rev. 21, 22 (2002).

One central difference has involved claims about performance. Many states prohibit testimonials, endorsements, specialty designations, or "self-laudatory" assertions, or require that they be accompanied by disclaimers. The mandatory disclaimers are often cumbersome or unfeasible in many advertising formats. For example, Iowa requires advertisements to include the following statement: "The determination of the need for legal services and the choice of a lawyer are extremely important decisions and should not be based solely upon self-proclaimed expertise. This disclosure is required by rule of the Supreme Court of Iowa."[6] Other jurisdictions provide that lawyers who advertise a specialty certification by organizations other than the state bar must include disclaimers that their state does not recognize or require such certification.[7]

Many legal ethics commentators and consumer protection experts raise concerns about such rules. In a submission to the ABA Commission on Advertising, the staff of the Federal Trade Commission noted:

> To be sure, testimonials and endorsements can be used in ways that mislead about likely outcomes, and it may be both appropriate and necessary to take action against those that do. But some aspects of professional services, unrelated to particular outcomes, might well be communicated truthfully and usefully by a report of a client's actual experience. Rather than a conclusive ban, an approach might be taken similar to that of the [FTC] Commission's guides on this subject, that seeks to ensure that client testimonials are truthful and not misleading. . . .
>
> Disclaimer and other disclosure prohibitions, which many jurisdictions require, tend to increase advertising costs, by requiring that messages be longer or by forcing advertisers to displace other information. Disclosure obligations may also discourage advertising if advertisers believe consumers will take the disclosure to reflect negatively on the advertiser, regardless of whether that imputation is justified. Because of these effects, disclosure requirements that are unnecessary can reduce the amount of useful information available to consumers. Disclosures and disclaimers can sometimes be necessary to

6. Iowa Code of Professional Responsibility, DR 2–101(A) (2001).

7. Illinois Rules of Prof'l. Conduct, Art. VIII, R. 7.4 (c); Texas Disciplinary Rules of Prof'l. Conduct, R. 704(b)(3). For online links to the specific state ethics provisions governing the communications of legal services, see ABA Comm'n. On Responsibility in Client Dev., Links to State Ethics Rules Governing Lawyer Advertising, Solicitation, and Marketing, ABA Network, at http://www.abanet.org/adrules.

prevent deception. It is important in evaluating disclosure requirements to weigh the costs against the expected benefits.[8]

On similar reasoning, the Eleventh Circuit Court of Appeals struck down a Florida prohibition on "self-laudatory statements" as applied to a Yellow Pages advertisement. That advertisement stated that the lawyer was " 'AV' Rated, the Highest Rating in Martindale Hubbell National Law Directory."[9] In the appellate courts' analysis, because the Florida bar failed to introduce any evidence suggesting that the statement would mislead the unsophisticated public, the state had not met its burden "to demonstrate that the harms it recites are real and that its restriction will in fact alleviate them to a material degree."[10]

A related area of controversy and inconsistency in state regulation involves prohibitions on "undignified" advertising techniques such as lyrics, jingles, animations, and dramatizations. To many judges and bar leaders, such techniques undermine lawyers' professionalism and cheapen their public image. According to Justice O'Connor, "fairly severe constraints on attorney advertising" are appropriate because they "act as a concrete day-to-day reminder to the practicing attorney of why it is improper for any member of this profession to regard it as a trade or occupation like any other." Shapero v. Kentucky Bar Association, 486 U.S. 466, 490–91 (1988) (O'Connor J., dissenting). Then Chief Justice Warren Burger put the point more emphatically. Selling law like laxatives was, in his view, " 'sheer shysterism,' and an outrageous breach of professional conduct." He personally would have preferred to "dig ditches" before placing an advertisement and he advised consumers "never, never, never, engage the services of a lawyer who finds it necessary to advertise in order to get clients."[11]

Yet most research, including ABA national surveys, finds that advertising is not a major factor in shaping public impressions of the legal profession.[12] Entertaining television commercials of the

8. Federal Trade Commission, Submission of the Staff of the Federal Trade Commission to the ABA Commission on Advertising 12 (June 24, 1994). See also Hornsby, supra note 4, at 66–69.

9. Mason v. Florida Bar, 208 F.3d 952, 954 (11th Cir.2000).

10. Id. at 957–58 (quoting Ibanez v. Florida Dept. of Bus. and Prof. Regulation, 512 U.S. 136, 146–47 (1994)).

11. David Margolick, "Burger Criticism Prompts Defense of Lawyer Ads," N.Y. Times, July 9, 1985, at A3; Warren

E. Burger, "The Decline of Professionalism," 63 Fordham L. Rev. 949, 953, 956 (1995).

12. See surveys cited in Hazard, Koniak and Cramton, supra note 2, at 1033; ABA Commission on Advertising, supra note 4, at 3; Hornsby, supra note 4, at 55; Richard J. Cebula, "Does Lawyer Advertising Adversely Influence the Image of Lawyers in the United States? An Alternative Perspective and New Empirical Evidence," 27 J. Legal Studies 503 (1998); Wiese Research Associates, kind that some states prohibit have a positive effect on viewers' perceptions of lawyers. Indeed, in one study, even sensational or cartoonish commercials improved audience evaluations of attorneys' professionalism, knowledge, helpfulness, and effectiveness.[13]

From a purely consumer protection standpoint, many states' restrictions on lawyer advertising are difficult to justify. Empirical research finds that advertising generally increases competition and reduces prices without diluting quality in professional services. Lower prices tend to heighten demand, expand volume, and encourage economies of scale. In a country where the average consumer receives close to a thousand messages a day, effective mass media advertising may depend on attention-getting devices of the sort that bar rules often condemn.

To a large extent, the debate over dignity in advertising involves a tradeoff between the public's interest in access to information and the bar's interest in maintaining decorum, status, and professional identity. That tradeoff emerged clearly in a dialogue published by the ABA Journal between Jeffrey Zuckerman, then director of the FTC Bureau of Competition, Consumer Protection, and Economics, and Adrian Foley, former Chair of the ABA Commission on Advertising. According to Zuckerman, requirements of dignity reflected a "bias against advertising" that restricted competition and the free flow of information.[14] By contrast, Foley considered such requirements to be crucial to the profession's self-image and acceptance of advertising. A Journal reporter then asked, "Is anyone really harmed if [a lawyer] pops out of a swimming pool in a television ad and asks 'if you're having trouble keeping your head above water?' Does this merely prick the profession's pomposity?" Foley responded, "To an extent, yes. But it also demeans the dedication of a great many lawyers whose professionalism is the result of years of study and hard work."[15]

To the extent that advertising regulation poses a conflict between professional and public interests, it also raises a more fundamental question: who should decide where to strike the balance. Should the organized bar play the dominant role, particularly given the low percentage of members with a personal stake in mass

Attorney Advertising Perception Study 10–11 (ABA 1994).

13.   Hazard, Koniak, & Cramton, supra note 2, at 1033. But cf. ABA Section of Litigation, Public Perception of Lawyers: Concerning Research Findings 32 (April 2002). (finding that 45% of consumers believe that changing the way lawyers advertise might improve the profession's reputation, but that it was the least important of various reform strategies proposed).

14.   "At Issue: Is Dignity Important in Legal Advertising?" 73 ABA J., Aug. 1987, at 52, 53.

15.   Id.

media communication? The ABA estimates that only about two to three percent of the nation's attorneys advertise on television or radio, and only about seven percent use direct mail. The majority of lawyers rely on brochures, yellow page listings, and internet websites.[16] Given the potential for bias within the organized bar, some commentators advocate placing oversight responsibility in more neutral authorities such as consumer protection agencies.[17]

A related issue involves the extent of discretion that regulatory agencies should exercise. Recent research suggests that advertising rules are grossly underenforced. Since *Bates*, surveyed jurisdictions have averaged fewer than one reported disciplinary case per year for advertising violations.[18] Formal enforcement actions are rare even in jurisdictions where noncompliance with specific rules is common.[19] A number of factors may account for this pattern:

- a lack of resources within disciplinary agencies;
- a lack of client complaints and demonstrable harm from violations;
- a lack of consensus within the bar about the appropriateness of advertising restrictions; and
- a lack of confidence among regulatory officials that rules can be fully and fairly enforced.

Yet however persuasive these explanations, the high visibility of unsanctioned rule violations raises obvious concerns. A refusal to enforce ethical standards erodes respect for bar regulatory processes and shields judgments about commercial speech from open debate and review. At the very least, some commentators argue, disciplinary authorities should define and defend their enforcement policies, and work to bring formal rules in line with actual practices.

A final area of controversy involves how to monitor advertising on the internet. The number of attorneys with website listings and promotional materials has been growing rapidly and bar regulatory

---

16. ABA Commission on Advertising, supra note 4, at 52.

17. Deborah L. Rhode, In the Interests of Justice: Reforming the Legal Profession 144–49 (2001); Linda Morton, "Finding a Suitable Lawyer: Why Consumers Can't Always Get What They Want and What the Legal Profession Should Do About It," 25 U.C. Davis L. Rev. 283, 303 (1992).

18. Fred C. Zacharias, "What Lawyers Do When Nobody's Watching: Legal Advertising As a Case Study of the Impact of Underenforced Professional Rules," 87 Iowa L. Rev. 971, 992 (2002).

19. In San Diego during a one year period, there were 257 cases of actual or presumptive noncompliance. In the entire state of California, there were only 3 disciplinary cases involving predominantly advertising violations. Id., at 978–88.

efforts have been unable to keep pace. These efforts have been limited by inadequacies in enforcement resources and authority over out-of-state lawyers.[20] In an era of increasingly multijurisdictional practice, state-based regulatory structures with inconsistent standards present obvious problems. As Louise Hill notes, many lawyers are faced with a difficult dilemma: full compliance with every jurisdiction's advertising requirements would unduly hamper promotional efforts and "limit [firms'] ability to compete in the global marketplace.[21]" As is clear from the discussion of unauthorized practice rules in Part C below, designing appropriate oversight structures for multijurisdictional practice is a central challenge for the contemporary legal profession.

B. Solicitation

Prohibitions on lawyers' personal solicitation of clients date to medieval England. During a time when tribunals were all too easily corrupted, the profession sought to discourage various practices associated with solicitation: maintenance (assisting others to prosecute or defend a suit without just cause); champerty (helping to maintain a suit in return for a share of the recovery); and barratry (continuing to stir up quarrels and litigation).

In this country, solicitation has been linked with similar practices and with invasions of the privacy of accident victims and their families. However, personal contact by lawyers has also had positive consequences in informing individuals of their legal rights, preventing exploitation by defendants, and enlisting plaintiffs in public interest litigation.[22]

Model Rule 7.3 attempts to strike a balance reflecting this mixed experience. It provides:

> (a) A lawyer shall not by in-person, live telephone or real-time electronic contact solicit professional employment from a prospective client when a significant motive for the lawyer's doing so is the lawyer's pecuniary gain, unless the person contacted:

20. Richard B. Schmitt, "Lowering the Bar: Lawyers Try In–Your–Face Pitches," Wall St. J., Jan. 12, 2001, at B1; Richard B. Schmitt, "Lowering the Bar: Lawyers Flood Web, But Many Ads Fail to Tell Whole Truth," Wall St. J. Jan. 15, 2001, at A1; ABA Commission on Advertising, White Paper: A Reexamination of the ABA Model Rules of Professional Conduct Pertaining to Client Development in Light of Emerging Technologies (July 1998); Hill, supra note 5.

21. Hill, supra note 5, at 50.

22. See Charles W. Wolfram, Modern Legal Ethics 786 (1986) (discussing, for example Abraham Lincoln, the Aaron Burr litigation, and the Dred Scott Case); Deborah L. Rhode, "Solicitation," 36 J. Legal Ed. 317, 325–29 (1986) (discussing Brown v. Board of Education).

(1) is a lawyer; or

(2) has a family, close personal, or prior professional relationship with the lawyer.

(b) A lawyer shall not solicit professional employment from a prospective client ... if:

(1) the prospective client has made known to the lawyer a desire not to be solicited by the lawyer; or

(2) the solicitation involves coercion, duress or harassment.

(c) Every written, recorded or electronic communication from a lawyer soliciting professional employment from a prospective client ... shall include the words "Advertising Material" on the outside envelope, if any, and at the beginning and ending of any recorded or electronic communication, unless the recipient of the communication is a person specified in paragraphs (a)(1) or (a)(2).

This Rule is consistent with the approach of two companion Supreme Court decisions: Ohralik v. Ohio State Bar Association, 436 U.S. 447 (1978), and In re Primus, 436 U.S. 412 (1978). *Ohralik* upheld the imposition of disciplinary sanctions on a lawyer who had personally solicited employment from a hospitalized accident victim and her family. *Primus* reversed the imposition of sanctions on a lawyer for the American Civil Liberties Union who had provided free legal advice and had written a letter offering pro bono representation to victims of abusive sterilization practices. In the Court's view, the potential for overreaching was sufficiently great to justify prohibitions on in-person solicitation in contexts involving potential financial gain for the lawyer. By contrast, a written solicitation by a lawyer with no monetary interest in the case posed far fewer risks. The Court did, however, leave open the possibility that states could fashion reasonable time, place, and manner restrictions on any form of solicitation. And, in Florida Bar v. Went For It, 515 U.S. 618 (1995), the Court sustained one such restriction—a prohibition on targeted mail by plaintiffs' lawyers to accident victims and their families within thirty days of the accident. According to the majority, the state has a substantial interest in improving the "flagging reputations" of lawyers and in preventing the "erosion of confidence in the profession that such repeated invasions [of privacy have fostered]." Id. at 625, 635.

Yet, as critics of that ruling noted, the Court has not permitted such restrictions on truthful speech to prevent overreaching or to salvage the reputation of other occupational groups. For example, in Edenfield v. Fane, 507 U.S. 761 (1993), the Court struck down a ban on personal solicitation by certified public accountants. Moreover, the main study supporting the Florida bar's concerns in *Went For It* found that only a quarter of consumers reported a lower regard for the legal profession as a result of such targeted solicitations. Although the state has a legitimate interest in protecting victims' privacy, many commentators agree with the dissenting Justices in *Went For It*, that such protection can be accomplished by narrower means. In the dissent's view, it is enough for states to follow the approach of Model Rule 7.3 and require disclosure on the outside of envelopes indicating that they contain a commercial solicitation.

The problem with broader thirty-day prohibitions on targeted mail by lawyers is that these bans generally do not apply to insurance agents as well. The result is that accident victims and their families may be pressured into accepting inadequate settlements before they have obtained legal advice. Victims who negotiate directly with an insurance company tend to receive substantially lower recoveries than those who are represented by lawyers.[23]

In order to address such problems, some legislators have enacted prohibitions on communications with victims by all potential litigants, including insurance companies, for a prescribed period. A representative example is the 1996 Federal Aviation Reauthorization Act, which bans unsolicited communication concerning legal action within thirty days of an air crash. Drawing on such examples, some commentators advocate solicitation rules that apply to a wider group of individuals than current prohibitions, but that cover a narrower range of conduct. So, for example, states could make all unsolicited communications to accident victims concerning potential litigation subject to reasonable time, place, and manner restrictions. Commonly proposed restrictions would prohibit in-person solicitation that:

- involves harassment, coercion, or undue influence;
- involves communication with persons who have expressed a desire not to be contacted; or
- occurs when a potential client is unable to exercise reasonable, considered judgment.[24]

23. Peter A. Bell & Jeffrey O'Conneal, Accidental Justice: The Dilemma of Tort Law 165–66 (1997); Richard Zitrin & Carol M. Langford, The Moral Compass of the American Lawyer, 129, 135–39 (1999).

24. FTC, supra note 8, at 151; James L. Kelley, Lawyers Crossing Lines: Nine Stories 157–58 (2001); Rhode, supra note 17, at 149.

Unlike the Model Rules, this approach would focus solely on harm to the potential recipient, not on the motives of the solicitor. Such a shift in emphasis would recognize that personal contact by a lawyer can sometimes be beneficial even if not disinterested. Indeed, some potential for financial gain is present even in most "public interest" litigation, given the possibility of enhanced reputation and statutory fee awards for prevailing parties.

Another way of meeting individual needs for legal advice while preventing abusive conduct is to maintain bans on personal solicitation but increase pro bono assistance. A growing number of bar associations have established mass disaster aid programs in which volunteer lawyers offer free advice or representation. For example, in the aftermath of the 9/11 terrorist attacks, thousands of attorneys volunteered free legal services for victims and their families. The Association of Trial Lawyers of America also asked attorneys representing those individuals to observe a temporary moratorium on filing suits. Widespread compliance with that request protected victims' privacy and gave them time to determine whether to seek compensation from a federal fund that required waiver of other legal remedies.[25] In the long run, such combinations of pro bono assistance and voluntary restraint may be among the best means of countering the problems traditionally associated with solicitation.

C. Multijurisdictional Practice

As the preceding discussion indicated, one of the greatest challenges in regulating the contemporary market for legal services involves multijurisdictional practice. The bar's longstanding position, codified in the Model Rules of Professional Conduct and the Code of Professional Responsibility, is that a "lawyer shall not . . . practice law in a jurisdiction where doing so violates the regulation of the legal profession in that jurisdiction." Model Rule 5.5. Accord DR 3–101(b). Under Model Rule 8.5, lawyers are subject to discipline in any jurisdiction where they provide legal services in violation of local ethics rules.

Attorneys who wish to represent a client outside of the jurisdiction where they are licensed generally must either limit themselves to extremely brief and occasional instances, affiliate local counsel, or, if the matter involves litigation, request the court to admit them temporarily, *pro hoc vice*. Courts are not constitutionally obligated to extend *pro hoc vice* admission, and may impose requirements

---

25. William Glaberson, "4 Suits Filed, Despite Calls for Restraint by Lawyers," N.Y. Times, Jan. 15, 2002, at A13.

such as affiliation of local counsel.[26] A few jurisdictions permit in-house lawyers to provide legal services on behalf of their employer from an office outside of the state if they register and submit to the local bar's regulatory authority.[27] Many states also allow members of a foreign bar to be licensed without examination as legal consultants, who may practice on a restricted basis. See ABA Model Rule for the Licensing of Legal Consultants.

The narrow exceptions to prevailing unauthorized practice rules do not, however, address the needs of most lawyers with multijurisdictional practices. For these lawyers, current licensing requirements are widely viewed as unworkable and unenforceable. Many legal matters and fields of specialization do not observe state boundaries. And many attorney communications by phone, email, fax, and internet websites do not remain within jurisdictions where the attorneys are licensed to practice law. As a recently appointed ABA Commission on Multijurisdictional Practice notes:

> Testimony before the Commission was unanimous in recognizing that lawyers commonly engage in cross-border legal practice. Further, there was general consensus that such practice is on the increase and that this trend is not only inevitable, but necessary. The explosion of technology and the increasing complexity of legal practice have resulted in the need for lawyers to cross state borders to afford clients competent representation. . . .

> The existing system of lawyer regulation is and should be a matter of serious concern for many lawyers. Even in contexts where jurisdictional restrictions clearly apply, as in state-court proceedings, problems are caused by the lack of uniformity among the *pro hoc vice* provisions of different states, unpredictability about how some of the provisions will be applied by the courts in individual cases, and, in some cases, the provisions' excessive restrictiveness. Of even greater concern, however, is that, outside the context of litigation, the reach of the jurisdictional restrictions is vastly uncertain as well as, potentially, far too restrictive. Lawyers may recognize that UPL [unauthorized practice of law] enforcement proceedings are infrequent, and that when UPL laws are invoked, courts have the ability to interpret them realistically to accommodate the interests of clients with interstate or multi-state legal problems. Nevertheless, some lawyers will turn down clients or take other steps to

26. Leis v. Flynt, 441 U.S. 956 (1979); Hazard, Koniak, & Cramton, supra note 2, at 1054–56.

27. ABA Report of the Commission on Multijurisdictional Practice (Aug. 2002) available at http://www.abanet.org/cpr/mjp/final_mjp_rpt_5-13.pdf.

avoid or reduce the risk of having to defend against UPL charges or of appearing to violate rules of professional conduct.

The existing system of lawyer regulation has costs for clients. For example, out of concern for jurisdictional restrictions, lawyers may decline to provide services that they are able to render skillfully and ethically.... Further, even if lawyers felt free to ignore UPL laws in areas where there is a professional consensus that the laws are outmoded and there appears to be a tacit understanding that they will not be enforced, it is undesirable to retain the laws as written, rather than amending them to accord with contemporary understandings and practices that serve clients well. Keeping antiquated laws on the books breeds public disrespect for the law, and this is especially so where the laws relate to the conduct of lawyers, for whom there is a professional imperative to uphold the law.[28]

The problems inherent in prevailing unauthorized practice rules are illustrated by a widely publicized California Supreme Court decision, Birbrower, Montalbano, Condon & Frank v. Superior Court, 949 P.2d 1 (Cal.1998). There, a New York lawyer represented a family corporation that had branches in New York and California in a dispute with a New York software manufacturer. The lawyer made several trips to California to confer with corporate officers, to negotiate with software representatives, and to initiate arbitration proceedings. The dispute was settled before arbitration but the client then sued the attorney for malpractice. The attorney cross claimed to recover his fee. In rejecting the cross claim, the California Supreme Court reasoned that the fee agreement was unenforceable because the attorney had engaged in the unauthorized practice of law. Under the court's analysis, the "primary inquiry is whether the unlicensed lawyer engaged in sufficient activities in the state, or created a continuing relationship with the California client that included legal duties and obligations." Id. at 5. Physical presence, according to the court, was a relevant but not conclusive factor. Lawyers could engage in unauthorized practice by providing legal advice by telephone, fax, or other means.

The *Birbrower* decision attracted widespread criticism. The California legislature partially addressed the concerns by creating a statutory exemption from unauthorized practice prohibitions for arbitration proceedings. But the broader problem of interstate practice calls for more fundamental solutions. Since *Birbrower*, about half the states' bar associations, as well as the ABA and

28. Id. at 10–12.

many local bar organizations, have formed groups to study the issue.[29]

On recommendation by a Commission on Multijurisdictional Practice, the ABA recently approved amendments to the Model Rules that would provide "safe havens" from unauthorized practice prohibitions. Under the proposed revisions to Model Rule 5.5, an out-of-state lawyer would be allowed to provide legal services on a temporary basis that:

- are undertaken in association with a lawyer who is admitted to practice in this jurisdiction and who actively participates in the matter;

- are in or reasonably related to a pending or potential proceeding before a tribunal in this or another jurisdiction, if the lawyer, or a person the lawyer is assisting, is authorized by law or order to appear in such proceeding or reasonably expects to be so authorized;

- are in or reasonably related to a pending or potential arbitration, mediation, or other alternate dispute resolution proceeding in [the] ... jurisdiction, if the services arise out of or are reasonably related to the lawyer's practice in a jurisdiction in which the lawyer is admitted to practice and are not services for which the forum requires *pro hoc vice* admission;
  . . .

- are provided to the lawyer's employer or its organizational affiliates and are not services for which the forum requires *pro hoc vice* admission; or

- are services that the lawyer is authorized by federal or other law to provide in this jurisdiction.

How workable this approach would prove in practice remains open to question. Some commentators believe that it is unduly complex and restrictive. A variety of other possibilities have been proposed. One option is to follow Section 3 of the Restatement (Third) of the Law Governing Lawyers, which permits legal work that "arises out of or is otherwise related to the lawyer's practice" in a jurisdiction in which the lawyer is licensed. Other possibilities include: a national system of bar admission, discussed in Chapter XI; more permissive state-based reciprocity rules modeled on the European Union system; and a national license to provide "cyber

29. Kenneth L. Carson, "Legalize It?
Lawyers Practicing Across State Lines,"
46 B.B.J. 18 (March/April 2002).

advice."[30] Under a national bar admission system, a license to practice law would be similar to a driver's license; the attorney's state of residence would test for competence, and other jurisdictions would honor its judgment as long as the non-resident attorney's presence was temporary. Under a system like the European Union, lawyers could provide legal services in another jurisdiction if they registered to do so, limited their practice to occasional activity, agreed to comply with local ethics rules and enforcement processes, and maintained legal malpractice insurance.[31] Under a cyber licensing system, lawyers could offer electronic advice in jurisdictions where they demonstrated some basic familiarity with the local laws.[32]

Although lawyers disagree about which approach to multijurisdictional practice makes most sense, there is broad agreement on two general points. First, as the ABA Commission has noted, multijurisdictional practice is an inevitable and necessary response to clients' needs. Second, current unauthorized practice rules require reform in order to take account of those needs and permit more effective service.[33]

D. Multidisciplinary Practice

Many of the same socioeconomic forces that have challenged the geographic boundaries of legal practice have also called into question its disciplinary boundaries, namely the barrier between law and other professional services. The bar's traditional approach, reflected in Model Rule 5.4 and DR 3–102(A), is that lawyers may not share fees or control over their practice with nonlawyers. Although attorneys have been allowed to work in-house for organizations owned by nonlawyers, they have not been permitted to form partnerships with nonlawyers to deliver legal services. The rationale for such prohibitions is that protection of the independence of lawyers is necessary to preserve the core values of the profession.

---

30. "Unauthorized Practice: ABA Panelists Explore UPL Ramifications Tied to Changing Nature of Law Practice," 16 ABA/BNA Lawyer's Manual on Professional Conduct 282 (June 7, 2000); Martha Neil, "Easing Up," ABA J., Feb. 2002, at 47, 49; Lance J. Rogers, "ABA Commission Hears Proposals, Concerns Over Expanded Multijurisdictional Law Practice," 17 ABA/BNA Lawyer's Manual on Professional Conduct 133 (2001). See also Anthony E. Davis, "Multijurisdictional Practice By Transactional Lawyers–Why the Sky Really Is Falling," 11 Prof. Law 1 (Winter 2000).

31. See Geoffrey C. Hazard Jr., "New Shape of Lawyering," Nat'l. L. J., July 23, 2001, at A21; Stephen Gillers, "Protecting Their Own," American Lawyer, Nov. 1998, at 118.

32. Katy Ellen Deady, Note, "Cyberadvice: The Ethical Implications of Giving Professional Advice Over the Internet," 14 Geo. J. Legal Ethics 891 (2001).

33. ABA Commission, supra note 27, at 1.

Over the last decade, that prohibition has become the focus of growing controversy. Faced with increasing competition for clients and increasing needs for cross-disciplinary expertise, many lawyers have sought to forge closer relationships with providers of other professional services. Disputes over how to structure such relationships have involved two organizational forms: (1) ancillary businesses, which are separate entities that work in collaboration with lawyers, such as firms offering financial, lobbying, and real estate services; and (2) multidisciplinary partnerships (MDPs), such as a law-and-accounting firms, which offer multiple professional services under one roof.

The current controversy began with ancillary businesses. It came to a head in the early 1990s when the District of Columbia adopted a rule allowing such businesses and permitting nonlawyers to become partners under specified circumstances.[34] This rule, and the broader trends it reflected, prompted considerable dispute and many reform proposals within other bar organizations. The American Bar Association's House of Delegates first voted to prohibit lawyers' ownership of ancillary non-legal businesses, then repealed the ban, and finally adopted Model Rule 5.4. That Rule permits such lawyer-owned businesses but does not allow nonlawyers to be partners. Only a few jurisdictions have adopted that rule.[35]

Underlying this controversy are a range of issues about quality, efficiency, commercialization, and professionalism. Proponents of lawyer-owned ancillary businesses argue that they encourage cost-effective collaborations between legal and nonlegal experts; decrease search costs in hiring such experts; and give lawyers incentives to monitor the performance of ancillary service providers. By contrast, critics worry that diversification into other business activity distracts lawyers from the practice of law; impairs their objectivity in recommending other professionals; invites misuse of confidential information; introduces too much profit-oriented, nonlawyer influence into law firm management; and erodes the distinctiveness of law as a profession rather than a business.

---

34. D.C. Rules of Professional Conduct, Rule 5.4 provides that lawyers may practice with nonlawyer partners who assist the organization in providing legal services, provided that these individuals abide by bar ethical rules and that lawyers undertake the same responsibility for these activities as if the participants were lawyers.

35. Ted Schneyer, "Policymakers and the Perils of Professionalism: The ABA's Ancillary Business Debate as a Case Study," 35 Ariz. L. Rev. 363 (1993); Mary C. Daly, "What the MDP Debate Can Teach Us about Law Practice in the New Millennium and the Need for Curricular Reform," 50 J. Leg. Ed. 521 (2000).

Similar issues underpin the current debate over multidisciplinary partnerships. That debate has attracted increasing attention largely due to increasing competition from accounting firms. Other western industrialized nations generally permit nonlawyers to provide some law-related services and to employ lawyers or to form partnerships with lawyers. As a consequence, the major accounting firms have a strong position in the global legal market. They have a presence in 138 countries and some employ over 60,000 workers.

These accounting firms are also making increased inroads in the American market. Federal law provides that federal tax advice and representation in federal tax court does not constitute the practice of law. This exception to traditional unauthorized practice prohibitions enables lawyers to provide services for clients of accounting firms as long as the work can be defined as tax, not legal, assistance. Lawyers may also provide legal advice to a professional who is giving nonlegal advice to a client. Over the past decade, the major accounting firms have pushed these boundaries between legal and nonlegal work, and have expanded their in-house legal staff to provide much the same services as law firms on matters such as tax, financial, and estate planning, intellectual property, ADR, and litigation support. The American legal profession faces growing difficulties in competing with these accounting organizations, which generally offer a wider range of services, more international networks and name recognition, greater economies of scale, and more effective marketing, information technology, and managerial capacities. Although bar leaders believe that many multidisciplinary organizations are violating unauthorized practice statutes, a lack of resources and public support has inhibited enforcement efforts.[36]

Supporters of liberalized rules on multidisciplinary practice stress the advantages to clients of "one stop" shopping, and the advantages to lawyers of being able to compete more effectively with other service providers. The benefits would extend not just to large firms and business clients, but also to small firms and solo practitioners with individual clients, such as senior citizens needing a range of legal, medical, and social services.

By contrast, opponents worry that lawyers will become accountable to supervisors from a different tradition with less rigorous standards governing confidentiality, conflicts of interest, and pro bono service. Particular concerns center on accounting firms' unwillingness to impute conflicts of interest; they rely rather on client consent and ethical screens. In critics' view, such safeguards

---

36. Daly, supra note 35, at 536; Philip S. Anderson, "Facing Up to Multidisciplinary Practice," 50 J. Leg. Educ. 473, 480 (2000).

are often ineffective, and allowing lawyers to become participants in these organizations will compromise core principles and blur the boundaries between law and business. Clients will reportedly pay the price as professional judgments are driven by the bottom line.[37]

In 1999, an ABA Commission on Multidisciplinary Practice issued a report acknowledging these ethical concerns but proposing strategies short of prohibition. The Commission recommended holding nonlawyers in multidisciplinary firms to the same ethical standards governing conflicts and confidentiality as those applicable to the bar generally. In addition, the Commission proposed special audit provisions to prevent nonlawyers from interfering with lawyers' professional judgments. Under this framework, the attorney-client privilege could be extended to cover nonlawyers, or clients could be warned about its unavailability.[38] An alternative approach, proposed by accounting firms, would be to follow their less stringent conflict of interest procedures. According to these firms, experience demonstrates the adequacy of this approach; sophisticated clients appear satisfied and have not pressed for reforms or alternatives.

The ABA House of Delegates overwhelmingly rejected the Commission's recommendations and declined to consider any less restrictive alternative. House members voted against relaxing prohibitions on multidisciplinary partnerships in the absence of evidence that they would serve the public interest and would not compromise lawyers' independence or loyalty to clients. Evidence to this effect was foreseeably unattainable. The Commission responded by reconsidering and supplementing the evidence that it had received from a broad range of professional and client groups. In the Commission's view, it would be impossible to measure the public interest in such arrangements until the "taint of illegality" was removed. In the interim, the support expressed by consumer groups and the market demand for lawyers in multidisciplinary settings was, from the Commission's perspective, evidence of the perceived social value of these arrangements.[39] Accordingly, the Commission submitted a revised proposal authorizing multidisciplinary partnerships under specified circumstances. The House of Delegates again rejected the Commission's recommendations.[40]

---

37. For an overview of these arguments, see David Luban, "Asking The Right Questions," 72 Temple L. Rev. 839 (1999).

38. ABA Commission on Multidisciplinary Practice, "Report of the Commission on Multidisciplinary Practice to the ABA House of Delegates," reprinted in 10 Professional Lawyer 1 (Spring 1999).

39. "MDP Rides Again," ABA J., Feb. 2000, at 96.

40. House of Delegates Resolution 10F (2000), reprinted in Daly, supra note 35, at 532.

Controversy then shifted to the states, and by the turn of the twenty-first century, virtually every jurisdiction was considering the issue.[41] A cottage industry of commentary also emerged. Analysis centered not simply on how to structure professional services, but also on how to define and pursue professional values in an increasingly competitive global market.[42] Recent scandals involving accounting practices fueled further disputes. To some commentators, the misconduct in cases like Enron reflected conflicts of interest between accountants' audit and consulting functions and demonstrated why lawyers should keep their distance.[43] To other commentators, these conflicts of interest underscored the need for tighter regulation of competing professionals who were employing a growing number of lawyers and supplying an increasing volume of law-related services.

Part of the difficulty in resolving these disputes involves the lack of systematic information about the extent of ethical problems in multidisciplinary organizations and the likely effectiveness of proposed responses. Lawyers who have worked in both law firms and MDPs testified before the Commission that there were not significant differences in the ethical cultures of the two kinds of organization, apart from the rules about imputed conflicts. Many of the MDPs that presented testimony also pointed to records of public service that rivaled those of law firms.[44] In any event, even if it could be established that conflicts and confidentiality problems were somewhat more likely to arise in multidisciplinary firms, and that those firms were somewhat less likely to provide institutional support for public service than law firms, it would not be self-evident that total prohibition is the best response. Many experts believe that clients should have the option of weighing the risks

---

41. John B. Attanasio, "The Brave New World of Multidisciplinary Practice: Foreword," 50 J. Leg. Ed. 469, 470 (2000). See also Daly, supra note 35, at 527. For an overview see ABA, Center for Professional Responsibility, Status of Multidisciplinary Practice Studies by State (and some local bars), Feb. 11, 2002, available at http://www.abanet.org/cpr/mdp-state_action.html

42. Symposia on the subject include: "The Brave New World of Multidisciplinary Practice," 50 J. Leg. Ed. 469 (2000); "Future of the Profession: A Symposium on Multidisciplinary Practice," 84 Minn. L. Rev. 1083 (2000); "New Roles, No Rules? Redefining Lawyers Work," 72 Temp. L. Rev. 773 (1999). For other overviews, see Mary C.

Daly, "Choosing Wise Men Wisely: The Risks and Rewards of Purchasing Legal Services from Lawyers in a Multidisciplinary Partnership," 13 Geo. J. Legal Ethics 217 (2000); and Report of the N.Y. State Bar Association Special Committee on the Law Governing Firm Structure and Operation (2000).

43. Geanne Rosenberg, "Scandal Seen as Blow to Outlook for MDP," Nat'l. L. J. , Jan 21, 2002, at A1; Steven C. Krane, "Let Lawyers Practice Law," Nat'l. L. J., Jan. 28, 2002, at A16.

44. Phoebe A. Haddon, "The MDP Controversy: What Legal Educators Should Know," 50 J. Leg. Ed. 504, 511–12 (2000).

and benefits of MDPs, and that ethical restrictions should be narrowly tailored to address demonstrated abuses.

However these issues are resolved, multidisciplinary collaborations of some form are obviously here to stay. There is a strong market demand and legitimate societal need for integrated legal and nonlegal advice. Where state bars prohibit multidisciplinary partnerships, multidisciplinary practice will take other forms. For example, New York now permits, and some American law firms are developing, "strategic alliances" with professional services firms. Under these arrangements, the firms agree to share clients and sometimes capital and marketing capacities.[45] Whether these arrangements can address client needs as effectively as "one stop shopping" MDPs remains to be seen. If experience is any guide, the only viable long term strategy for regulating the legal services market is one that can adequately adapt to competitive forces.

E.   Attorneys' Fees

Of all the public's complaints about lawyers, expense is at the top of the list. Most Americans believe that legal assistance costs too much, and fewer than five percent believe that they get good value for the price of lawyers' services.[46] Such perceptions are longstanding. Virtually all societies have, at least intermittently, made efforts to restrict attorneys' fees.[47] Many countries now set these fees by detailed statutes that graduate the amount of payment for specified services. America's regulatory structure reveals a more complicated combination of bar oversight, deference to market forces, and sporadic legislative and judicial intervention.

Practices involving legal fees have long aroused discomfort among both lawyers and clients. In England, early tradition had it that gentlemen did not pay other gentlemen for their services, so more discrete forms of remuneration were required. Barristers, the elite of the profession, never discussed fees with their clients; all matters of compensation were handled through solicitors and clerks.[48] In this country, many attorneys also attempted to avoid "haggling" over money by adherence to bar-established minimum

---

45. Daly, supra note 35, at 542.

46. Public Perceptions of Lawyers, supra note 13, at 14 (2002); Gary A. Hengstler, "Vox Populi: The Public Perception of Lawyers," ABA J., Sept. 1993, at 63.

47. William Howard Taft, Ethics in Service 4-8, 15 (1915); Charles Warren, A History of the American Bar 112–13 (1911); Dennis R. Nolan, Readings in the History of the American Legal Profession 103–05 (1980).

48. W. J. Reader, Professional Men: The Rise of the Professional Classes in Nineteenth–Century England 36–37 (1966); R. E. Megarry, Lawyer and Litigant in England 56–60 (1962).

fee schedules. The Canons of Ethics encouraged this practice and condemned any form of "underbidding."[49] In 1975, the Supreme Court struck down minimum fee schedules as a restraint of trade in violation of the Sherman Antitrust Act.[50] However, some information concerning standard charges has remained accessible through various publications for practitioners.

Lawyers have also looked for other ways to avoid fee disputes. In cases where they anticipate or experience reluctance by clients to settle accounts, practitioners can employ a variety of measures apart from litigation: substantial non-refundable retainers, refusal to complete work or relinquish client papers, informal modifications of their bills, or threats to reveal confidential information in the course of suing to recover payment.

Four types of fee arrangements are now common. The predominant billing method is the hourly fee. Other options are a flat fee for a particular matter; a proportional fee (such as a percentage of an estate or property involved in a transaction); or a contingent fee, which gives the lawyer a flat fee or a proportion of the recovery if the matter is successfully resolved. Such billing methods can also be used in combination, such as a flat fee with a bonus contingent on a particular result.

Regulation of these fees takes several forms. Rule 1.5 of the Model Rules of Professional Conduct prohibits lawyers from charging "unreasonable" fees, and DR 2–106 of the Code prohibits fees that are "clearly excessive." However, bar ethics committees and disciplinary authorities generally have not enforced these rules in individual cases unless the amount charged is so excessive as to be unconscionable or equivalent to a misappropriation of funds.[51] Rather, bar authorities have largely confined their focus to the general propriety of certain billing practices. For example, in Formal Opinion 93–379 (1993), the ABA Ethics Committee ruled that a lawyer should not double bill by charging more than one client for the same hours or work product; should not bill a client for overhead expenses generally associated with equipping an office; and should not impose surcharges on services such as photocopying beyond the costs actually incurred.

On the whole, however, bar regulatory authorities have viewed the appropriate remedy for unreasonable charges to be nonpayment of fees, malpractice claims, or breach of contract actions. To most

49. ABA Canons of Ethics, Canons 27 and 28.

50. Goldfarb v. Virginia State Bar, 421 U.S. 773, 787 (1975).

51. American Bar Foundation, Annotated Code of Professional Responsibility 101–02, 104–05 (1979).

disciplinary committees, the criteria for deciding what constitutes an excessive fee are too indeterminate to justify disciplinary proceedings except in egregious cases, and bar disciplinary systems generally lack sufficient resources to handle ordinary fee disputes.

However, as Chapter XII notes, malpractice and contractual litigation is often an inadequate means of deterring or remedying excessive fees. For individuals with fee-related grievances, paying a second attorney to challenge the charges of the first is seldom an appealing option, particularly if the amount at issue is modest. Although corporate clients may have sufficient knowledge, experience, and leverage to protect themselves from excessive charges, many individual clients do not. And even sophisticated clients may not always have adequate information to insure fairness, as is clear from the frequency of problems concerning excessive charges, nonrefundable retainers, and contingent fees noted below.

Excessive Charges

Model Rule 1.5 lists the following factors as relevant in determining the reasonableness of a fee:

(1) the time and labor required, the novelty and difficulty of the questions involved, and the skill requisite to perform the legal service properly;

(2) the likelihood, if apparent to the client, that the acceptance of the particular employment will preclude other employment by the lawyer;

(3) the fee customarily charged in the locality for similar legal services;

(4) the amount involved and the results obtained;

(5) the time limitations imposed by the client or by the circumstances;

(6) the nature and length of the professional relationship with the client;

(7) the experience, reputation, and ability of the lawyer or lawyers performing the services; and

(8) whether the fee is fixed or contingent.

Courts and commentators generally agree with this list, although some would add the client's ability to pay and two further considerations set forth in the Restatement (Third) of Law Governing Lawyers: "when the agreement was made, did the lawyer afford the client a free and informed choice?; [and] ... was there a subsequent change in circumstances that made the fee agreement unreasonable?"[52]

Although there is widespread consensus about the relevant standards in assessing a fee, there is widespread difficulty in applying them in particular cases. Fee-related abuses fall across a spectrum, reflecting everything from flagrant fraud and "creative timekeeping" to sloppy accounting and inefficient staffing. The frequency of such abuses is difficult to gauge, since many constitute the "perfect crime." Although sophisticated business clients have become increasingly adept at monitoring charges, it is often impossible to verify whether certain tasks were essential and whether they required, or actually consumed, the time that lawyers charged for completing them. Auditors find demonstrable fraud in about five to ten percent of the bills they review and questionable practices in another twenty-five to thirty-five percent. Such practices include inflating hours, overstaffing cases, performing unnecessary work, and double billing multiple clients for the same task or time. Forty percent of surveyed lawyers acknowledge that some of their work is influenced by a desire to bill additional hours.[53]

The basic problem arises from the obvious divergence in lawyers' and clients' interests. An attorney's goal, so far as compensation is concerned, is to maximize profits; a client's goal is to maximize value and minimize costs. If lawyers are charging by the hour and lack other equally profitable uses for their time, they have an incentive to prolong projects or to accept matters beyond their expertise that will require substantial learning at clients' expense. The problem is compounded by the amount of billable work that firms increasingly demand, and its importance in determining lawyers' status, promotion, and compensation. Current billable hour quotas generally range between 1800 and 2000 a year, and the averages are higher in many firms. Most estimates indicate that about a third of lawyers' office time cannot be billed honestly to clients; administrative matters, firm meetings, personal needs, and keeping current with legal developments all occupy a substantial

---

52. Restatement (Third) of Law Governing Lawyers § 46 Comment. For a summary of cases finding clients' lack of resources relevant, see Wolfram, supra note 22, at 518–22. See also former Canon 12 of the ABA Canons of Ethics, which provided that a client's ability to pay could not justify charges in "excess of the value of ... services," but that poverty could justify lower charges.

53. William G. Ross, The Honest Hour: The Ethics of Time–Based Billing

by Attorneys 65 (1996); John J. Marquess, "Legal Audits and Dishonest Legal Bills," 22 Hofstra L. Rev. 637, 643–44 (1994); Ralph Nader & Wesley J. Smith, No Contest: Corporate Lawyers and the Perversion of Justice in America 233–42 (1996); Darlene Ricker, "Greed, Ignorance and Overbilling," ABA J., Aug. 1994, at 62. Some lawyers have double billed for the same time if, for example, while traveling for one client they do work for another.

chunk of time. To generate 2000 billable hours, attorneys typically need to work ten hours a day, six days a week. As Chief Justice Rehnquist has noted, if lawyers are expected to bill at current levels, "there are bound to be temptations to exaggerate the hours actually put in."[54]

In the face of such pressures, rationalizations for padding hours and relabeling expenses come readily to hand. Studies of billing abuses find that lawyers often insist that their work really was "worth more" than the time that it required. Others use upward "adjustments" to compensate for hours and expenses that they assume they have forgotten to claim or for tasks that clients will not reimburse. In egregious cases, lawyers have billed over 6,000 hours a year for several years, have charged running shoes as "ground transportation," and have classified dry cleaning for a toupee as a litigation expense.[55] Such forms of fee-related deception erode client trust and attorney integrity. They also deflect attention from the problems that contribute to overbilling, such as poor time management or excessive overhead expenses.

Bar disciplinary processes are not well structured to police such fee-related misconduct. As noted earlier, most enforcement agencies are unwilling to intervene except in extreme cases, and even these may be difficult for clients to prove. Most lawyers are reluctant to second-guess their colleagues' charges, or to support a regulatory approach that might subject everyone's fees to more frequent oversight. Only a minority of jurisdictions have arbitration systems for fee disputes. Even fewer require lawyers to participate.[56] Model Rule 1.5 provides only that lawyers should "conscientiously consider" submitting to arbitration programs. Most of these programs also exclude issues regarding the quality of services, even though such issues underlie many fee disputes.

The absence of alternative dispute resolution procedures compromises lawyers' interests as well as those of clients. Litigation is seldom a desirable strategy for collecting unpaid fees; it is likely to prove highly unpleasant, impose significant financial and reputational costs, and encourage malpractice counterclaims. Particularly where the unpaid bills are modest and clients' assets are limited,

54. William H. Rehnquist, "The Legal Profession Today: Dedicatory Address," 62 Ind. L. J. 151, 153 (1987). See Ross, supra note 53, at 3, 27.

55. Hazard, Koniak & Cramton, supra note 2, at 504; Lisa G. Lerman, "Blue–Chip Bilking: Regulation of Billing and Expense Fraud by Lawyers," 12 Geo. J. Legal Ethics 205 (1999); Barbara A. Serrano, "Lawyers Who Flouted Ethics Rules Escape Reprimand," Seattle Times, March 31, 1996, at A1; Gerald F. Phillips, Reviewing a Law Firm's Billing Practices, Professional Lawyers 2001 at 2.

56. Rhode, supra note 17, at 181.

attorneys may end up providing services pro bono, but not by choice.

An obvious way to improve fee-related enforcement structures is for all states to establish alternative dispute resolution programs and require lawyers to participate. These programs should address issues of performance as well as charges, and should be as independent as possible of the organized bar. They should include qualified nonlawyer representatives and should be publicized through media outreach and disclosure requirements. Bar ethical codes should require that lawyers provide clients with a standard "bill of rights," including information about fee-related rules and remedies. Systematic efforts to assess participants' evaluation of alternative dispute resolution processes should also be a high priority, because the limited evidence available reveals substantial client dissatisfaction with current programs.[57]

Not only do we need better remedies for consumers, we also need better responses from law firms. Studies of attorneys convicted of billing fraud illustrate common patterns of institutional indifference. When the issue is padding or meter running, supervising lawyers often look the other way or fail to look at all. And when significant misconduct comes to light, significant responses too seldom follow. Studies of fraudulent billing find that firms typically fail to report criminal conduct of their members to bar disciplinary authorities or prosecutors.[58] In most cases, the only penalty for excessive fees is a reduction of charges or reimbursement for overpayments, coupled with a loss of future business from the client. Given the low probability of detection, such sanctions provide inadequate deterrence.

To change these incentive structures, more severe penalties are necessary. In cases of serious ethical abuses, lawyers should be required to forfeit their fees and should be subject to discipline for failure to report fraud by other attorneys. Firms in which significant billing abuses occur should be required to develop appropriate oversight procedures, including internal training programs and random audits.[59]

Finally, the profession could encourage more realistic billable hour quotas and more alternatives to hourly rates. Over the last decade, interest in innovative billing structures has substantially

---

57. Id.

58. Kelly, supra note 24, at 182; Lerman, supra note 55, at 278; Ross, supra note 53, at 199–219.

59. Lerman, supra note 55, at 297–300; Erin White, "More Law Firms Are Auditing Themselves to Catch Billing Errors," Wall St. J., July 14, 1998, at B8; Joanne Pitulla, "Excessive Fees Bite Back," ABA J., April 1997, at 82.

increased. Common alternatives include fixed fees for routine tasks, reduced hourly fees plus a contingency bonus based on results, and blended fees, involving flat rates with adjustments based on hours or results. Such arrangements can accommodate client concerns such as the desire to increase predictability, encourage efficiency, compare risks, or share risks.[60] Of course, these alternative structures also carry certain disadvantages. If flat fees are set too low, lawyers have an incentive to cut quality. The risk of insufficient preparation is especially pronounced for unsophisticated clients or for those who are not paying for the lawyers' services. For example, inadequate quality has been a chronic problem in the context of indigent criminal defense contracts, where lawyers submit competitive bids to cover a jurisdiction's entire caseload for a fixed fee.[61] However, in matters involving experienced corporate clients, where attorneys have a strong economic interest in maintaining their reputation for quality, a fixed fee or blended fee can be an attractive option.[62]

Nonrefundable Retainer Fees

Nonrefundable retainer fees generally take two forms. One is an "engagement" fee or "general retainer." An engagement fee is earned when attorneys lend their names to the case, and it bears no relation to the charge for hours spent on the matter. Such a fee is intended to compensate for the attorney's reputation, commitment to a specific client, unavailability to an opponent, and reservation of future time to be spent on that client. A second type of nonrefundable fee is a "special" retainer; services are billed against that initial amount but at the conclusion of the case, the attorney keeps any part of the retainer that has not yet been charged.

Some jurisdictions prohibit use of certain types of non-refundable fees. For example, the New York Court of Appeals disallowed "special retainer" agreements in a case in which a divorce lawyer had attempted to collect substantial sums for little or no work. In the Court's view, if such agreements were "allowed to flourish, clients would be relegated to hostage status," because they would

---

60. See Ronald D. Rotunda, "Moving from Billable Hours to Fixed Fees: Task–Based Fees and Legal Ethics," 47 U. Kan. L. Rev. 819 (1999). The ABA has created a Commission on Billable Hours, which is exploring alternative structures. See http://www.aban-et.org/careerCounsel/billable.html. See also Donald C. Massey & Christopher A. D'Amour, "The Ethical Considerations of Alternative Fee Billing," 28 S. U. L. Rev. 111 (2001); The Committee on

Lawyer Business Ethics, "Business and Ethics Implications of Alternative Billing Practices: Report on Alternative Billing Arrangements," 54 Bus. Law. 175 (1998).

61. See Rhode, supra note 17, at 61.

62. See Robert E. Litan & Steven C. Salop, "Reforming the Lawyer–Client Relationship Through Alternative Billing Methods," 77 Judicature 191 (1994).

find it prohibitively expensive to fire their counsel.[63] That same logic argues for broader bans on nonrefundable fees, or modifications if the attorney-client relationship ends before the object of representation is completed.

Contingent Fees

Fees that are conditional on a successful outcome are a matter of longstanding controversy. Contingent fees are now virtually universal in personal injury litigation, and widespread in other areas such as professional malpractice, tax refunds, employment discrimination, eminent domain, debt collection, shareholders' derivative claims, and private antitrust actions. The size of the fee often varies, but one-third of the total client recovery is a common rate.

Such arrangements have prompted continuing criticism and intermittent restrictions. Early English common law banned contingent fees entirely as a form of unlawful maintenance, barratry, and champerty (i.e., selling shares in the subject matter of a lawsuit and stirring up frivolous litigation). Although some American jurisdictions initially replicated such prohibitions, by the early twentieth century, contingency arrangements under court supervision were generally permissible.[64] By contrast, many other countries have banned contingent fees, not only because of concerns about nonmeritorious suits but also because of potential lawyer-client conflicts of interest.

Defenders of contingent fees generally emphasize three main advantages of America's more permissive rules. Such arrangements:

- give lawyers an incentive to pursue a case vigorously in contexts where clients would have difficulty evaluating the quality of professional services;

- allow clients with limited financial resources to afford competent legal assistance by trading upon the value of their claims; and

---

63. In re Cooperman, 633 N.E.2d 1069, 1072 (N.Y.1994). The court did not, however, prohibit general retainer agreements. For other state rules, see P. Thomas Thornbrugh, "The Nonrefundable–Fee Minefield," 80 ABA J., April 1994, at 105. Section 34 of the Restatement (Third) of the Law Governing Lawyers views engagement retainer fees as legitimate to the extent that they bear a reasonable relationship to income that lawyers sacrifice or expenses that they incur.

64. After heated debate, the ABA adopted that position in its 1908 Canons of Ethics. For a critical analysis of the organized bar's hostility toward contingent fees, and the class, religious, and ethnic biases that helped explain such animosity, see Jerold Auerbach, Unequal Justice: Lawyers and Social Change in Modern America 45–51 (1976).

- enable clients to shift most of the risk of an unsuccessful suit to attorneys, who can spread the costs among other claimants.

Critics of prevailing contingency agreements, however, object to the conflict of interest that they create between lawyers and clients. Attorneys' economic interest lies in maximizing the return on their work; clients' interest lies in gaining the highest possible settlement. Depending on the amount of effort and expense that lawyers invest in preparing a case, the alternative uses of their time, and their attitude toward risk, they may be more or less inclined to settle than their clients. Most commentators have concluded that for claims with low or modest stakes, contingent fee lawyers have inadequate incentives to prepare a case thoroughly and to hold out for the highest possible settlement. Conversely, in high-stakes cases, once lawyers have spent substantial time in preparation, they may be more inclined than their economically-pressed clients to gamble for a large recovery.

In addition, critics of contingency arrangements object to fee structures in which a lawyer's return bears no necessary relationship to the amount of work performed or to the risk actually assumed. In cases with easy facts and large damages, a standard one-third percentage recovery will provide windfalls for the attorney. In some widely publicized examples, the amount of work done was so insignificant that it would amount to hourly returns estimated at between $12,500 and $30,000 an hour.[65]

Lawyers defend such recoveries as essential to subsidize other cases with higher risks. Evidence on this point is mixed. One study of California litigation found that personal injury plaintiffs were successful in only about one-third of the cases, as compared with an average plaintiff success rate of about one-half. The authors of the study observe that this is precisely what one would expect if personal injury plaintiffs' lawyers, who generally use contingency fees, were accepting the riskier cases that justify contingency arrangements.[66] At least some evidence also suggests that outside the large metropolitan areas where most high-stakes litigation occurs,

---

65. Lester Brickman, Michael Horowitz, & Jeffrey O'Connell, Rethinking Contingency Fees: A Proposal to Align the Contingency Fee System with Its Policy Roots and Ethical Mandates 20–23 (1994). According to some commentators, lawyers' windfalls are becoming a greater problem because the percentage of cases settling and the size of the payouts is rising, while fee arrangements are remaining the same. Peter Passell, "Windfall Fees in Injury Cases Under Assault," N.Y. Times, Feb. 11, 1994, at A1 (quoting Yale professor George Priest).

66. Samuel R. Gross & Kent D. Syverud, "Getting to No: A Study of Settlement Negotiations and the Selection of Cases for Trial," 90 Mich. L. Rev. 319, 337 (1991).

the average earnings of continent fee attorneys are not significantly higher than those of counsel who bill hourly.[67] But as critics also note, in too many cases, lawyers' windfall recoveries may far exceed a reasonable return and a necessary incentive to bring socially useful lawsuits.[68] And too many clients are presented with standard contingent fee contracts on a take-it-or-leave-it basis, without information about possible alternatives.

The potential for abuse is especially great in class action litigation because most members of large plaintiff classes lack sufficient information or incentive to monitor lawyers' fees. The same deficiency of information hampers trial judges, despite their formal responsibility to ensure the fairness of settlements and the reasonableness of fees. Effective oversight of compensation often requires more time-consuming review than overburdened judges can readily supply. Many courts face staggering caseloads, and the prospect of prolonging a case by overturning a fee agreement is seldom appealing.[69] Adequate judicial review is particularly difficult when defense counsel agree to fee requests. Although defendants sometimes have an interest in challenging such requests in order to discourage nonmeritorious claims, the path of least resistance in other contexts is a cheap settlement with generous fees. Where mass torts are at issue, the judgments are so enormous that a standard contingency arrangement may deliver returns out of all proportion to the work performed or the risks assumed. A case in point involves the settlement of a Texas tobacco lawsuit, in which plaintiffs' counsel received an effective rate of $92,000 per hour.[70] In other consumer cases, class members may end up with nominal damages or largely worthless product coupons; the lawyers are the real parties in interest.[71]

To address the problem of windfall fees, a number of approaches are possible. One strategy is to set statutory caps on fees, with advancing percentage formulas. Under this approach, lawyers

67. Herbert M. Kritzer, "The Wages of Risk: The Returns of Contingency Fee Legal Practice," 47 DePaul L. Rev. 267, 302 (1998); Lester Brickman, "Contingency Fee Abuses, Ethical Mandates and the Disciplinary System: The Case Against Case-by-Case Enforcement," 53 Wash. & Lee L. Rev. 1339, 1345 (1996).

68. Alison Frankel, "Why People Hate the System: Greedy, Greedy, Greedy," American Lawyer Nov. 1996, at 71; Lester Brickman, "Lawyers' Ethics and Fiduciary Obligation in the Brave New World of Aggregative Litigation," 26 Wm & Mary Envtl. L. & Pol'y

Rev. 243 (2001); Brickman, supra note 67; and Brickman, Horowitz, & O'Connell, supra note 65.

69. John C. Coffee, Jr., "The Corruption of the Class Action: The New Technology of Collusion," 80 Cornell L. Rev. 851, 855 (1995); Samuel Issacharoff, "Class Action Conflicts," 30 U.C. Davis L. Rev. 805, 829 (1997).

70. Lester Brickman, "Will Legal Ethics Go Up in Smoke?" Wall St. J., June 16, 1998, at A18.

71. Rhode, supra note 17, at 175–76.

receive a larger portion of the total recovery as the case progresses and presumably becomes more time consuming. So, for example, in a matter settled without filing suit, the lawyer receives twenty-five percent of the recovery; in a case settled after filing, thirty-three percent, in a case that goes to trial, forty percent; and in a case won on appeal, fifty percent. An obvious problem with such a formula, however, is that it may encourage lawyers to prolong proceedings where the stakes are sufficiently high. An alternative that some jurisdictions have adopted sets a graduated scale giving lawyers a smaller percentage of recovery as clients' claims grow larger. This approach prevents windfall fees, but at the cost of discouraging lawyers from accepting large, complex claims.

Another strategy for curbing windfall recovery has been developed by the Manhattan Institute. Under its proposal, a defendant in a civil suit would have an opportunity to make an early settlement offer within sixty days of a plaintiff's demand for such an offer. If the defendant chooses not to make an offer, the proposal would not apply and the plaintiff's lawyer would be free to negotiate a contingent fee, subject to general requirements of reasonableness. However, if an offer was made and accepted, the compensation to the plaintiff's attorney would be limited to a reasonable hourly rate or a modest share of the recovery, such as ten percent of the first $100,000 and five percent of any greater amounts. If a settlement offer was made and refused, that offer would set a baseline for later assessing the reasonableness of contingency fees.[72]

Opponents of this approach claim that it would prove both under- and over-inclusive; it would offer no protection in the absence of a settlement offer, and it could deny lawyers a reasonable recovery in some settled cases. The ultimate effect might be to reduce attorneys' willingness to take contingent cases, restrict clients' access to legal services, and decrease the deterrent value of liability claims. But only through experience with such a formula can these concerns be accurately assessed. The effects may differ across different categories of cases. However, the limited evidence now available indicates that some lawyers already take lower contingent fees in cases that settle early and nonetheless manage a reasonable return. Even if restrictions on windfall fees somewhat diminished other attorneys' ability to subsidize speculative cases, the trade-off might still be worthwhile.[73]

---

72. Brickman, Horowitz, & O'Connell, supra note 65.

73. Id.; Peter Passell, "Contingency Fees in Injury Cases under Attack by Legal Scholars," N. Y. Times, Feb. 11, 1994, at 1; Lawrence Fox, "Contingent Fees," ABA J., July 1995, at 44; Kritzer, supra note 67.

Courts and bar associations could also do more to protect clients, and to enable clients to protect themselves in class action proceedings. Steering committees that are representative of the entire class can help select attorneys and negotiate competitive fee arrangements. Greater reliance on special masters to review compensation agreements could also prove useful.

A related reform proposal worth consideration involves contingent fees for expert witnesses. DR 7–109(C) of the Code explicitly bans such payments, and Model Rule 3.4(b) bans any "inducement ... prohibited by law", which often covers witness compensation beyond expenses. In rejecting constitutional challenges to such bans, the Second Circuit Court of Appeals nonetheless noted that there might be sound policy reasons for changing these rules:

> Cross-examination would reveal whatever financial stake a witness has in the outcome of litigation.... [Moreover] experts often have ongoing business relationships with the parties who retain them and therefore, in an indirect sense, frequently have a stake in the outcome of litigation although their fee is not contingent and thus not covered by DR 7–109(C). Other experts, although retained on a "fixed fee" basis, often do not expect to receive payment unless the party for whom they testify is successful.[74]

The prevailing system not only disadvantages litigants of limited means, it also does a poor job of exposing expert bias because it may encourage de facto rather than explicit contingency arrangements. Such tacit understandings are harder to discover and to expose in cross examination, which suggests reasons for modifying current rules.[75]

Some commentators propose more fundamental reforms that would allow third parties to help finance lawsuits in exchange for a share of the recovery. Such investment in litigation, long condemned as "champerty" at common law, remains impermissible in all but a few jurisdictions.[76] Advocates of reform argue that permitting such financial arrangements would increase access to the courts and enable litigants of modest means to obtain adequate recoveries. The current system, by allowing investment only by

74. Person v. Association of Bar of City of New York, 554 F.2d 534, 539 (2d Cir.1977).

75. Jeffrey J. Parker, Note, "Contingent Expert Witness Fees: Access and Legitimacy," 64 S. Cal. L. Rev. 1363, 1387 (1991).

76. Saladini v. Righellis, 687 N.E.2d 1224 (1997); Ari Dobner, Comment, "Litigation for Sale," 144 U. Pa. L. Rev. 1529 (1996); Susan Lorde Matin, "Financing Plaintiffs' Lawsuits: An Increasingly Popular (and Legal) Business," 33 U. Mich. J. L. Reform 57 (2000).

lawyers under contingent fee arrangements, limits the investment market and permits lawyers to earn an inflated "economic rent."[77]

A final area of debate concerning compensation arrangements involves the degree of protection appropriate for sophisticated clients. In one such case, the court enforced a $1 million fee for services that turned out to involve only filing one petition for *certiorari*. The case arose from antitrust proceedings in which Telex obtained a $259 million judgment against IBM, but lost an $18 million counterclaim. On appeal, IBM won reversal of the judgment and affirmance of its counterclaim. In the face of liability substantial enough to bankrupt the company, Telex sought the best available lawyer for its petition to the Supreme Court. The company settled on a partner at Brobeck Phleger & Harrison, and agreed to a complicated contract specifying different fees contingent on different outcomes. After the Supreme Court granted certiorari, Telex and IBM reached a settlement in which each dropped their claims. In rejecting Telex's claim that the $1 million fee was unconscionable, the court concluded that the contract must be reviewed "with reference to the time [it was made] and cannot be resolved by hindsight."[78]

As a practical matter, such fee-related litigation with sophisticated clients is rare. These clients take the relevant risk factors into account if they resort to contingency arrangements, and lawyers frequently adjust their bills to avoid charges that become unreasonable in light of the results obtained. But where unanticipated circumstances arise and lawyers fail to reduce excessive fees, even sophisticated clients may need protection. In the long run, neither the profession nor the public is well served by a system that overlooks serious overcharging, whatever the reason.

---

77. Rudy Santore and Alan D. Viard, "Legal Fee Restrictions, Moral Hazard and Attorney Rents," 44 J. L. & Econ. 549 (2001); Peter Charles Choharis, "A Comprehensive Market Strategy for Tort Reform," 12 Yale L. J. on Reg. 435, 465–87 (1995).

78. Brobeck, Phleger & Harrison v. Telex Corp., 602 F.2d 866, 875 (9th Cir. 1979).

Chapter XI

QUALIFICATIONS FOR THE BAR

A. Introduction

For much of its history, the American bar made relatively little effort to ensure adequate qualifications among its members. As Chapter III noted, the courts traditionally asserted inherent power to regulate the practice of law. However, until the twentieth century, formal admission standards were lax. Courts required applicants to demonstrate "fitness to practice" law, but generally required only perfunctory oral exams and some limited period of preparation. What occurred during that period generally left much to be desired. The dominant method of qualification was through "reading law" independently and serving as an apprentice. Under the conventional apprenticeship arrangement, aspiring attorneys offered their services plus a fee to established lawyers in exchange for "instruction" and the right to use the lawyers' legal forms later in practice. In an era before typewriting, preprinted forms, and duplicating services, students often spent much of their apprenticeships copying documents.[1]

During the late nineteenth century, the growth of bar associations and the general cultural trend toward stronger occupational standards encouraged a corresponding formalization of qualifications for legal practice. Ever since, the structure of legal education and bar admission has been a matter of continuing attention and periodic reform.

B. Legal Education

During the late eighteenth and early nineteenth centuries, formal legal education typically centered in small for-profit schools. Although a few applicants to the bar traveled to England for instruction in the Inns of Court, or took some undergraduate legal courses at an American university, the most accessible training was in one of the nineteen or twenty specialized institutions taught by practitioners.[2] However, these independent schools, along with uni-

---

1. See generally Charles R. McKirdy, "The Lawyer as Apprentice: Legal Education in Eighteenth Century Massachusetts," 28 J. Legal Educ. 124 (1976); Lawrence M. Friedman, A History of American Law 97–98 (2d ed. 1985).

2. J. Willard Hurst, The Growth of American Law: The Law Makers, 277–93 (1950); Robert Stevens, Law School:

201

versity law courses, dwindled during the populist Jacksonian era, when admission standards were exceptionally lax.[3]

The characteristic features of modern legal education emerged at Harvard Law School after the Civil War. The impetus came largely from Dean Christopher Columbus Langdell, who, like many of his academic colleagues, had great faith in scientific methodology. In their view, law was a science that could be taught through the Socratic case method. Just as rules of nature could be discovered from examining biological specimens, legal principles could be deduced from parsing judicial decisions. Yet the seeming "objectivity" of this case method was achieved only by excluding a broad array of other critical issues, such as legislation, lawyering skills, and the operation of the justice system in practice. Proponents of this approach, however, viewed it as a means of making the educational curricula more "rigorous." To that end, they also attempted to extend its duration into a three-year post-graduate program.

This effort coincided with a period of increased support for higher educational standards within most professions, including law. The American Bar Association, formed in 1870, soon recommended tighter admission requirements. As Chapter II noted, much of the organized bar's concern was driven by an influx of new applicants from lower class and immigrant backgrounds, who were graduating in increasing numbers from for-profit night programs.[4] Similar reform recommendations emerged from the Association of American Law Schools (AALS), which formed in 1900 to support and strengthen legal education.

This campaign for heightened academic standards was not without its critics. Among the most prominent was sociologist Thorstein Veblen, who argued that "vocational" schools like law "belong[ed] in the modern university no more than a school of fencing or dancing."[5] Other commentators, although sympathetic towards efforts to make legal education more rigorous, were concerned about changes that would reduce its accessibility. During the early 1900s, about a third of the nation's law students were enrolled in night programs. A requirement of three years of full-

Legal Education in America from the 1850s to the 1980s 7–10 (1983).

3. Stevens, supra note 2, at 7–8. In 1860, only nine of thirty-nine states required any specific period of legal study. Id.

4. Jerold S. Aurbach, Unequal Justice: Lawyers and Social Change in Mod-

ern America 62–87 (1976); Herb D. Vest, "Felling the Giant: Breaking the ABA's Stranglehold on Legal Education in America," 50 J. Legal Educ. 494 (2000).

5. Thorstein Veblen, The Higher Learning in America: A Memorandum on the Conduct of Universities by Businessmen 211 (1918).

time training would exclude many of these individuals. And such an extended period of study was not self-evidently necessary for the routine matters that dominated most lawyers' practice. These concerns were reflected in an influential 1921 Report for the Carnegie Foundation, Training for the Public Profession of Law. It recommended a divided bar with different exams and educational requirements. The more highly trained graduates could serve business and government clients, and the graduates of night and part time programs could remain available to meet more routine individual needs.

Both the ABA and the AALS flatly rejected that recommendation. Rather, they pushed for more stringent admission requirements for all lawyers and more demanding accreditation standards for all law schools. These efforts were largely successful, but controversies persist over the appropriate form of education for an increasingly diverse profession. Who should teach what, to whom, for how long, and by what methods, all remain matters of dispute. Discussion here focuses on the most contested issues: educational structure; law school curricula, methodology, and climate; professional responsibility and pro bono service; and diversity in student admissions, faculty appointments, and institutional culture.

Educational Structure

Law schools are subject to multiple regulatory systems. The United States Department of Education recognizes the ABA's Council of the Section of Legal Education and Admission to the Bar as the nation's accrediting authority for professional training in law. Under that authority, the Council has developed detailed accreditation standards governing matters such as classroom hours, student-faculty ratios, library resources, and so forth. Once a school has established its compliance with these standards, it is subject to a site visit every seven years to insure its continued adherence to accreditation requirements. Forty-five states and the District of Columbia require applicants to the bar to graduate from an ABA accredited school. The other states have developed their own accreditation systems, and California also permits practice by graduates of unaccredited schools who pass the bar exam.

Current accreditation requirements have been subject to frequent criticism. Many commentators believe that the diversity of legal practice should be matched by diversity in educational structure. The day-to-day work of a Wall Street securities specialist bears little resemblance to that of a solo practitioner handling matrimonial cases, and it is not obvious that they should be trained in the same way. Nor is it clear that the time and expense of a three year program is necessary for all fields of practice. Federal judge and law professor Richard Posner puts the case for more diversity in law school structures. As he notes:

> We have no experimental or otherwise empirical basis ... for believing that law school has to take so long, at enormous cost.... Graduate schools of business grant an M.B.A. after only two years, and the business world seems not to be suffering as a result of the "abbreviated" education that their students receive.... It will be argued that law students can't make a judgment whether they need a third year of law school; they are too immature and too ignorant about law. Maybe so. But employers know whether a third year of law school is necessary. If they think it is, they will not hire students who have not completed a third year of law school, or they will pay students who leave earlier much less.... There is no need for government to do the insisting.
>
> I am willing to concede the case for some paternalism. Some newly graduated lawyers hang out their own shingle rather than going to work for a law firm or other knowledgeable employer.... If consumer protection is needed in this area, it can be provided by stiffening the bar exam, or perhaps by giving a special bar exam to students who don't complete the third year, or perhaps by confining the title "lawyer" to the three-year graduate and assigning another title, such as "legal advocate" or "legal counselor," to practitioners who have not had three years of law school.
>
> Courts, too, need protection from lawyers who lack the skills or experience to handle a trial. But the necessary protection can be obtained by court rules requiring demonstrated skills and experience, not completion of an artificially determined period of schooling.[6]

An approach somewhat different from Judge Posner's leads to a similar conclusion. The three-year curriculum was initially envisioned as covering everything a new lawyer needed to know: Contracts, Property, Torts, Procedure, and so forth. But since 1900, and particularly in the last half century, the subject matters of practice have grown exponentially and specialization within legal fields has intensified. A three-year curriculum cannot begin to cover everything that all lawyers need to know over the course of their careers. Dean William Prosser, of torts fame, once reviewed all the demands that legal education was expected to satisfy and

---

6. Richard A. Posner, "Let Employers Insist if Three Years of Law School is Necessary," Los Angeles Daily J., Dec. 15, 1999, at A6.

sardonically suggested that a 10-year curriculum might be adequate.[7]

Yet the logic of this analysis leads in quite the opposite direction. Law school can aspire only to serve as an introduction to basic legal skills and information, and that might well be accomplished in under three years. For example, a two or two-and-a-half year program could leave room for some electives, interdisciplinary courses and skills training, along with coverage of basic subjects, such as Property, Contracts, Torts, Civil Procedure, Tax, Criminal Law, Constitutional Law, Administrative or Regulatory Law, and Corporate Law.

More specialized course work often would be most useful later in lawyers' careers, after they have established fields of concentration. For many practitioners, specialization is determined partly by design but also by fortuity. Early assignments and opportunities shape careers in ways that individuals cannot fully anticipate while in law school. So too, a basic survey course taken while a student will not provide practitioners with all that is necessary for competent representation in that area many years later. As a consequence, many lawyers could benefit from short intensive postgraduate courses in their specialty. They should be short because most practitioners could not spare an entire semester, and intensive because they would have strong incentive to focus on subjects directly related to their job. This is, in fact, the format of some of the most successful Continuing Legal Education programs, such as one sponsored by the National Institute of Trial Advocacy.

In any event, it is only through greater experimentation with alternatives that the relative merits of the current three-year curriculum can be assessed. A competitive process might well produce effective two-year programs, as it has in other professional and business contents.

A similar argument has been advanced by the Massachusetts School of Law as part of its widely publicized accreditation campaign. In the late 1990s, after failing to satisfy accreditation requirements, MSL sued the ABA and the AALS on antitrust grounds. According to the MSL complaint, the current accreditation system functions as a cartel by setting unnecessary and burden-

---

7. The demands included instruction not only in basic doctrine and legal skills but also in jurisprudence, philosophy, ethics, legal history, political science, economics, sociology, psychology, international and comparative law, "Ameri-canism," (i.e., patriotic values) and the legal profession (with special focus on the "value of bar associations"). William I. Prosser, "The Ten Year Curriculum," 6 J. Legal Educ. 149, 152–55 (1953).

some standards that unjustifiably raise the cost of legal education.[8] Although courts rejected the MSL claims on both procedural and substantive grounds, similar concerns have emerged from mainstream educators.[9] In their view, the accreditation process is overly intrusive and inflexible, and stifles innovation in favor of a "one size fits all" model of legal education.[10]

By contrast, defenders of the current structure typically respond that at a time when the law is becoming "more complex than ever before and occupying more areas of economic and social life, we should [not] acquiesce in the notion that lawyers can be trained in two-thirds of the time."[11] Many bar leaders would like to tighten, not loosen, educational standards in certain areas involving fundamental skills and values. An influential 1992 report by an ABA Task Force on Law Schools and The Profession, Narrowing the Gap (the MacCrate Report), identified ten core skills and four central values necessary for any "well-trained generalist to practice law competently and professionally." The "Fundamental Lawyering Skills" describe functions common to nearly all areas of practice: (1) problem solving; (2) legal analysis and reasoning; (3) legal research; (4) factual investigation; (5) communication; (6) counseling; (7) negotiation; (8) litigation and alternative dispute-resolution procedures; (9) organization and management of legal work; and (10) recognition and resolution of ethical dilemmas. The "Fundamental Values of the Profession" formulate norms of ethical lawyering that call upon lawyers to: (1) provide competent representation; (2) strive to promote justice, fairness, and morality; (3) improve the profession; and (4) undertake professional self-development.[12] This ambitious agenda contemplates enriching, not shortening, current educational requirements.

---

8. Margo Slade, "A Little Law School Does Battle with the ABA," N.Y. Times, Feb. 4, 1994, at A19; Courtney Leatherman, "Rebellion Brews in Tight–Knit World of Law Accreditation," Chron. of Higher Educ., June 1, 1994, at A14, A16.

9. Massachusetts School of Law at Andover v. ABA, 107 F.3d 1026 (3d Cir. 1997).

10. Deborah L. Rhode, In the Interests of Justice: Reforming the Legal Profession, 190–91 (2000); Leatherman, supra note 8, at A14, A16 (quoting a letter from deans of fourteen law schools); Vest, supra note 4, at 497–501. Some commentators have also claimed that the current accreditation structure restricts access to law school by students of color because it excludes schools targeted at that applicant pool, which have lower tuitions and GPA/LSAT requirements. See George Shepherd, "No African–American Lawyers Allowed: The Inefficient Racism of the ABA's Accreditation of Law Schools," J. of Legal Educ. (Forthcoming, 2002).

11. See sources quoted in Rhode, supra note 10, at 190–91; Preble Stolz, "The Two Year Law School: The Day The Music Died," 25 J. Legal Educ. 37, 42–44 (1973).

12. American Bar Association Section of Legal Education and Admissions to the Bar, Legal Education and Professional Development—An Educational

So too, some law school administrators support stringent accreditation standards as a way to maintain leverage in resource negotiations with central university decision makers. Historically, many university administrations have viewed law schools as "cash cows"—money makers with relatively low costs and high tuitions, which can subsidize other educational programs that are less well off. Law schools' need to comply with accreditation requirements governing libraries, faculty size, and so forth has enabled them to hold onto resources that might otherwise go to poorer academic cousins.

Consensus in this area is difficult partly because legal education has multiple constituencies with competing agendas. Law schools are expected to produce both "Pericles and plumbers"-lawyer statesmen and legal scriveners.[13] The most direct consumers–students–have interests that are not necessarily identical with those of the ultimate consumers–clients and the public. Education is one of the rare contexts where many buyers want less for their money.[14] Some students would like to earn a degree with the minimal effort required to pass a bar examination and land a job; others find too much of law school classwork impractical or irrelevant. In the absence of strict accreditation standards, law schools might need to reduce costs and quality standards in order to compete for applicants who view "less as more." By contrast, for many practitioners and professors, "less is more" has different and far less appealing connotations. Less rigorous educational standards means more graduates competing for business and more constraints on law school resources.

Not only are there competing concerns within the profession, there are competing demands from the clientele served by the bar. The constituencies directly affected—students, faculty, and practitioners—all have interests that are not entirely consistent with those of the public. Consumers' overriding concern is access to reasonably competent assistance at a price they can afford. Clients at different income levels with different needs are likely to make different cost/quality tradeoffs. A central challenge for legal education lies in striking an appropriate balance among these competing public and professional concerns. A structure that permitted more variation and innovation in educational structure might at least provide a more informed basis for finding that balance.

Continuum, Report of the Task Force on Law Schools and the Profession: Narrowing the Gap (1992) [MacCrate Report].

13. William Twining, "Pericles and the Plumber," 83 L. Q. Rev. 396 (1967).

14. Rhode, supra note 10, at 188–92.

Educational Content, Climate, and Methodology

Questions concerning the structure of legal education are related to other issues about curricula, teaching, scholarship, and climate, all of which have been equally controversial. Part of the dispute stems from the schizophrenic role that law schools attempt to play. In seeking to advance legal knowledge as well as convey practical skills, legal education runs the risk of doing neither very well. According to many critics, the contemporary curriculum offers too little practice and too little theory. It provides too little training in basic skills and too little grounding in related disciplines such as philosophy, psychology, history, finance, and management. Other criticisms focus on the dominant instructional methods of casebooks and Socratic dialogue; the lack of support for legal ethics and public service; and the overly competitive, stressful aspects of law school culture.

Although modern legal education has largely rejected Langdell's assumptions about law as a science, his approach is often said to "rule us from the grave." A diluted case method and quasi-Socratic style remain common in many law school classrooms. The reasons have less to do with educational quality than with the adaptability of this method to large classes, its corresponding low costs, and its perceived ability to maintain analytic rigor while accommodating different intellectual approaches.

Yet the case approach is of limited value and somewhat of a misnomer. It does not in fact require study of actual cases. It relies rather on published judicial opinions, which leave out much of the living process of the law: the translation of a dispute into a legal grievance; the investigation and presentation of parties' claims; the unstated factors influencing judicial decisions; the consequences of those decisions on the individuals involved; and the social, political, and economic implications of the legal process. In effect, students often get law without lawyering, perhaps a legal analogue of "geology without the rocks."[15]

Also absent is any sustained effort to address the practical skills and interpersonal dimensions of lawyers' work. These capabilities are largely relegated to clinical courses, which are still treated as poor relations in most academic communities.[16] Between two-thirds and four-fifths of surveyed graduates believe that skills such

---

15. Lawrence Friedman, quoted in Rhode, supra note 10, at 198.

16. ABA Section of Legal Education and Admissions to the Bar, Legal Education and Professional Development: An Educational Continuum: Report of the Task Force on Law Schools and the Profession–Narrowing the Gap (1992); see also Rhode, supra note 10, at 197–98.

as negotiation, fact gathering, and document preparation could be taught effectively in law school, but only about a quarter feel that those subjects receive sufficient attention. Similar disparities are reported for problem solving, oral communication, counseling, and litigation.[17] So too, despite recognition of the importance of cross-cultural and cross-disciplinary perspectives, the core curriculum stubbornly resists intruders. With the exception of law and economics approaches, which have managed to infiltrate many law school courses, these perspectives generally remain at the margins of law school curricula. At most schools, a "bit of borrowed intellectual finery dresses up the standard legal wardrobe, but the fashion remains the same."[18] The consequence is to deprive students of approaches that could prove useful in their future work, from fields such as finance, management, psychology, organizational behavior, and international relations. In an era of increasing multidisciplinary and global practice, future lawyers need exposure to insights from a broad range of fields.[19]

Corresponding limitations are apparent in legal scholarship. Law schools' curricular focus on reported cases and inadequate support for interdisciplinary or empirical work have constrained research agendas. Legal academics write increasingly for each other, in forms insufficiently informed by other fields and insufficiently intelligible to practitioners, judges, and policy makers.[20]

The quasi-Socratic style of law school teaching also has limitations. In Ralph Nader's phrase, it offers students only freedom to "roam in an intellectual cage."[21] At its best, the Socratic method promotes critical reflection and facility in oral argument. At its worst, it can lead to a controlled dialogue in which the professor first invites the student to "guess what I'm thinking," and then finds the response inevitably lacking. The result is what Professor Anthony Amsterdam once labeled MOPIE: Maximum Obtainable Passivity in Education.[22] Critics argue that such an atmosphere can

17. Joanne Martin & Bryant G. Garth, "Clinical Education as a Bridge Between Law School and Practice: Mitigating the Misery," 1 Clinical L. Rev. 443, 448 (1994).

18. Rhode, supra note 10, at 198.

19. Mary C. Daly, "What the MDP Debate Can Teach Us About Law Practice in the New Millennium and the Need for Curricular Reform," 50 J. Legal Educ. 521, 543–44 (2000); Judith Welch Wegner, "The Curriculum: Patterns and Possibilities," 51 J. Legal Educ. 431 (2001).

20. Deborah L. Rhode, "Legal Scholarship," 115 Harv. L. Rev. 1327 (2002); Harry T. Edwards, "The Growing Disjunction Between Legal Education and the Legal Profession," 91 Mich. L. Rev. 34 (1992).

21. Ralph Nader, "Law Schools and Law Firms," New Republic, Oct. 11, 1969, at 20–21, 23.

22. Anthony Amsterdam, Address Before the Society of American Law Teachers, quoted in Geoffrey C. Hazard, Jr., Susan P. Koniak, & Roger C. Cram-diminish students' self-confidence, erode conviction, and encourage corrosive skepticism. By depersonalizing and decontextualizing inquiry, it may also foster an impoverished understanding of the lawyer's role.[23]

A related concern is the effect of law school culture on student values and career choices. A frequent critique is that legal education undermines the commitments that attract students to law in the first instance: they enter law school talking of justice but leave talking of jobs.[24] Critics believe that several aspects of the educational experience contribute to this shift in perspective. First, the high tuition and limited financial aid and loan forgiveness programs at most law schools discourage students from taking poorly-paid public interest positions. Although some research suggests that the core problem is not debt levels but pay disparities between public interest and private practice careers, debt burdens obviously heighten the significance of those disparities.[25] In addition, law school culture often provides relatively little support for public interest work through pro bono programs, placement priorities, or other initiatives.[26]

However, most empirical research finds that law school does not have a large measurable effect on attitudes, including attitudes toward public interest law, and that market forces are a much stronger influence.[27] For example, an in-depth study of Harvard Law students found that they reported becoming more interested in public interest and social justice issues while in law school, although only a tiny percentage ended up taking jobs in this area. What appeared to account for the disparity between interest and

ton, The Law and Ethics of Lawyering 972 (3rd ed., 1999).

23. Rhode, supra note 10, at 197; Deborah L. Rhode, "Missing Questions: Feminist Perspectives on Legal Education," 45 Stan. L. Rev. 1547 (1993); Roger C. Cramton, "The Ordinary Religion of the Law School Classroom," 29 J. Legal Ed. 247 (1978).

24. See Robert Granfield, Making Elite Lawyers: Visions of Law at Harvard and Beyond 38–39 (1992); Robert V. Stover, Making It and Breaking It: The Fate of Public Interest Commitment During Law School (Howard S. Erlanger ed., 1989).

25. See Lewis A. Kornhauser & Richard L. Revesz, "Legal Education and Entry into the Legal Profession:

The Role of Race, Gender, and Educational Debt," 70 N.Y.U. L. Rev. 829 (1995); Bruce Buckley, "Public Interest Honor Roll," 9 National Jurist, Jan/Feb 2000, at 28 (In the late 1990s, the median public interest job paid half as much as the median private practice position).

26. See Granfield, supra note 24, at 8; Stover, supra note 24; and text accompanying note 40, infra.

27. See surveys discussed in Deborah L. Rhode & David Luban, Legal Ethics 876 (3d ed. 2001); Hazard, Koniak, & Cramton, supra note 22, at 975; E. Gordon Gee & Donald W. Jackson, "Current Studies of Legal Education: Findings and Recommendations," 32 J. Leg.Ed. 471, 494–501 (1982).

employment was the comparatively low salary and prestige associated with most public interest options available.[28]

Empirical research does, however, suggest that law school has a significant impact on other aspects of student life. Of greatest concern is its link with stress-related dysfunctions including obsessive-compulsive behavior, depression, severe anxiety, and isolation. Between twenty and forty percent of students in any given law school class report such symptoms. Another significant proportion develop substance abuse problems.[29] The most systematic research available indicates that the problem lies more with the law school experience than with the characteristics of students who choose law. Although the individuals who apply to law school do not differ from the population generally in their mental health, those who are enrolled in law in school do differ. For example, their rates of depression are about three times higher than the population generally.[30]

Although the exact causes of stress-related dysfunctions are difficult to measure, most research identifies the following factors:

- excessive workloads and lack of assistance with time-management problems;

- high student-faculty ratios leading to limited interactions and feedback;

- overly competitive reward structures with too much emphasis on grades as the measure of status and self-worth;

- inadequate information, counseling, and treatment programs concerning psychological and substance abuse problems; and

- inadequate assurances of confidentiality for students who would benefit from counseling and treatment.[31]

28. Granfield, supra note 24, at 38–48, 88–90. See also Kornhauser & Revesz, supra note 25.

29. Mariam Alikhan, Note, "The ADA is Narrowing Mental Health Inquiries on Bar Applications: Looking to the Medical Profession to Decide Where to Go from Here," 14 Geo. J. Legal Ethics 159 (2000); Andrew H. Benjamin et al., "The Role of Legal Education in Producing Psychological Distress Among Law Students and Lawyers," 1986 Am. B. Found. Res. J. 225, 246, 248-52. See Ann L. Iijima, "Lessons Learned, Legal Education and Law Student Dysfunction," 48 J. Legal Educ. 524 (1998);

Lawrence S. Krieger, "What We're Not Telling Law Students–and Lawyers–That They Really Need to Know: Some Thoughts–In–Action Toward Revitalizing the Profession from its Roots," 13 J. L. & Health 15 (1998–99); "Report of the AALS Special Committee on Problems of Substance Abuse in Law Schools," 44 J. Legal Educ. 35, 44 (1994).

30. Benjamin, et al., supra note 29; Alikhan, supra note 29, at 159.

31. Report of the AALS Special Committee, supra note 29; Krieger, supra note 29, at 18.

None of these issues are readily resolved. As commentators have often noted, innovation in legal education comes hard and dies young.[32] Talk is cheap and many educationally desirable initiatives are not. There are obvious limits to how much time-intensive or specialized training can be provided without increasing tuition, which may further restrict access and raise student debt burdens to intolerable levels.[33] Yet not all curricular initiatives require extensive additional resources. Many of the inadequacies noted above could be ameliorated through greater use of adjuncts, interdisciplinary collaboration, on-line technology, interactive exercises, and cooperative out-of-class projects. More support should be available for curricular development as well as empirical and cross disciplinary research. Students should receive multiple forms of feedback and greater access to confidential support services.

The problem with many of these strategies is not that they are unaffordable but rather that they are insufficiently rewarded. Improvements in the curriculum and support structures for students are not adequately reflected in law school rankings and guides for applicants. Nor is excellence in teaching the path to greatest recognition for individual faculty.

Significant changes in law school curricula and climate will thus require significant changes in law school incentive structures. A crucial first step is to develop more systematic ways of assessing educational effectiveness and holding institutions and individual faculty members accountable. At a minimum, more information needs to be available comparing and monitoring law schools on curricular issues and support structures. And educators need more prodding to educate themselves about effective teaching, and to respond accordingly.

Professional Responsibility and Pro Bono Service

A further limitation in legal education involves its treatment of professional responsibility. In 1974, largely in response to lawyers' involvement in illegal Watergate activities, the ABA mandated that accredited schools provide some instruction in professional responsibility. A growing number of states also began to require such instruction as a condition of admission to practice, and bar examinations increased their coverage of ethical issues.

Although these initiatives resulted in substantial improvements, current approaches still fall short. Most law schools relegate professional responsibility to a single required course, which focus-

---

32. Thomas Shaffer & Robert S. Redmount, Lawyers, Law Students, and People 24 (1977).

33. Rhode, supra note 10, at 199.

es largely on rules of conduct. This approach often leaves out crucial issues, such as those concerning access to justice, the conditions of practice, and the adequacy of bar regulatory processes. Moreover, ethical issues arise in every legal field, and the failure to address them throughout the curricula sends a negative message that no single course can counteract. Faculty who treat professional responsibility as someone else's responsibility encourage future practitioners to do the same.[34]

Part of the resistance to more extensive legal ethics coverage rests on an assumption that moral conduct cannot be effectively taught in professional schools. Many faculty and students assume that ethics instruction at the graduate level offers too little too late; a few classroom hours are unlikely to reshape values that individuals have acquired over long periods from family, friends, schools, churches, and other cultural influences. Moreover, even if course exposure has some impact on moral views, it is by no means clear how much effect it will have on moral conduct. Both historical experience and psychological research make clear that ethical behavior is highly contextual, and that situational pressures often undermine individuals' professed principles.[35]

Such evidence reveals important limits on the potential contributions of professional responsibility courses, but it is not a reason to avoid integrated coverage of the subject in law school curricula. Most psychological research finds that, despite the importance of situational pressures, moral judgment has some impact on moral behavior.[36] How individuals evaluate the consequences of their actions can be critical in shaping conduct, and education can affect those evaluative processes. It can also make individuals aware of how economic and peer pressures, structures of authority, and diffusion of responsibility skew moral judgment.

So too, a substantial body of evidence suggests that ethical values are by no means as fixed as is often assumed. Psychological research indicates that during early adulthood, significant changes occur in people's basic strategies for dealing with moral issues.[37]

34. Deborah L. Rhode, "The Professional Responsibilities of Professors," 51 J. Legal Educ. 158, 165 (2001); Deborah L. Rhode, "Ethics by the Pervasive Method," 42 J. Legal Educ. 31 (1992).

35. See research surveyed in Rhode, Ethics By the Pervasive Method, supra note 34, at 45; David L. Rosenhan, Bert S. Moore & Bill Underwood, "The Social Psychology of Moral Behavior," in Moral Development: Advances in Research and

Theory 241 (James R. Rest, et al. eds., 1986).

36. See sources cited in Rhode, "Ethics By the Pervasive Method," supra note 34, at 45 n. 67.

37. James R. Rest, "Can Ethics Be Taught in Professional Schools? The Psychological Research," Easier Said Than Done, Winter 1988, at 22, 23–24; James R. Rest, Muriel Bebeau, & Joseph

More than a hundred studies evaluating ethics courses find that well-designed curricula can significantly improve capacities for moral reasoning among individuals in their twenties and thirties.[38] So too, many issues in professional ethics and regulation call for the same skills of legal and policy analysis that are standard fare throughout the curriculum. Although the classroom experience cannot fully simulate, or insulate, individuals from the pressures that lead to unethical practices, it can provide a setting to explore their causes and appropriate institutional responses.

Similar points can be made about public service. In 1996, the American Bar Association amended its accreditation standards to call on schools to "encourage students to participate in pro bono activities and to provide opportunities for them to do so." The revised ABA standards also encourage schools to address the obligations of faculty to the public, including participation in pro bono activities. However, fewer than ten percent of schools require pro bono work by students, and almost none impose such obligations on faculty.[39] Even at schools with mandatory pro bono programs, the amounts required are sometimes very modest: some demand fewer than eight hours per year. Although most institutions offer voluntary public service programs, only a minority of students are involved. In short, most law students graduate without pro bono legal work as part of their educational experience. As a report by the Association of American Law Schools Commission on Public Service and Pro Bono Opportunities succinctly concluded: "law schools should do more."[40]

The inadequacy of support for pro bono programs is a missed opportunity for both the profession and the public. Such work offers law professors and students a range of practical benefits, including trial experience, problem solving skills, and professional contacts. For many participants, this involvement provides their most direct exposure to what passes for justice for the poor and to the need for legal reforms. In addition to these educational benefits, positive pro bono experiences in law school may also inspire long-

Volker, "An Overview of the Psychology of Morality," in Moral Development, supra note 35, at 3, 14.

38. Rest, supra note 37. See also James S. Leming, "Curricular Effectiveness in Moral–Values Education: A Review of Research," 10 J. Moral Educ. 147 (1981).

39. AALS, A Handbook on Law School Pro Bono Programs 9 (2001); Deborah L. Rhode, "Cultures of Commitment: Pro Bono for Lawyers and Law Students," 67 Fordham L. Rev. 2415 (1999); AALS Commission on Pro Bono and Public Service Opportunities in Law School, Learning to Serve: A Summary of the Findings and Recommendations of the Commission on Pro Bono and Public Service Opportunities in Law Schools 4 (1999).

40. AALS Commission, supra note 39 at 2.

term personal commitments that will continue throughout practitioners' legal careers. For these reasons, the AALS Commission recommended that schools seek to make available for every law student at least one well-supervised, law-related pro bono opportunity, and either require student participation or find ways to attract the great majority of students to volunteer.[41]

Some commentators have also recommended that law schools do more to foster pro bono service by faculty. If an important goal of legal education is to inspire a commitment to public service among future practitioners, then encouraging professors to act as role models makes obvious sense. As research on altruism makes clear, individuals learn more by example than exhortation.[42] Pro bono work also offers experience that can enrich classroom teaching. In short, providing more rewards and recognition for public service could encourage more faculty and students to connect with the values of social justice that brought many of them to law in the first instance.

Diversity

A final challenge for legal education is to ensure diversity among law faculties and student bodies, and to foster values of equal opportunity and mutual respect within the law school community. Here again, great progress has been made over the last quarter century, but substantial progress also remains to be made.

As Chapter II indicated, most law schools long discriminated on the basis of sex, race, ethnicity, and religion. Part of the impetus for tighter educational standards during the late nineteenth and early twentieth centuries reflected such biases. For example, Columbia Law School was urged to require that applicants have a college diploma or pass an examination including Latin as a way to "keep out the little scrubs whom the school now promotes from grocery counters.... "[43] Discrimination against immigrants and Jewish students continued throughout the early twentieth century, while racial barriers were more enduring. Although the first black graduated from law school in 1869 and some black institutions formed graduate programs in law around the same period, few of these programs survived after the Reconstruction era. Those that did had grossly inadequate resources.

---

41. AALS Commission, supra note 39.

42. Rhode, supra note 39, at 2443; David Luban, "Faculty Pro Bono and the Question of Identity," 49 J. Legal Educ. 58 (1999).

43. D. Kelly Weisberg, "Barred from the Bar: Women and Legal Education in the United States 1870–1890," in 2 Women and the Law 231, 252 (D. Kelly Weisberg ed., 1982); Stevens, supra note 2, at 100–101.

The barriers confronting racial minorities are apparent from the Supreme Court's landmark decision in Sweatt v. Painter, 339 U.S. 629 (1950), which held Texas' racially segregated law schools unconstitutional. At the time of the litigation, the Texas legal profession included approximately 7500 white attorneys and 22 blacks. When a qualified black applicant sought admission at the University of Texas Law School, the state responded first by adding law classes at Prairie View University, an impoverished black institution that offered college credit for mattress and broom-making. Two of the three law classrooms lacked chairs and desks. Yet, in the *Sweatt* litigation, the state court had concluded that the Prairie View facility was "substantially equal" to the University of Texas Law School.[44] After the Supreme Court's reversal of that decision, the AALS passed a resolution designed to encourage, but not to require, member schools to abolish racially discriminatory practices. It was only in 1964 that all schools did so. Even after removal of formal prohibitions against non-white applicants, the absence of financial aid, affirmative action, active recruiting strategies, and supportive academic environments worked against minorities. Until the 1960s, they represented under two percent of the profession.[45]

For white women, the situation was better, but even the most intellectually qualified and economically privileged applicants faced significant discrimination. Throughout the first half of the twentieth century, female students never constituted more than 3% of law school classes except during World War II. Not until 1972 did all ABA-accredited schools remove bans on women students. Sol Linowitz, a prominent Washington practitioner, recalls that "[t]here were only two women in my class at Cornell Law School, and to tell the truth we felt somewhat uncomfortable when they were around. It never occurred to us to wonder whether *they* felt uncomfortable."[46]

Beginning in the 1960s, formal racial, ethnic and gender barriers declined, partly in response to the civil rights and women's

44. Douglas L. Jones, "The Sweatt Case and the Development of Legal Education for Negroes in Texas," 47 Tex. L. Rev. 677, 678–85 (1969); Richard Kluger, Simple Justice: The History of Brown v. Board of Education and Black Americas' Struggle for Equality, 261 (1975); Edward J. Littlejohn & Leonard S. Rubinowitz, "Black Enrollment in Law Schools: Forward to the Past?," 12 T. Marshall L. Rev. 415, 431 n. 81 (1987).

45. See Geraldine Segal, Blacks in the Law: Philadelphia and the Nation, 212–13 (1983); Karen Berger Morello, The Invisible Bar: The Woman Lawyer in America, 1638 to the Present 143–47 (1986).

46. Sol M. Linowitz with Martin Mayer, The Betrayed Profession: Lawyering at the End of the Twentieth Century 6 (1994).

movements. Increased financial aid packages, expanded recruitment strategies, and law student organizations for women and minorities also encouraged greater diversity. By the turn of the twenty-first century, women constituted about half of entering classes and twenty percent of full professors.[47] Racial and ethnic minorities, which accounted for about thirty percent of the nation's population, constituted about twenty percent of law schools' student population and ten percent of full professors.

However, despite substantial increases in law school representation, students of color and women of all racial and ethnic backgrounds confront several persistent barriers to full inclusion. One involves minorities' underrepresentation in the eligible applicant pool of college graduates, in part because of inadequate financial assistance and educational preparation. A second major hurdle involves the racially disproportionate impact of objective law school admission criteria. A final barrier to full inclusiveness involves disproportionate minority attrition rates, and lack of support for the perspectives and concerns of traditionally underrepresented groups.

How law schools should respond to these problems has been a matter of continuing controversy. To increase racial and ethnic diversity, the most widely accepted strategies involve proactive recruitment and retention programs. These programs identify talented candidates from under-represented groups and provide adequate financial aid and educational support services. A more controversial approach involves affirmative action policies that give preferential treatment to applicants of color. In Regents of the University of California v. Bakke, 438 U.S. 265 (1978), the Supreme Court held that educational institutions may consider ethnicity and race in order to achieve a diverse student body as long as they do not employ rigid quotas. Subsequent challenges to law school admission processes have involved the exclusion of white applicants with GPAs and test scores higher than those of racial and ethnic minorities. Voter initiatives in two states, California and Washington, have prohibited race-based preferences by state schools, and federal appellate courts have divided on the constitutionality of such preferential treatment.

In the two most far reaching decisions, the Fifth Circuit Court of Appeals, in Hopwood v. Texas, 78 F.3d 932 (1996), struck down an affirmative action program at the University of Texas Law School, while the Sixth Circuit, in Grutter v. Bollinger, 288 F.3d

---

47. ABA, The Unfinished Agenda: Women and the Legal Profession 27 (Report Prepared by Deborah L. Rhode, 2000).

732 (6th Cir.2002), upheld a somewhat differently structured program at the University of Michigan Law School. *Hopwood* involved an admission process that operated with different cut off scores for minority and non-minority applicants. The Fifth Circuit regarded this process as the functional equivalent of an unconstitutional quota system. By contrast, *Grutter* involved a unitary program aimed at producing a "critical mass" of targeted minorities. To the Sixth Circuit, this program was a legitimate means of furthering the law school's interest in insuring a diverse learning environment.

Defenders of affirmative action argue that it is appropriate for law schools to take into account factors other than quantitative measurements such as test scores and grade point averages. As these commentators note, formulas based on such criteria account for only sixteen to thirty-six percent of the variance in law school grades, and grades measure only some of the skills necessary for effective legal practice.[48] The most systematic attempt to follow students after graduation has not found a significant correlation between law school grades and later achievements. In a longitudinal survey by Michigan Law School, LSATs and GPAs did not correlate with graduates' earned income, career satisfaction or contributions to the community. Minorities admitted under affirmative action criteria did at least as well on these measures as other graduates, and better concerning community service.[49]

Moreover, a diverse law school community is necessary to reflect the diverse make-up of the population it serves. A class of students with varied backgrounds and perspectives can enrich the learning environment for all participants. Empirical research indicates that students who experience racial diversity in education

48. The correlation between law school grades and undergraduate test scores and GPAs is statistically significant. However, its predictive power is still quite limited, which points up the risks in admission systems that give almost conclusive importance to such formulas in admitting or excluding some group of applicants. Rhode, supra note 10, at 196; Lani Guinier & Gerald Torres, The Miner's Canary: Enlisting Race, Resisting Power, Transforming Democracy 272–74 (2002); Beth Cobb O'Neil, New Models to Assure Diversity, Fairness, and Appropriate Test Use in Law School Admissions (Law School Admissions Council, 1999); Elizabeth Chambliss, Miles to Go: Progress of Minorities in the Legal Profession, (ABA Commission on Racial and Ethnic Diversity, 2000); Jess Bravin, "Law School Admission Council Aims to Quash Overreliance on LSAT," Wall St. J., March 29, 2001, at B1; Linda F. Wightman, "The Threat to Diversity in Legal Education: An Empirical Analysis of the Consequences of Abandoning Race as a Factor in Law School Admission Decision," 72 N. Y. U. L. Rev. 1 (1997).

49. David L. Chambers, Richard O. Lempert & Terry K. Adams, "Michigan's Minority Graduates in Practice: The River Runs Through Law School," 25 Law & Soc. Inq. 395, 401 (2000); Lani Guinier, "Confirmative Action," 25 Law & Soc. Inq. 565, 568 (2000).

show less prejudice, more ability to deal with conflict, better cognitive skills, clearer understanding of multiple perspectives, and greater satisfaction with their academic experience.[50] The record in *Grutter* included a comprehensive statistical study in which students who experienced the most diversity in classroom and informal peer interactions showed the greatest growth in intellectual and academic skills. Similar arguments have been made to justify affirmative action for law school faculty. Professors from diverse backgrounds enrich the learning environment and provide mentors and role models for students of color.

Opponents of affirmative action, while not necessarily disagreeing about the value of diversity, believe that preferential treatment in student admissions and faculty appointments reinforce the stereotypes of inferiority that the legal profession should be seeking to challenge. Many opponents also believe that affirmative action violates a moral principle of color-blindness and fails to address the core problem, which is inadequate educational preparation well before law school. According to Clint Bolick of the Institute of Justice, which has brought a number of the lawsuits challenging university affirmative action policies, "so long as we have a regime of racial preferences [the underlying] problem is not going to be addressed head-on.... The way affirmative action is practiced today is cosmetic and superficial. It does not offer a systemic cure for serious social problems. It simply reshuffles the deck [among applicants]." In his view, current policies simply enable the most privileged nonwhite candidates to obtain better faculty positions, or to attend better law schools, than their objective credentials justify.[51]

These controversies over affirmative action raise broader issues about what qualities are most important for membership in the bar and how they can be assessed. Many schools are experimenting with reduced reliance on quantitative measures and greater emphasis on other characteristics such as leadership ability, employment experience, community service, and persistence in the face of economic or other disadvantages. Whether giving weight to such factors can insure adequate diversity without producing unduly idiosyncratic decisions is a matter of ongoing evaluation.

50. Daryl G. Smith, et al., Diversity Works: The Emerging Picture of How Students Benefit (Assoc. of American Colleges and Universities, 1997); Maureen T. Hallinan, "Diversity Effects on Students: Social Science Evidence," 59 Ohio St. L. J. 733, 746-50 (1998); Gary Orfield & Dean Whitla, Diversity and Legal Education: Student Experiences in Leading Law Schools 14-16 (1999).

51. Tim Wells, "Affirmative Action in Law Schools: Is It Necessary?–Interview with John Payton and Clint Bolick," Washington Lawyer, Jan/Feb 2000, at 46, 48 (quoting Clint Bolick).

In the interim, however, both sides in the debate over affirmative action have a stake in improving the law school environment for students of color. More curricular integration of materials on race and ethnicity, along with more proactive steps to combat bias and intolerance, should be educational priorities.

Similar initiatives are necessary for women. Although gender disparities in admissions have been largely eliminated, similar progress has not been made in faculty, administrative, and student leadership positions. Only twenty percent of full professors and ten percent of law school deans are female, and only about five percent of those in either position are women of color. Women faculty are still clustered in the least prestigious academic specialties and positions, such as librarians, research and writing instructors, and non-tenured clinicians.[52] At many schools, women students are also underrepresented in leadership positions such as law review editors, class officers, and members of academic honor societies. The limited research available finds that these sex-based disparities cannot be entirely explained by objective factors such as academic credentials or experience.[53] Such findings are consistent with research on other legal settings, which documents persistent gender biases and lack of accommodation of women's disproportionate family obligations.[54] Another factor of indeterminate, and probably indeterminable, dimension is the extent to which women law students hold not only professional-vocational ambitions but also commitments to a "traditional" family role.

Failure to address gender-related barriers not only compromises equal opportunity for individual women, it also deprives the law school community of valuable role models, scholars, and teachers. Without adequate gender as well as racial diversity, prospective lawyers will lack the informed interchanges and understanding of multiple perspectives that are critical to legal practice.

A true commitment to equal opportunity will also require broader changes in the educational culture. Research over the last decade consistently finds that women, particularly women of color, are more likely than men to be silenced in the classroom. Female students are less likely to volunteer, and their comments are more likely to be overlooked, devalued, or misattributed.[55] The highly

---

52. Chanbliss, supra note 48, at 27.

53. Id.; Lani Guinier, Michelle Fine & Jane Balin, Becoming Gentlemen: Women, Law School, and Institutional Change (1997).

54. See ABA Commission, supra note 47; Deborah L. Rhode, "Gender and the Profession: The No Problem Problem," 30 Hofstra L. Rev. 1001 (2002); discussion in Chapter II, supra.

55. See e.g., Guinier, Fine, & Balin, supra note 53, at 28–29; Linda F. Wightman, Law School Admission Council Research Report Series, Women in Legal

competitive atmosphere of many law school classrooms also tends to silence students with lower self-confidence, who are disproportionately women. The marginalization of women's classroom participation is compounded by the marginalization of issues concerning gender and sexual orientation in core curricula, as well as the disparaging treatment of students and faculty who introduce such concerns. Most institutions have experienced racist, sexist, and homophobic backlash in e-mails, graffiti, or anonymous flyers, and many have experienced other egregious forms of sexual harassment. In Law School Admission Council surveys, discrimination is reported by about two-thirds of gay and lesbian students, a majority of African–American students, and a third of women, Asian-American, and Hispanic students.[56] Given these patterns, it is scarcely surprising that women express greater dissatisfaction and disengagement with the law school experience than men, and that women of color report the greatest alienation.[57]

Some women's rights advocates have also raised other challenges to contemporary legal education. Building on work such as that popularized by Carol Gilligan, many feminists have argued that women bring a distinctive perspective to legal issues. These perspectives, which are especially attentive to care, cooperation, and context, are devalued in many traditional legal educational approaches.[58] Other feminists, however, worry that such critiques oversimplify and overclaim. They overlook the ways that gender difference is experienced differently across race, class, ethnicity, age, and sexual orientation, and they make sweeping generalizations based on small statistical differences. Psychological research finds few characteristics on which men and women consistently differ along gender lines, and even on these characteristics, gender

Education: A Comparison of the Law School Performance and Law School Experience of Women and Men 25, 36, 72–74 (1996); Deborah L. Rhode, "Whistling Vivaldi: Legal Education and the Politics of Progress," 23 N.Y.U. Rev. L. & Soc. Change 217, 223 (1997); Elizabeth Mertz, Wamucii Njogu & Susan Gooding, "What Difference Does Difference Make? The Challenge for Legal Education," 48 J. Legal Educ. 1, 6–7 (1998); ABA Commission, supra note 47, at 16–17.

56. ABA Commission, supra note 48, at 27–9, 35, 56; Guinier, Fine & Balin, supra note 53, at 56, 28–29, 68; Rhode, supra note 55, at 220; Lorraine Dusky, Still Unequal: The Shameful Truth About Women and Justice in America

28–39 (1996); Janice L. Austin et al., "Results from a Survey: Gay, Lesbian, and Bisexual Students' Attitudes About Law School," 48 J. Legal Educ. 157, 166 (1998).

57. ABA Commission supra note 47, at 29; Guinier, Fine, & Balin, supra note 53, at 28–29, 51–62; Wightman, supra note 55, at 25, 36, 72–74; Rhode, supra note 55, at 217.

58. Carol Gilligan, In a Different Voice: Psychological Theory and Women's Development (1982); Rand Jack & Dana Crowley Jack, Moral Vision and Professional Decisions: The Changing Values of Men and Women Lawyers (1989).

typically accounts for only about five percent of the variance.[59] Many feminists accordingly argue for a more contextual approach that avoids sweeping claims about women's essential nature, but that also acknowledges the influence of gender in professional life.

This approach argues for recasting educational priorities along the lines suggested earlier. Law schools committed to more cooperative, collaborative, and empathetic lawyering should place less reliance on large lectures or quasi-Socratic discussion, and should provide more feedback and student support services. Greater emphasis should be given to seminars, clinics, simulations, pro bono programs, and other settings for interactive discussion and experiential learning. Dimensions such as gender, race, class, ethnicity, and sexual orientation should become more central categories in legal analyses.

This is not a modest agenda. But whatever the flaws in current educational programs, it is also important to acknowledge their strengths. Over the last half century, law schools have grown considerably in terms of applicants, resources, prestige, and diversity. Their graduates are among the nation's most influential leaders in both the public and private sector. If legal education is this successful by conventional measures, it must be doing something right.

C. Admission to the Bar

Competence

Bar examinations have an extended history, but their early forms bear little resemblance to their modern versions. Before the Civil War, exams were typically oral, and were administered by state judges or attorneys appointed by the court on an ad hoc basis. The process was often quite informal, as the following description of an examination by Abraham Lincoln suggests. The candidate, Jonathan Birch, encountered his examiner in a hotel room, in the process of taking a bath, which continued during the interview. According to Birch,

> [Lincoln] asked in a desultory way the definition of a contract, and two or three other fundamental questions, all of which I answered readily, and I thought, correctly. Beyond these meager inquiries, as I now recall the incident, he asked nothing more. Meanwhile, sitting on the edge of the bed he began to entertain me with recollections—many of them characteristi-

---

59. Deborah L. Rhode, *Speaking of Sex: The Denial of Gender Inequality,* 37–38 (1997); ABA Commission, *supra* note 48, at 30–32.

cally vivid and racy—of his own practice and the various incidents and adventures that attended his start in the profession. The whole proceeding was interesting yet so unusual, if not grotesque, that I was at a loss to determine whether I was really being examined or not.[60]

Eventually Lincoln sent Birch off with a note to the other member of the bar examining committee, who admitted him without further inquiry. The note read: "The bearer of this is a young man who thinks he can be a lawyer. Examine him if you want to. I have done so and am satisfied. He's a good deal smarter than he looks to be. Yours, Lincoln."[61]

In the late nineteenth century, states attempted to upgrade standards by establishing boards of bar examiners and requiring written exams. However, most early examiners were part-time or short-term employees, with limited expertise. The tests that they devised usually demanded only rote learning and basic literacy skills. What limited information is available leaves doubt that these examinations effectively measured competence. Almost all candidates ultimately passed.[62] Moreover, in many jurisdictions, a major impetus for screening candidates was not competence *per se*, but public image. Elite members of the bar often saw examinations as a means of stemming the tide of lower-class applicants, particularly religious and ethnic minorities, whose admission might threaten the profession's status.[63] In 1931, a National Conference of Bar Examiners formed to upgrade standards and to promote more uniformity among state examinations. The later development of a multi-state, multiple choice test in core subjects reflected and accelerated this trend. Yet whether current bar exams are an appropriate means of assessing competence remains a matter of considerable dispute.

Opponents of bar examinations generally raise three arguments. The first and most fundamental claim is that the skills that existing exams measure do not adequately predict performance as a lawyer. As critics have long noted, standardized testing procedures place a high premium on rote memorization, which is likely to be less critical in practice than various other untested skills such as research, negotiation, interviewing, drafting, imagination, and

---

60. Len Young Smith, "Abraham Lincoln as a Bar Examiner," B. Examiner, Aug. 1982, at 35, 37.

61. Id.

62. See e.g., Esther Lucile Brown, Lawyers and the Promotion of Justice 117 (1938) (80–90% of applicants ulti-

mately passed); Hurst, supra note 2, at 292–93 (90% passed).

63. See Auerbach, supra note 4, at 49, 112–14 (1976); Randall Collins, The Credential Society: An Historical Sociology of Education and Stratification 149–56 (1979).

working effectively with others. A little knowledge can be a dangerous thing, and that is what bar examinations demand.[64] This
screening method is both over-and under-inclusive. It excludes
individuals with experience and skills essential in many areas of
practice, while providing no assurance that candidates who pass
are, or will, remain competent in their chosen fields. The result,
according to opponents, is to encourage a superficial acquaintance
with a broad span of substantive areas, which creates a false sense
of assurance to the profession and to the general public.

A second problem involves grading procedures.

Although bar exams do measure some relevant skills, the
current grading system does not capture relevant distinctions.
No effort has been made to correlate performance on admission
exams with performance in practice. The most that bar officials
can establish is a correlation between examination scores and
law school grades. That relationship is scarcely surprising,
since both measure similar skills. How well either predicts
success as a lawyer is something else again, and has yet to be
demonstrated. Charles Evans Hughes failed the New York bar
exam six times and later became Chief Justice of the United
States Supreme Court, and the list of less celebrated failures is
extensive.

The inadequate link between exam and job performance is
of special concern because minority applicants have disproportionately low passage rates. Part of the problem is that these
applicants are least able to afford the time and expense of bar
review courses and multiple attempts at passing. Although
courts have rejected claims that the exam process is racially
discriminatory and insufficiently predictive of competence in
practice, their reasoning has relied on evidence that they have
found deficient in other occupational contexts: unsupported
testimony by administrators who believe that their questions
are unbiased and relevant. But even assuming that exam
performance demonstrates some necessary lawyering skills, the
current grading process is arbitrary at best. One California
study found that a third of bar examiners disagreed about

---

64. Rhode, supra note 10, at 150;
Chief Justices Committee on Professionalism and Lawyer Competence, A National Action Plan on Lawyer Conduct
and Professionalism 15 (1998); See ABA
Task Force on Law Schools and the Profession, supra note 16, at 273, 277–82
(noting that bar exams traditionally test
only substantive knowledge and to a
lesser extent skills in legal analysis and
writing; only three states include efforts
to test other performance skills); Frances Kahn Zemans & Victor G. Rosenblum, The Making of a Public Profession
(1981) (finding that the skills practitioners rated as most important were ne-
glected in law schools and bar exams).

whether a particular set of answers failed or passed, and that a quarter of examiners, when presented with the same paper a second time, reversed their earlier decision.

The selection of passing scores raises further difficulties. States that use the same multiple choice tests vary considerably in their selection of passing scores and in their ratios of successful to unsuccessful applicants. The percentage of candidates who pass ranges from the 30s to the 90s. Unsurprisingly, success rates tend to be lowest in the states with the greatest concentrations of lawyers, where new competitors are particularly unwelcome. By contrast, other jurisdictions pass a high proportion of candidates.... No evidence suggest that these states experience exceptional problems with lawyer performance. If states swapped cut-off scores, the majority of applicants passing the bar in permissive jurisdictions would fail, and the majority of those failing in stringent jurisdictions would pass. So too, as statisticians point out, higher grading standards do not guarantee higher competence in a system where about 95 percent of candidates who keep taking the exam eventually pass. In states with low success rates, students simply "study harder" and more applicants have to take the test multiple times.[65]

The problems of justifying state passing scores and ratios emerged clearly in an antitrust suit against the Arizona Board of Bar Examiners. In Hoover v. Ronwin, 466 U.S. 558 (1984), an unsuccessful bar applicant claimed that the Board's practice of setting passing scores after exams were graded constituted an anticompetitive effort to limit the number of licensed attorneys in violation of the Sherman Antitrust Act. The United States Supreme Court rejected that claim. In the majority's view, because bar admission occurred under Arizona Supreme Court auspices, it fell within the state action exemption to the Sherman Act. However, the majority also acknowledged the subjectivity involved in the choice of passing scores: "By its very nature, therefore, grading examinations does not necessarily separate the competent from the incompetent or—except very roughly—identify those qualified to practice and those not qualified. At best, a bar examination can identify those applicants who are more qualified to practice law than those less qualified." 466 U.S. at 578 n. 31.

A third and final criticism of bar exams involves their costs. Critics point to the disproportionate exclusion of minority candi-

---

65. Rhode, supra note 10, at 151–52 (2000); Douglas J. Besharov & Terry W. Hartle, "Here Come the Mediocre Law-yers," Wall St. J., Feb. 22, 1985, at 30 (describing California grading disagreements).

dates, the time and effort spent on cram courses, the inadequate accommodation of students with learning disabilities, the inhibition of innovative law school curricular approaches that do not aid exam preparation, and the barriers to practitioners' mobility across state lines.[66] If the bar exam system is justifiable despite these costs because it measures basic competence, critics question why graduation from an accredited school is also required. Conversely, if the test does not adequately screen for competence, why require it in addition to law school?[67]

In response to such arguments, supporters of the bar examination make two primary claims. First, they defend standardized tests as a useful incentive for students to synthesize their knowledge and to recognize legal issues in areas outside their own expected speciality. To the extent that current bar exams do not provide a useful learning experience, supporters wish to improve, not eliminate, testing procedures. Second, these proponents fear that the likely alternative to bar exams would be worse. If, for example, all graduates of accredited law schools were entitled to practice, states might interfere more extensively with those schools' curricular offerings, graduation requirements, or admission standards. Given the current unwillingness of most faculty to fail students, elimination of the bar exam might leave no significant screening device for minimal competence.[68] Nor would an apprenticeship program be a better solution. The systems that most other countries employ vary considerably in quality, and their history in this country offers little basis for optimism that they would prove successful in insuring basic competence. These concerns, together with a sense of hard-won entitlement among admitted practitioners, have impeded significant change.

There have, however, been some modest reform efforts. A few states, including California and Maine, have sought ways to expand the range of skills tested. Several other jurisdictions have waived exam requirements for graduates of in-state law schools. Bar lead-

---

66. For racial and ethnic differences in bar pass rates, see Law School Admission Council, National Longitudinal Bar Passage Study (Newtown, Pennsylvania: National Law School Admission Council, 1998). For cases rejecting challenges to bar exams as racially discriminatory, see Delgado v. McTighe, 522 F.Supp. 886 (E.D.Pa.1981); Richardson v. McFadden, 540 F.2d 744 (4th Cir.1976); Parrish v. Board of Commissioners of Alabama State Bar, 533 F.2d 942 (5th Cir.1976); Harper v. District of Columbia Comm. on Admissions, 375 A.2d 25 (D.C.App.

1977). For a critique, see Cecil J. Hunt II, "Guests in Another's House: An Analysis of Racially Disparate Bar Performance," 23 Fla. St. U. L. Rev. 721 (1996). For cases involving students with learning disabilities, see Hazard, Koniak, & Cramton, supra note 22, at 889.

67. See Vest, supra note 4, at 502.

68. Erwin Griswold, "In Praise of Bar Examinations," 42 B. Examiner 136 (1973).

ers and judges in Vermont, Maine, and New Hampshire have formed a Tri–State Task Force on Bar Admissions that has recommended a pilot program that would replace the bar exam. Instead, applicants would complete a comprehensive educational program designed to improve lawyer competence through in-depth skills training and evaluation.[69] Another recent proposal involves supervised post-graduate pro bono work as an alternative to the exam.[70]

The prospects for such reform efforts remain unclear. According to ABA polls, about eighty-five percent of surveyed lawyers believe that bar exams should continue. Although seventy percent also agree that the tests do not measure ability to practice law, about eighty percent felt that this screening requirement at least insures some minimum legal knowledge. Slightly over half of those surveyed preferred a national exam, with character assessments by individual states.[71] Given these views, along with all the problems previously discussed in connection with multijurisdictional practice, some further reform in admission procedures might well be possible.

Character and Fitness

Every bar in this country makes moral fitness a prerequisite for practice. Such requirements have an extended history; similar standards were applicable in ancient Rome and thirteenth-century England.[72] Yet what qualifies as moral character has been a matter of equally longstanding dispute, and the requirement has served to exclude a diverse and changing constituency, including immigrants and racial minorities as well as former felons, adulterers, political radicals, and bankrupts.[73] In what may have been the high water mark of exclusivity, one 1929 Pennsylvania board rejected candidates deemed "dull," "colorless," "subnormal," "unprepossessing," "shifty," "smooth," "keen," "shrewd," "arrogant," "conceited," "surly," and "slovenly." Also rejected were those who lacked "well defined ideas on religion," or who had family members with "unsavory" backgrounds or a "poor business reputation."[74]

69. Chief Justices Committee on Professionalism and Lawyer Competence, supra note 64.

70. Kristin B. Glen, "When and Where We Enter: Rethinking Admission to the Profession," Colum. L. Rev. (forthcoming 2002).

71. Paul Reidinger, "Law Poll: Bar Exam Blues," ABA J., July 1, 1987, at 35; Law Poll: Learning and Licensing: Law School and Bar Exams, 68 ABA J. 544 (1982).

72. Deborah L. Rhode, "Moral Character as a Professional Credential," 94 Yale L. J. 491 (1985).

73. Id. at 500–03.

74. Walter C. Douglas, Jr., "The Pennsylvania System Governing Admission to the Bar," 54 Rep. ABA 701, 703–05 (1929).

During the Cold War and Vietnam eras, the exclusion of applicants with leftist political views led to a series of Supreme Court decisions imposing some constitutional constraints on character requirements. In Schware v. Board of Bar Examiners of New Mexico, 353 U.S. 232 (1957), the Court reversed the rejection of a candidate based on his membership in the Communist Party thirteen years before his application. Under the governing standard of *Schware*, which remains applicable to current proceedings, "any qualification must have a rational connection with the applicant's fitness or capacity to practice law." Id. at 246–47. In subsequent cases, the Court held that character committees could question applicants about whether they were "knowing member[s]" of organizations advocating violent overthrow of the government, and could exclude applicants who refused to answer.[75] Committees could not, however, ask about all organizations that an applicant had joined since becoming a law student.[76] Since the early 1970s, the United States Supreme Court has issued no further rulings on issues of moral character. In the absence of such guidance, state courts and committees have interpreted requirements in an inconsistent, idiosyncratic, and sometimes highly intrusive fashion.

In principle, moral character requirements make perfect sense; the public has an obvious interest in protection from unethical lawyers. In practice, however, bar screening processes are ill suited to provide such protection. An inherent problem involves timing; the current process comes both too early and too late. Screening takes place before most applicants have faced circumstances comparable to those arising in practice, but after candidates have invested so much time and money in legal training that examiners are reluctant to deny admission. The most systematic research available suggests that about ninety-nine percent of bar applicants eventually gain entrance.[77] However, the process also imposes substantial burdens on candidates, and a significant number are delayed, deterred, or demeaned. Some evidence also suggests that Ivy League graduates receive more cursory investigation than other applicants, and that candidates of color receive more stringent review than white counterparts.[78]

75. Konigsberg v. State Bar of California, 366 U.S. 36 (1961); In re Anastaplo, 366 U.S. 82 (1961); Baird v. State Bar of Arizona, 401 U.S. 1 (1971); Application of Stolar, 401 U.S. 23 (1971).

76. Law Students Civil Rights Research Council, Inc. v. Wadmond, 401 U.S. 154 (1971).

77. Rhode, supra note 72, at 516.

78. Id., at 513–15; Mike Allen, "Beyond the Bar Exam," N. Y. Times, July 11, 1999 § 4, at 3; Abdon M. Pollasch, "Screening Process May Become Screaming Process for Bar Applicants," Chicago Lawyer, Sept. 1997, at 4; M. A. Cunningham, Comment, "The Professional Image Standard: An Untold Stan-

States generally have lengthy questionnaires concerning any incidents of dishonesty, disrespect for law, mental health difficulties, or "dishonorable," "immoral," or "improper" conduct. Bar inquiry frequently extends to juvenile offenses, parking violations, child support payments, and civil disobedience. Violation of a fishing license statute ten years before application was sufficient to cause one local Michigan committee to decline certification. But in the same state at about the same time, other examiners admitted individuals convicted of child molesting and conspiracy to bomb a public building.[79] Decisions have been particularly inconsistent concerning drug and alcohol offenses, sexual orientation, bankruptcy, and mental health treatment.[80]

There are, of course, some cases clearly justifying denial or deferral of admission, particularly where applicants make a bad situation worse by trivializing prior misconduct. Recent examples from California involve a candidate who explained theft while a bank teller as a "youthful indiscretion" (she thought the bank would "never miss the money"), and a candidate with half a dozen undisclosed convictions who could not be bothered to recount such "ancient history."[81] But in other cases, the degree of culpability and the appropriate response are subject to dispute.

One of the most controversial recent rulings involved Illinois' denial of admission to white supremacist Mathew Hale. Hale was the leader of World Church of the Creator, and was responsible for a Church web site that demonized Jews and "other mud races," and claimed that Hitler had the right idea.[82] Although some members of his organization had been convicted of violent hate crimes, Hale stated that he did not advocate violence, and his only criminal convictions involved minor charges in connection with protest activities like burning an Israeli flag. According to the Illinois committee panel, Hale was free

> to incite as much racial hatred as he desires and to attempt to carry out his life's mission of depriving those he dislikes of their legal rights, but in our view, he cannot do this as an officer of the court. Under any civilized standards of decency, the incitement of racial hatred for the ultimate purpose of depriving selected groups of their legal rights shows a gross

dard of Admission to the Bar," 66 Tul. L. Rev. 1015, 1037–39 (1992).

79. Rhode, supra note 72, at 538.

80. Id. at 537–542, 574; Rhode & Luban, supra note 27, at 788–92.

81. Debra Murphy Lawson, "Tales From the Character and Fitness

Trenches," The Bar Examiner, May, 2002, at 31, 33–34.

82. Pam Bellick, "Avowed Racist Banned from Practicing Law," N.Y. Times, Feb. 10, 1999, at A12.

deficiency in moral character, particularly for lawyers who have a special responsibility to uphold the rule of law for all persons.[83]

By contrast, many other bar leaders and examiners believe that excluding individuals like Hale on the basis of their moral beliefs compromises the principles that the system is designed to serve.[84]

Taken together, these admission decisions raise concerns not only of inconsistency but also of inaccuracy. Psychological research makes clear that moral behavior is highly situational. While individuals differ in their responses to temptation, contextual pressures have a substantial impact on moral conduct. Attorneys' compliance with ethical rules depends heavily on factors that cannot be anticipated at the time of admission, such as client pressures, collegial practices, and health or family difficulties. Prior behavior is relevant but also sometimes misleading; it is necessary to know a great deal about how and why individuals responded to earlier situations in order to predict how they will react in somewhat different future circumstances. Examiners seldom have that kind of knowledge.[85]

The same is true for predictions based on mental health and related difficulties. Many jurisdictions include broad questions about almost any mental health treatment and require applicants to release all medical records.[86] These requirements have been subject to increasing challenge under the Americans with Disabilities Act, which requires occupational licensing bodies to treat disabled individuals as "qualified" if they can meet the essential eligibility requirements for practice.[87] In these cases, bar examiners have been unable to show that past mental health assistance predicts future professional problems.[88] In general, about half of all individuals who seek such assistance do not have a diagnosable

83. Committee on Character and Fitness for the Third Appellate District of the Supreme Court of Illinois (1998). The Montana bar also denied admission. See Montana Human Rights Network Newsletter, March, 2001, at 1.

84. George Anastaplo, "Lawyers, First Principles, and Contemporary Challenges: Explorations," 19 N. Ill. U. L. Rev. 353 (1999).

85. Rhode, supra note 72, at 556–62; Walter Mischel & Yuichi Shoda, "A Cognitive–Affective System, Theory of Personality: Reconceptualizing Situations, Dispositions, Dynamics, and Invariance in Personality Structure," 102 Psychol. Rev. 246 (1995).

86. Alikhan, supra note 29.

87. Department of Justice Analysis, 28 C.F.R. § 35.104 (1991), interpreting 42 USC § 12132 (1991).

88. Rhode, supra note 10, at 156; Stanley S. Herr, "Questioning the Questionnaires: Bar Admissions and Candidates with Disabilities," 42 Vill. L. Rev., 635, 669–674, 721, nn. 65–69 (1997); Hilary Duke, "The Narrowing of State Bar Examiner Inquiries into the Mental Health of Bar Applicants: Bar Examiner Objectives Are Met Better Through Attorney Education, Rehabilitation, and Discipline," 11 Geo. J. L. Ethics 101, 105–07 (1997); Clark v. Virginia Bd. of Bar Examiners, 880 F.Supp. 430, 436 (E.D.Va.1995).

illness. Those who do may pose fewer risks than candidates with undisclosed and untreated problems.[89] Except in extreme cases, even mental health experts cannot reliably predict future difficulties based on past treatment. Untrained bar examiners are scarcely likely to do better. Their intrusive, often ill-informed inquiries during character proceedings have proved highly humiliating to applicants.[90] The potential psychological and financial costs of these proceedings, and the risk of being delayed or denied admission, also discourages many students from seeking appropriate professional services.[91]

A comparison of bar admission and disciplinary processes raises a final set of doubts about current character requirements. Bar disciplinary officials do not require practicing lawyers to report their parking violations, overdue child support payments, or mental health treatment. Yet if such conduct is relevant for applicants, why is it not even more relevant for licensed attorneys? Even more to the point, why doesn't the bar devote more of its resources to sanctioning misconduct involving clients? Behavior occurring after individuals become officers of the court surely is a more relevant indication of fitness to practice than behavior occurring before admission to practice. Yet the reverse double standard now prevails: applicants must satisfy higher requirements than practicing attorneys.[92] This disparity in standards is impossible to justify in terms of the stated rationale of bar admission processes: protection of the public.

How best to respond to these concerns is a matter of dispute. Defenders of the current process argue that a high percentage of lawyer disciplinary violations are linked to moral turpitude, mental health difficulties, and substance abuse.[93] Given the costs of detecting and remedying such violations after the fact, examiners believe that the public has a legitimate interest in character screening

89. Phyllis Coleman & Ronald A. Shellow, "Ask About Conduct, Not Mental Illness: A Proposal for Bar Examiners and Medical Boards to Comply with the ADA and Constitution," 20 J. Legis. 147, 162 n. 83 (1994); see also sources cited in note 88, supra.

90. Jon Bauer, "The Character of the Questions and Fitness of the Process: Mental Health, Bar Admissions and the Americans With Disabilities Act," 49 UCLA L. Rev. 93, 164 (2001).

91. See sources cited in notes 88 and 89, supra; Stephen T. Maher & Lori Blum, "A Strategy for Increasing the

Mental and Emotional Fitness of Bar Applicants," 23 Ind. L. Rev. 821, 830–61 (1990).

92. Rhode, supra note 72, at 546–51; Frasher v. West Virginia Bd. of Law Examiners, 408 S.E.2d 675 (W.Va.1991) (holding that higher standard of conduct for bar applicants than admitted attorneys is permissible).

93. Erica Moeser, "Personal Matters: Should Bar Applicants be Asked About Treatment for Mental Health? Yes: The Public Has the Right to Know About Instability," ABA J., Oct. 1994, at 36.

processes, however imperfect their implementation. Many experts argue, however, that this interest could be served by a narrower range of inquiries, in a system that is less idiosyncratic and intrusive. In the view of these commentators, applicants should have earlier and clearer notice about the conduct that could justify denial or deferral. Inquiry should be limited to recent histories of serious misconduct or current mental health impairments, and should avoid overbroad questions, particularly on matters such as psychological counseling, political beliefs, and sexual orientation. For example, with respect to mental health treatment, some jurisdictions make no inquiries or ask only about hospitalization. Other states limit their questions to a specific time period such as two or five years, or decline to act on disclosures unless the record reveals related facts—such as financial mismanagement or commission of a crime—indicating that the applicant would present a threat to clients.[94]

Whatever approach states choose, it would make sense to redirect some of the resources now spent on ineffective efforts to predict misconduct into disciplinary programs that could deter or remedy it. Only a more constrained and consistent administration of moral character requirements can avoid compromising the values at issue.

94. Mary Elizabeth Cisneros, "A Proposal to Eliminate Broad Mental Health Inquiries on Bar Examination Applications; Assessing an Applicant's Fitness to Practice Law By Alternative Means," 8 Geo. J. Legal Ethics 401 (1995); Herr, supra note 88, at 641–42 ; Duke, supra note 88, at 107.

Chapter XII

COMPETENCE AND DISCIPLINE

A. Introduction

Lawyers' conduct is subject to multiple forms of regulation. The most significant are informal: they flow from the rights of clients to select a lawyer of their choice, to discharge a lawyer with or without cause, and to share opinions about a lawyer with others. More formal regulations include: sanctions by courts and administrative agencies for misconduct in proceedings under their supervision; sanctions by disciplinary agencies acting under judicial authority; internal oversight by employers; civil liability for malpractice or breach of contract; and standards established by insurance companies as conditions of malpractice coverage. This chapter focuses primarily on discipline and malpractice proceedings since these regulatory structures are the most official, the most criticized, and the most readily reformed. However, as the following discussion makes clear, the limitations of these formal remedial procedures make other oversight structures equally critical.

Courts have long asserted authority to discipline lawyers as part of their inherent power to regulate the practice of law. The tradition of disbarment has its roots in thirteenth century England, where attorneys guilty of misconduct were literally cast over the "bar," a wooden barrier separating judges from lawyers, litigants, and witnesses.

In this country, eighteenth and nineteenth century courts seldom exercised their disciplinary power. Community disapproval was the primary sanction for professional misconduct, and the inadequacy of this approach was a major impetus for the formation of bar associations during the early twentieth century. Most associations accordingly established grievance committees to handle attorney misconduct. However, these committees proved inadequate for the task. As part of a voluntary governance system, the committees lacked power to compel attendance of witnesses or to impose sanctions. The committees could recommend discipline to the court, but their members were often reluctant to incur the animosity that such reports could trigger. Given the infrequency of bar action, few attorneys or clients made efforts to file complaints.[1]

1. See generally James Willard Hurst, The Growth of American Law: The Law Makers 286–93 (1950); George Martin, Causes and Conflicts: The Cen-

233

As the early twentieth century progressed, bar associations gradually acquired authority to investigate misconduct and impose sanctions, subject to judicial oversight. The procedures now governing lawyer discipline vary from state to state, although they all must meet constitutional requirements. Because current disciplinary proceedings are "quasi-criminal" in nature, they must incorporate basic due process safeguards, such as the opportunity to confront evidence and cross-examine witnesses, and the privilege against self-incrimination. However, lawyers granted immunity from criminal proceedings may be obligated to supply information to disciplinary authorities concerning possible misconduct; failure to do so may give rise to adverse inferences. So too, incriminating testimony given by an attorney under a grant of immunity from criminal prosecution is admissible in disciplinary proceedings.[2] Other procedural requirements are set forth in state statutes, rules of court, and bar ethical codes. A majority of jurisdictions require that disciplinary charges be proven by clear and convincing evidence; a minority require a fair preponderance of the evidence.

According to the ABA Standards for Lawyer Discipline and Disability Proceedings, Standard 1.1:

> [t]he purpose of lawyer discipline and disability proceedings is to maintain appropriate standards of professional conduct in order to protect the public and the administration of justice from lawyers who have demonstrated by their conduct that they are unable or are likely to be unable to properly discharge their professional duties.[3]

Another remedy for professional misconduct is a civil malpractice action by the injured party. An essential element of a malpractice claim is the lawyer's noncompliance with recognized standards of professional conduct. Those standards are memorialized in ethical codes. As noted below, the terms of the codes are therefore centrally significant in malpractice litigation, even though the violation of an ethical rule is not, of itself, a basis for civil liability.

Neither disciplinary nor malpractice proceedings are fully effective in upholding professional standards. The same is, of course, true of all law enforcement, and as with other regulatory systems, the limitation of bar oversight processes are matters of longstand-

tennial History of the Association of the Bar of the City of New York 1870–1970 (1970).

2. Willner v. Committee on Character and Fitness, 373 U.S. 96 (1963); Spevack v. Klein, 385 U.S. 511 (1967); In re Ruffalo, 390 U.S. 544 (1968). See Geoffrey C. Hazard, Jr. & Cameron Beard,

"A Lawyer's Privilege Against Self–Incrimination in Professional Disciplinary Proceedings," 96 Yale L.J. 1060 (1987).

3. The most current standards are in the Model Rules for Lawyer Disciplinary Enforcement (1999).

ing concern. Only about a quarter of surveyed Americans believe that the legal profession does a good job of disciplining its members.[4] "Too slow, too secret, too soft, and too self-regulated" is how the public views the disciplinary system.[5] Lawyers also have reservations about the current process, although their dominant concerns are the opposite of those of the public. According to ABA studies, lawyers generally see the process as too severe and too responsive to frivolous complaints.[6] Moreover, even attorneys who are critical of the current system oppose fundamental changes in its structure. For example, only twenty percent of California lawyers think that the disciplinary system is effective, but some ninety percent want the bar to continue its disciplinary activities.[7]

This disjuncture between the public's and the profession's view of disciplinary processes raises broader questions about self-regulation such as those addressed in Chapter III. Are there inherent problems in a regulatory structure controlled by the group to be regulated? If so, what follows from that fact? Commentators have often noted that

> lawyers have interests that overlap but are not coextensive with those of the public. Most attorneys want a process that is sufficiently responsive to clear abuses to protect clients and the profession's public image, as well as forestall more intrusive state regulation. But few lawyers have supported a system that would require major increases in their own bar dues, that would significantly expand oversight of their own conduct, or that would impose substantial risks of serious sanctions.[8]

This tension between professional and public interests accounts for many of the limitations in oversight structures identified below. The challenge remaining is how to design appropriate correctives without compromising the independence of the bar.

B.   Disciplinary Standards and Structures

The Definition of Misconduct

Rule 8.4 of the Model Rules of Professional Conduct sets forth the basic standard on lawyer misconduct.

4. ABA, Perceptions of the U.S. Justice System 77 (1999),

5. ABA Commission on Evaluation of Disciplinary Enforcement, Lawyer Regulation for a New Century 12–16 (1992). See also "Lawyer Disciplinary Hearings," ABA J., Jan. 1990, at 109.

6. "Lawyer Disciplinary Hearings," supra note 5, at 109.

7. Nancy McCarthy, "Pessimism for the Future," Calif. B. J., Nov. 1994, at 1.

8. Deborah L. Rhode, "Institutionalizing Ethics," 44 Case W. L. Rev 665, 694 (1994). See also Rhode, supra note 10, at 158–65.

It is professional misconduct for a lawyer to:

(a) violate or attempt to violate the Rules of Professional Conduct, knowingly assist or induce another to do so, or do so through the acts of another;

(b) commit a criminal act that reflects adversely on the lawyer's honesty, trustworthiness or fitness as a lawyer in other respects;

(c) engage in conduct involving dishonesty, fraud, deceit or misrepresentation;

(d) engage in conduct that is prejudicial to the administration of justice. . . .

DR 1–102 of the Code imposes similar prohibitions.

Reporting Requirements

Because law is intended to be a self-regulating profession and lawyers are often the only individuals with knowledge of other lawyers' misconduct, both the Model Rules and the Code include reporting requirements. Model Rule 8.3 provides: "A lawyer who knows that another lawyer has committed a violation of the Rules of Professional Conduct that raises a substantial question as to that lawyer's honesty, trustworthiness or fitness as a lawyer in other respects, shall inform the appropriate professional authority," unless the information is protected as a client confidence. DR 1–103 of the Code is more comprehensive: it requires reporting by lawyers with unprivileged knowledge of any violation of the rules.

These requirements are widely ignored and almost never enforced. According to some commentators, the infrequency with which attorneys report fellow professionals is inevitable and in some measure justifiable. For example, Gerald Lynch, a former law professor and now federal judge, has argued that the same values underpinning society's unwillingness to impose reporting requirements on citizens generally also apply in lawyer disciplinary contexts. In his view, the "impulse to protect one's friends and associates from harm, even from deserved punishment, is a moral and socially useful impulse precisely because it reaches beyond individual self-interest; it assimilates another's well-being to that of oneself."[9] According to Lynch, if disciplinary agencies are inadequate, "the bar should certainly act to strengthen them" rather

---

9. Gerald E. Lynch, "The Lawyer as Informer," 1986 Duke L.J. 491, 531 (1986).

than attempt to impose reporting requirements that professionals will routinely evade in practice.[10]

By contrast, other commentators, including the ABA's Commission on Professionalism, believe that reports of serious collegial misconduct are essential to protect clients and the public from abuses that would otherwise be impossible to detect or deter.[11] Even disclosure obligations that are not consistently observed can provide essential support for those who would like to come forward but fear collegial hostility or retaliation. There is, moreover, an inherent contradiction in the rationale for self-regulation and the refusal to enforce reporting obligations that are necessary for its effectiveness. In justifying a disciplinary process controlled by the profession, bar leaders have emphasized the importance of insuring that individuals who "pass judgment on attorney conduct be knowledgeable regarding the practice of law."[12] If so, it makes no sense to have a disciplinary complaint process that proceeds on precisely the opposite basis, and that relies almost exclusively on clients as a source of information about ethical violations.

Yet Illinois is the only jurisdiction that has made serious (if sporadic) attempts to enforce reporting requirements. In re Himmel, 533 N.E.2d 790 (Ill.1988), is the first published decision imposing discipline solely for a lawyer's failure to report collegial misconduct. The lawyer, James Himmel, was retained on a contingent fee basis by a woman whose former lawyer had withheld her share of a personal injury settlement. Himmel's initial strategy was to negotiate an agreement for payment under which his client would not initiate criminal, civil, or disciplinary charges. When the lawyer failed to honor that agreement, Himmel brought a successful legal claim for the amount due. However, he was also suspended for a year for not reporting the lawyer's misconduct to the bar's disciplinary authority. That decision has been highly controversial. Some commentators note with approval that Illinois lawyers' reports of misconduct have increased substantially after the court's judgment in *Himmel*.[13] Other commentators find that to be an ominous development, particularly in light of the risks of retaliation that whistleblowing may trigger.

10. Id. at 537–38.

11. ABA Commission, supra note 5.

12. Commission on the Future of the Legal Profession and the State Bar of California, The Future of the California Bar 103 (1995).

13. See Laura Gatland, "The Himmel Effect," ABA J., April 1997, at 24–28; Darryl van Duch, "Best Snitches: Illinois Lawyers," The Nat'l. L. J., Jan 27, 1997, at A1.

Whistleblowing Protections

Those risks are compounded by the absence of adequate protections for attorneys who report collegial misconduct. In a widely publicized example, Bohatch v. Butler & Binion, 977 S.W.2d 543 (Tex.1998), the Texas Supreme Court reversed a jury award to a lawyer whose partnership was terminated after she reported a colleague's suspected overbilling to firm management. In the court's view, "[o]nce such charges are made, partners may find it impossible to continue to work together to their mutual benefit and the benefit of their clients.... The threat of tort liability for expulsion would tend to force partners to remain in untenable circumstance–suspicious of and angry with each other–to their own detriment and that of their clients...." However, the court also made clear that its "refusal to create an exception to the at-will nature of partnerships in no way obviates the ethical duties of lawyers" to report misconduct. Id. at 547.

Most ethics experts have found such reasoning highly problematic. Lawyers already face substantial disincentives to "snitch" on a colleague. Why should they run the risks of retaliation when any benefit is likely to redound not to them personally but to the profession as a whole? The failure to provide wrongful discharge remedies for attorneys compounds these risks. For that reason, a growing number of courts and commentators support increased whistleblower protection.[14] As they recognize, such protections are necessary to alter lawyers' incentive structures. A passage from The Adventures of Huckleberry Finn, quoted by the dissent in *Bohatch,* makes the point directly: "[W]hat's the use you learning to do right when it's troublesome to do right and ain't no trouble to do wrong, and the wages is just the same?" Id. at 558.

Structural Problems and Reforms

Other, more fundamental, changes are also essential to make the disciplinary structure responsive to client needs. Studies by bar associations and legal ethics experts generally find three structural problems in current processes: the low percentage of consumer grievances that ever reach regulatory agencies; the failure of agencies to address minor misconduct such as negligence or fee disputes for which civil remedies are theoretically available; and the low percentage of reported complaints that result in significant sanctions.

Not only do few lawyers and judges report misconduct, relatively few clients are willing or able to initiate disciplinary proceedings.

---

14. Wieder v. Skala, 80 N.Y.2d 628 (N.Y.1992). See Stephen Gillers, "Protecting Lawyers Who Just Say No," 5 Ga. St. U. L. Rev. 1 (1988).

Many unsophisticated consumers are unaware of hard-to-detect abuses, such as billing for duplicative or unnecessary work. Clients who have knowledge often lack confidence that an effective response will be forthcoming from bar agencies, or are discouraged by the complexity of complaint structures and the lack of financial remedies for their own injuries. Misconduct from which a client may have benefitted, such as discovery abuse or misrepresentation in negotiations, is even less likely to trigger reports to disciplinary agencies.

The disciplinary system also fails adequately to address many grievances that are in fact reported. Resource constraints have led to a mismatch between client needs and regulatory responses. The problems that consumers are most likely to experience, such as neglect and overcharging, are least likely to fall within agency jurisdiction. As subsequent discussion suggests, malpractice litigation is too expensive for most of these matters and only a minority of states have alternative dispute resolution systems for client grievances. The programs that are available usually are voluntary. Clients most in need of assistance seldom find their attorneys willing to cooperate.[15]

Even cases that fall within bar disciplinary jurisdiction often receive inadequate attention or sanctions. Over ninety percent of complaints are dismissed without investigation; only about two percent result in public discipline.[16] Part of the reason for the high dismissal rate is that many complaints are inherently implausible or reflect dissatisfaction with outcomes rather than professional misconduct. However, inadequate enforcement resources and jurisdictional limitations are responsible as well. Funding constraints also prevent agencies from undertaking proactive, independent investigations, and limit their capacity to assist clients who need help in filing grievances.

So too, procedural delays and the requirement of clear and convincing proof result in dismissals of a significant number of complaints. Many jurisdictions have no time limits for resolving cases, and will "abate" disciplinary proceedings during the pen-

---

15. "ABA Committee Proposes Rules for Lawyer Client Mediation," 13 ABA/BNA Lawyers' Manual on Professional Conduct 398 (Dec. 1997); ABA Commission, supra note 5, at 129; Ken Armstrong & Maurice Possley, "The Verdict: Dishonor," Chi. Trib., Jan. 10, 1999, at A1.

16. See sources cited in Deborah L. Rhode, In the Interests of Justice: Re-

forming the Legal Profession, 159–60 (2000); Geoffrey C. Hazard, Jr., Susan P. Koniak, & Roger C. Cramton, The Law and Ethics of Lawyering 915 (1999); Leslie C. Levin, "The Emperor's Clothes And Other Tales About the Standards for Imposing Lawyer Disciplinary Sanctions," 48 Am. U. L. Rev. 1, 20 (1998).

dency of civil actions. Yet individuals are often reluctant to pursue bar complaints after the termination of a civil suit that was itself bitter and protracted. Extended delays also can result in the loss of crucial evidence and expose more clients to misconduct. Except in a few states, bar disciplinary agencies will not disclose the existence of a complaint unless they have found a disciplinary violation or probable cause to believe that a violation has occurred. Lawyers with as many as 20 complaints under investigation have received a clean bill of health when a consumer has asked for information about their records.[17] Potential clients also lack a ready way of discovering sanctions even after the process is completed. Not all states publish information concerning disciplinary actions, and none do so in publications designed to reach the general public.

These limitations in the current disciplinary process have prompted reform proposals along several lines. First, many commentators advocate making the process more proactive. Rather than relying almost exclusively on complaints and felony prosecutions, regulatory officials should initiate investigations based on malpractice filings, judicial sanctions, and random audits of trust funds. More steps should be taken to publicize the complaint process, to assist individuals in filing complaints, and to develop low-cost alternative dispute proceedings, including mandatory fee arbitration. Adequate resources should be available to support such initiatives.

A second set of proposals should focus on increasing the public's knowledge about the ethical records of attorneys. Some commentators advocate data banks and toll-free hotlines that would provide information about judicial sanctions, disciplinary actions, and malpractice judgments. Disciplinary processes should be open to public scrutiny from the time that complaints are filed. Although many lawyers oppose such open processes on the ground that disclosure of unfounded complaints would unjustly prejudice their reputations, Oregon's extended experience with public proceedings does not disclose such problems. Because consumer surveys have found deep suspicion about closed-door systems, the ABA Commission on Evaluation of Disciplinary Enforcement recommended public disclosure of complaints.[18]

A third cluster of proposals involves increasing the independence of disciplinary agencies. Although all states place such agencies under the authority of the state supreme court, only about half

---

17. Rhode, supra note 16, at 161.

18. ABA Commission, supra note 5; Mary Devlin, "The Development of Law-yer Disciplinary Procedures in the United States," 7 Geo. J. Legal Ethics 911, 931–32 (1994).

make them independent of the organized bar.[19] The ABA Commission recommended such autonomy as a means of avoiding the fact and appearance of conflict of interest. Some commentators have proposed further strategies to insure that disciplinary bodies are not unduly hostage to professional concerns. One possibility would be to require that the officials responsible for the disciplinary process be appointed by a diverse group, such as the chief judge of the state supreme court, the governor, and the speaker of the state legislature. Criteria for selection would be expertise in consumer protection and professional regulation.[20] Such an approach could secure greater public accountability than the current system in most states, which is to limit nonlawyer involvement in the disciplinary process to a few members chosen by lawyers.

C. Disciplinary Sanctions

Reforms are equally necessary concerning disciplinary sanctions. The sanctions currently available include:

- disbarment–a permanent or indefinite withdrawal of the license to practice law;

- suspension–a temporary prohibition on practice either for a specified period (usually ranging from several months to several years) or until compliance with certain specified conditions and an order of the court;

- public or private censures, reprimands, admonitions, warnings, and cautions–expressions of disapproval that establish a record of misconduct admissible in subsequent cases;

- rehabilitative sanctions–probation, mandatory education, and requirements of participation in substance abuse programs designed to correct specific conduct.

Some jurisdictions permit lawyers under investigation to resign, but treat such resignations as an admission of guilt. Attorneys who later seek reinstatement following resignation must make the same showing of rehabilitation as disbarred attorneys who seek reinstatement.

At an abstract level, there is general agreement about the factors most relevant in imposing disciplinary sanctions. Those factors include: (1) the extent to which the lawyer's conduct injured others; (2) the "blameworthiness" of that conduct; (3) the lawyer's

---

19. "Supreme Court Team to Study ABA Finding," Cal. St. B. J., Oct. 2001, at 5.

20. For such a proposal, see Rhode, supra note 16, at 162.

general character, demeanor, and prior disciplinary history; (4) the need for incapacitation; and (5) general or specific deterrence.[21] But in particular cases, there is often no comparable consensus about the degree of blameworthiness and the appropriate remedy.

The Severity of Sanctions

One longstanding dispute involves the stringency of sanctions. Courts and disciplinary agencies are generally reluctant to withdraw a lawyer's means of earning a living, either through disbarment or suspension. By contrast, commentators and the public repeatedly criticize the leniency of discipline, particularly in cases involving powerful government officials, attorneys from leading firms, or repeated instances of neglect, misrepresentation, or incompetence. For example, prosecutors have positions in which unprofessional conduct can have dire consequences, but they are rarely subject to disciplinary proceedings. A recent study of several hundred cases of serious prosecutorial misconduct found that none resulted in public disciplinary action.[22] Other commonly cited examples of leniency include Wall Street partners who have been only suspended, not disbarred, for offenses such as lying under oath about the destruction of documents, or falsifying billing records. Similar criticisms have focused on the light sanctions for government officials such as Richard Kleindienst, who testified falsely before Congress while serving as Attorney General, and William Clinton, who made what a federal trial court found to be "false and evasive" statements in a sexual harassment lawsuit during his term as President.[23] Kleindienst received a thirty-day suspension; Clinton received a five-year suspension and a $25,000 fine, which represented well under one evenings' speakers' honorarium.

A related issue involves permanent disbarment. In all but a few states, disbarred attorneys may apply for reinstatement after a prescribed period, generally between three and six years. About half of those who apply are readmitted. Critics of the process believe that the frequency of reinstatement compromises the deterrent value of sanctions, undermines public respect, and permits unacceptable levels of recidivism. In one study, a quarter of lawyers who

21. Charles W. Wolfram, Modern Legal Ethics, 110–11 (1986); see also ABA Joint Commission on Professional Sanctions, Standards for Imposing Lawyer Sanctions (1986).

22. Armstrong & Possley, supra note 15, at A1.

23. James B. Stewart Jr., "Kodak and Donovan Leisure," in The Partners: Inside America's Most Powerful Law Firms (1983); In re Cooper, 586 N.Y.S.2d 250 (App.Div.1992); Levin, supra note 16, at 83 n. 57; District of Columbia Bar v. Kleindienst, 345 A.2d 146 (D.C.1975) (per curiam); Jones v. Clinton, 36 F.Supp.2d 1118 (E.D.Ark. 1999).

were disciplined but not disbarred for financial violations were subsequently found guilty of further financial misconduct.[24] In other surveys, some attorneys have been disbarred multiple times for serious misconduct.[25]

Other commentators, however, believe that reinstatement should remain an option. Ronald Rotunda, for example argues:

> Because the purpose of discipline is to protect the public, if the court finds that the reason to impose the discipline has changed, and no longer exists, or that the risk to the public of future harm no longer exists, then the court should also reevaluate the need for continued discipline. Wisdom never comes to some people; we should not reject it in others merely because it comes a little late.... The possibility of reinstatement is a good policy because it serves the laudable purpose of giving the lawyer an incentive to mend his or her old ways. To take away this possibility is to take away an incentive to reform.... Proponents of permanent disbarment often claim that we should agree with their proposal because it will improve the public image of lawyers. We should resist that temptation: the organized bar should propose legal reforms because they are right, not because they might improve our public image.[26]

Mitigating Circumstances

Further controversy centers on the role of mitigating circumstances. The ABA Standards for Imposing Lawyer Sanctions list relevant factors including: remorse, cooperation with the disciplinary process, the absence of a prior record, timely efforts to make restitution, participation in a rehabilitation program, personal or emotional problems, mental health impairments, and the imposition of other penalties. How to weigh these factors in particular cases provokes considerable dispute. Some courts and commentators are sympathetic toward offenses that appear attributable to personal problems and disabilities.[27] Other courts and commentators, primarily concerned with client protection, have been reluctant to view such difficulties as adequate mitigation. The significance of lawyers' feelings of remorse and willingness to provide

24. David E. Johnson, Jr., "Permanent Disbarment: The Case For ...," The Professional Lawyer, Feb. 1994, at 22.

25. Id. at 27.

26. Ronald D. Rotunda, "Permanent Disbarment: The Case Against," The Professional Lawyer, Feb. 1994, at 23–24.

27. See Wolfram, supra note 21, at 96–97 (discussing cases involving, e.g., emotional disorders, stress of trial practice, burnout, family illness, compulsive gambling, and traumatic love affairs); Levin, supra note 16, at notes 49–50.

client compensation is equally controversial. According to Americans for Legal Reform, it is the job of disciplinary agencies to make sure that the risk of clients is "eliminated or minimized, not excused. The kind of leniency [granted to lawyers] is not accorded elsewhere—one can hardly imagine a bank forgiving a teller's theft of thousands of dollars and keeping them on the job based on excuses such as alcoholism, mental disability, or willingness to pay it back."[28] By contrast, other commentators can readily imagine such compassion. History, they note, reveals countless celebrated examples where "the quality of mercy [was] not strained...."

Similar controversies involve questions about whether the attorney has "suffered enough." Some courts and commentators maintain that disbarment is gratuitous for a prominent lawyer who has undergone the humiliation of public disciplinary proceedings, particularly those accompanied by criminal investigations or involuntary resignation from employment. Such considerations influenced the decisions concerning Clinton, Kleindienst, and the Wall Street partners noted above. Other courts and commentators are disturbed by the class bias underlying such decisions. In their view, lawyers who have attained positions of wealth and status should be held to a higher standard of conduct, particularly since their cases are likely to attract more attention than the usual proceedings and they have fewer extenuating financial circumstances. To the extent that the profession is concerned with general deterrence and the appearance of even-handedness, no special allowance should be made for the "mighty who are fallen."

Financial Sanctions

Another contested issue involves the appropriateness of financial sanctions. Unlike the disciplinary systems in other countries, American proceedings generally do not allow monetary fines.[29] The stated rationale is that such sanctions constitute punishment, and the purpose of disciplinary procedures is protection. A related concern has been that fines would make disciplinary procedures resemble those of the criminal justice system, and might accordingly require comparable due process safeguards such as proof beyond a reasonable doubt. Some commentators, however, argue that fines are an appropriate mechanism of deterrence and one commonly employed in civil as well as criminal cases. As these commentators note, the American justice system is premised on the assumption

---

28. HALT (Americans for Legal Reform), Attorney Discipline 16 (1988).

29. Only a few states, such as California and Nevada, explicitly permit fines and less than a dozen fines per year are reported to the ABA's National Lawyer Regulatory Data Bank. By contrast, fines have long been available in British and Canadian proceedings.

that individuals contemplating misconduct are influenced by the severity of sanctions and the probability of their imposition. Lawyers are even more likely than the average person to have information about the low risks of penalties. Adding the possibility of significant financial sanctions might alter some attorneys' cost-benefit calculations. In addition, courts may be less reluctant to impose fines than suspension or disbarment, which involve the loss of an individual's livelihood.[30] And if financial penalties were used to compensate injured parties, more of those victims might report misconduct and feel fairly treated by the disciplinary process.

Organizational Liability

A related issue is whether disciplinary sanctions should be directed at law firms as well as individuals. Bar leaders have led campaigns for organizational liability in other contexts (such as those involving securities, antitrust, and environmental regulation), and many commentators believe that the reasons for institutional accountability are just as relevant for legal workplaces. In some cases, it is impossible or inequitable to single out particular individuals for sanctions. Collective liability could encourage development of appropriate mechanisms for preventing or responding to misconduct, and could avoid the need to scapegoat particular lawyers in circumstances of diffuse or shared responsibility.[31]

Two states, New York and New Jersey, have pioneered rules permitting discipline of law firms, and other jurisdictions are considering the approach. The impact of such rules is difficult to gauge. In the first two years after the rule went into effect in Manhattan and the Bronx, only two law firms were sanctioned, and they received only private admonitions. According to one New York bar disciplinary counsel, sanctioning firms may be counterproductive because it enables regulators to take the "easy way out" and avoid identifying the lawyers immediately responsible for misconduct.[32] Because organizations can't be disbarred or suspended, penalties like admonitions or modest fines may be inadequate to insure compliance .

---

30. See generally, Steven G. Bené, Note, "Why Not Fine Attorneys? An Economic Approach to Lawyer Disciplinary Sanctions," 43 Stan. L. Rev. 907 (1991).

31. The Committee on Professional Responsibility, "Discipline of Law Firms," 48 The Record of the Association of the Bar of the City of New York 628 (1993); Ted Schneyer, "Professional Discipline for Law Firms?," 77 Cornell L. Rev. 1 (1991).

32. "Law Firm Discipline: Easy Way Out or Getting More Bang for the Buck," 15 ABA/BNA Lawyer Manual on Professional Conduct 401 (1999) (quoting Robert J. Saltzman).

Such considerations led the ABA's Ethics 2000 Commission to drop recommendations of discipline for law firms. Many lawyers who testified before the Commission maintained that such sanctions would "undermine the principle of individual responsibility that runs through the Model Rules."[33] Supporters of organizational liability have responded that fines and admonitions can be supplemented by requirements that firms' establish review bodies to oversee compliance with ethical standards. In their view, such an approach could strengthen principles of individual responsibility by putting teeth into the Model Rules concerning obligations of supervising attorneys. Model Rule 5.1 requires that lawyers with management authority make "reasonable efforts to ensure that the firm has in effect measures giving reasonable assurance that all lawyers in the firm conform to the Rules of Professional Conduct." The disciplinary process would obviously be strengthened by enforcement of this Rule in contexts such as discovery abuse, overbilling, or failure to implement adequate policies governing conflicts of interest and client funds.[34]

Conduct Outside Professional Relationships

Cases involving discipline for conduct occurring outside a lawyer's professional relationships raise a somewhat different set of concerns. As Chapter XI's discussion of admissions notes, the bar has been much more active in policing moral character among applicants than among admitted attorneys. From a public policy standpoint, this double standard is hard to justify. It is, of course, true that practicing lawyers have a greater vested interest in their professional licenses than applicants to the bar. But acts committed after admission are more probative of future threats to the public than acts committed before becoming an officer of the court. The difficulty, however, is that there is considerable disagreement within and across jurisdictions about how probative certain nonprofessional offenses in fact are. Particular dispute has centered on offenses such as those involving marijuana, driving while intoxicated, tax evasion, and sexual activity.[35]

---

33. "Ethics 2000 Commission Unveils Late Changes to Recommendations," 69 U.S.L.W. 2780 (2001).

34. For a case history of the kind of deficient supervisory mechanisms that could be subject to sanctions, see James L. Kelly, Lawyers Crossing Lines: Nine Stories 183 (2001).

35. Barrie Althoff, "Ethics and the Law: Lawyer Disciplinary Sanctions,"

Wa. St. B. News, Jan. 2002, at 1; Carrie Menkel-Meadow, "Private Lives and Professional Responsibilities? The Relationship of Personal Morality to Lawyering and Professional Ethics," 21 Pace L. Rev. 365 (2001); Deborah L. Rhode, "Moral Character as a Professional Credential," 94 Yale L.J. 491, 551–54 (1985).

A number of proposals have been made to foster greater consistency in responses to nonprofessional misconduct. One approach would be for states to set forth presumptive sanctions for specific acts, and to require justifications for any departure.[36] Another approach would be to require some "nexus between misconduct and job function."[37] So, for example, acts involving dishonesty would stand on different footing than those involving sexual misconduct or personal drug use.

Mental Health and Substance Abuse

When mental health or substance abuse affect professional performance, the disciplinary process must obviously respond. An estimated one-third of lawyers suffer from depression or from alcohol or drug addiction. Attorneys have about three times the rate of depression and almost twice the rate of substance abuse as other Americans.[38] These problems figure in a large percentage of disciplinary and malpractice cases; some estimates place the number between sixty and eighty percent.[39] Given the frequency of the issue, it is striking to find little consensus in reported decisions concerning the effect that addiction and other psychological difficulties should have in disciplinary cases.

One area of disagreement involves the extent to which disciplinary processes should be concerned not only with fitness to practice, but also with culpability and deterrence. Some courts and bar agencies have viewed addiction primarily as a mitigating factor; others see it as an indication of unfitness. Related disagreements involve causation. Some decisions assume a relationship between addiction and misconduct; others have demanded a showing that but for the addictive behavior, the misconduct would not have occurred.[40] Underlying these disputes are more fundamental issues. Professor David Luban observes:

36. See Levin, supra note 16, at 61–68 (advocating such an approach for all misconduct, modeled on the ABA's Sentencing Guidelines for criminal conduct).

37. Menkel–Meadow, supra note 34, at 388.

38. Blane Workie, Note, "Chemical Dependency and the Legal Profession: Should Addiction to Drugs and Alcohol Ward Off Heavy Discipline?," 9 Geo. J. Legal Ethics 1357 (1996); Michael J. Sweeney, "It's About Time: Lawyer Assistance Programs," Compleat Law., Spring 1996, at 17.

39. John Mixon & Robert P. Schuwerk, "The Personal Dimension of Professional Responsibility," 58 Law and Contemp. Probs. 87, 96 (1995); John Rogers Carroll & Vincent J. Rinella, Jr., "Attorneys and Alcohol: How to Help Impaired Lawyers," Trial, July 1994, at 28.

40. Workie, supra note 38; Compare In re Kersey, 520 A.2d 321, 326 (D.C. 1987) (holding alcoholism to be a mitigating factor) with In the Matter of Crowley, 519 A.2d 361, 363 (N.J.1987) (refusing to hold alcoholism a mitigating factor); see ABA Commission, supra note 21, at Standard 9.3(h) (allowing "physical or mental disability or impairment" as a mitigating factor in the de-

> Though alcoholism is a disease, it is unlike most diseases in that it does not just happen to the victim. He brings it on himself by drinking alcohol, behavior which ... is voluntary.... Even a purely medical judgment of whether the lawyer is recovered to the point of being fit to practice is therefore partly a judgment of will power, and thus of character. Medical [experts] try as best they can to base their prognoses on external factors—the quality of the lawyer's support group (such as Alcoholics Anonymous), his responses to counseling, the changes he has made in his environment to protect himself from stresses to which he has in the past responded by drinking, the stability and happiness of his life, etc. But in the end ... although alcoholism is a disease, not a defect of character, recovery from it will be a perpetual test of character....[41]

Although many courts and disciplinary bodies agree, they divide on how best to respond. Some are willing to give lawyers an opportunity for probation if their substance abuse was the primary cause of misconduct and they are in a structured rehabilitation program. By contrast, other tribunals impose suspension or disbarment, with the option of reinstatement after a suitable period of recovery.[42]

Similar variations occur in cases involving lawyers with mental health impairments. A widely noted example involves Joel Greenberg, disbarred in New Jersey in July 1998, and admitted in Pennsylvania in July 1999. Greenberg lost his New Jersey license after stealing almost $35,000 from his law firm. Neither the state's disciplinary review board nor its supreme court accepted Greenberg's claim that his misconduct was a self-destructive act fueled by depression, not greed, and that his subsequent psychiatric treatment left him fit for legal practice. According to the New Jersey Supreme Court, failure to impose disbarment would impair public confidence and exonerate other attorneys who misappropriated funds in response to personal hardship. In the court's view, attorneys suffering from mental health or substance abuse should seek help before they engaged in activities that would irreparably damage their own reputation and seriously compromise the profession's public standing. By contrast, Pennsylvania bar examiners obviously accepted Greenberg's claims of rehabilitation, but refused to make

---

gree of discipline imposed, but noting in the commentary that this factor has been treated inconsistently by state courts and does not excuse the misconduct).

41. David J. Luban, "Commentary: A Professional Tragedy," Nat. Rep. Legal Ethics and Prof. Resp. (1988).

42. See sources cited in note 38, supra.

any public comment about their decision due to confidentiality concerns.[43]

However such cases are resolved, virtually all experts in the field advocate greater reliance on treatment programs. Referral to such programs is particularly helpful at the early stages of addiction before social stigma, physiological problems, and professional impairment become pronounced. Recovery rates among professionals who obtain adequate treatment are encouragingly high.[44] Some type of program is available in every state, and many jurisdictions have implemented diversion systems for cases not involving serious misconduct. Under these programs, disciplinary action will be stayed pending successful completion of a rehabilitation program. Encouraging greater participation in these programs should be a key priority for the profession.

Increased emphasis should also be given to prevention of disciplinary problems and accountability for bar agency performance. To make the remedial process more consistent and responsive to public concerns is likely to require structural reforms along the lines noted earlier.

D. Competence

Competence in legal practice is something "everyone wants more of, but no one has a very clear sense of what exactly 'it' is, how best to promote it, or which efforts will be worth the cost."[45] The contemporary campaign for increased competence began in the early 1970s, when Chief Justice Burger asserted that between one-third and one-half of lawyers appearing in serious cases were "not really qualified to render fully adequate representation."[46] Although the empirical basis for that assertion remained unclear, other commentators began offering similar assessments. Over the next quarter century, various bar organizations considered appropriate responses.

Defining the Problem

A threshold challenge in responding to professional incompetence lies in identifying the problem to be addressed. Definitions of competence in bar ethical rules and reported decisions are

---

43. In re Greenberg, 714 A.2d 243 (N.J.1998); Wendy Davis, "Advice for the Disbarred, Go West," 157 N.J. L. J. 217 (1999).

44. See sources cited in notes 38 and 39, supra. See also Michael J. Sweeney, "A Return to Counselor," 18 GP Solo 57 (2001).

45. Deborah L. Rhode, "The Rhetoric of Professional Reform," 45 Md. L. Rev. 274, 288–93 (1986).

46. Id. (quoting Chief Justice Burger).

formulated at high levels of abstraction. The ABA's Code of Professional Responsibility prohibits "neglect" and mandates "preparation adequate in the circumstances" DR 6–101(A). The Model Rules of Professional Conduct require "reasonable diligence and promptness" and "the legal knowledge, skill, thoroughness, and preparation reasonably necessary for the representation." Rule 1.1 and Rule 1.3. Both the Model Rules and the Code also provide that lawyers who lack sufficient expertise in the field may accept employment if they associate an experienced lawyer or expect to become qualified through necessary study. Rule 1.1, Comment; DR 6–101; EC 6–3. The Code's Ethical Considerations add the qualification, missing in the Disciplinary Rules and Model Rules, that the additional preparation should not result in "unreasonable delay or expense to the client." EC 6–3.

How often lawyers' performance falls beneath these standards is a matter of frequent speculation but no hard data. The fragmentary research available reveals that most qualities rated highly relevant by practitioners and employing organizations are not learned in law school or tested on bar examinations: for example, investigation, effective oral expression, maintaining client and collegial relations, document drafting, diligence, judgment, and supervisory capability.[47] According to the report of the ABA Task Force on Law Schools and the Profession, Narrowing the Gap (the MacCrate Report), lawyers are not adequately prepared for their first jobs in practice; their deficiencies are also increasing as law becomes more complex and the range of necessary skills becomes more diverse.[48]

To address these problems, bar leaders generally propose: additional skills-oriented bar exams, law school courses, and continuing legal education; "bridging the gap" training and mentoring programs for new attorneys; special assistance for solo and small firm practitioners; and improved in-house education by employers. Almost no effort has been made to assess the effectiveness of such initiatives. Moreover, the most clearly identifiable incompetence is attributable less to inadequate knowledge and skills than to attitudinal problems and financial considerations. To the extent that poor representation results from greed or indifference, or from inadequate stakes and client resources, the conventional proposals are not much of a solution.

---

47. See Joanne Martin & Bryant G. Garth, "Clinical Education as a Bridge Between Law School and Practice: Mitigating the Misery," 1 Clinical L. Rev. 443 (1994); see also discussion in Chapter XI supra.

48. ABA, Section on Legal Education and Admission to the Bar, Legal Education and Professional Development: An Educational Continuum: Report of the Task Force on Law Schools and the Profession–Narrowing the Gap (MacCrate Report) (1992).

Continuing Legal Education

Continuing legal education (CLE) for practicing lawyers began a half century ago, to help armed forces veterans get up to speed in the law practices to which they were returning. Attention resurfaced in the 1970s in the aftermath of the Watergate scandals, in which a substantial number of prominent lawyers were involved. About four-fifths of all states now require practicing lawyers to participate in CLE programs, generally ranging from ten to twelve hours. In most jurisdictions, part of the coursework must focus on ethics. Some states demand coverage of other topics such as bias in the profession and substance abuse.

These requirements have been relatively uncontroversial. It is hard to object to having lawyers make minimal efforts to stay current in their fields and knowledgeable about ethical rules. But an analysis of CLE as currently implemented raises several concerns. Few jurisdictions impose meaningful quality control, and none have compiled evidence of the effectiveness of CLE programs. In order to gain acceptance from the bar, most educational requirements are minimal and some are exceptionally user-friendly. For example, courses on substance abuse and emotional distress have focused on stress reduction and relaxation methods, while courses on sports law have occurred at sporting events, complete with complementary hot dogs and peanuts.[49] The problem is not simply that some classes stretch the concept of "legal education"; the more fundamental difficulty, as a District of Columbia task force noted, "is that there have been no reliable, scientific demonstrations of the efficacy of continuing legal education." Research in other professions such as medicine and engineering has found no relationship between performance and participation in continuing education.[50] Neither is it self evident that passive attendance at ungraded courses will significantly increase competence in legal practice.

That is not to suggest that all CLE is unproductive. But as one expert notes, the "major benefit appears to be skill enhancement of already motivated and relatively competent practitioners."[51] To make CLE more useful to those who need it most, commentators have proposed a range of reforms.

49. Rhode, supra note 16, at 156.

50. Task Force on Mandatory Continuing Legal Education, Report to the Board of Governors of the District of Columbia Bar 26–28 (1995); Rhode, supra note 16, at 156.

51. Susan R. Martyn, "Lawyer Competence and Lawyer Discipline: Beyond the Bar?," 69 Geo. L. J. 705, 725–32 (1981).

One possibility might be to require both less and more. States could demand fewer hours but impose greater quality controls. Bar officials should require passage of an exam and deny credit for courses that bear little demonstrated relationship to performance in practice. More programs should target the deficiencies that cause the greatest disciplinary problems, such as client neglect and financial improprieties. Providers could themselves be held to educational requirements that insured some basic level of effectiveness. . . .

Alternatively, states could combine required and voluntary approaches. CLE could be mandatory for new lawyers and for other practitioners who have violated ethical rules. Attorneys who are subject to disciplinary, judicial, or malpractice sanctions could be required to take appropriate courses. Other attorneys who voluntarily complete CLE classes and pass a basic test could receive certification of their coursework. . . . An increasing number of lawyers are now willing to complete demanding educational requirements in order to become certified as specialists in particular fields of practice. States could encourage this trend by expanding specialization programs, publicizing their value to consumers, and improving their educational quality.[52]

Disciplinary Diversion Programs

A further competence-related strategy involves educational programs in lieu of lawyer discipline. The ABA Commission on Disciplinary Enforcement recommended that all jurisdictions adopt such programs for matters in which a lawyer's action constitutes minor misconduct, incompetence, or neglect. These programs could include arbitration, mediation, practice management courses, and substance abuse or psychological counseling.

Implementation of this recommendation has been uneven. Most states have some form of substance abuse diversion, a minority have arbitration or mediation systems, and several have practice management "ethics schools." Under these approaches, lawyers accused of minor violations who might otherwise receive a private reprimand have the option of participating in alternative programs. The effectiveness of these programs is unclear. One of the few systematic efforts to evaluate alternative dispute resolution found that thirty to forty percent of clients who participated in bar-sponsored fee arbitration were not satisfied with the experience. Their dissatisfaction was substantially higher than that of attor-

52. Rhode, supra note 16, at 156–58.

neys, who generally felt well-served by the programs.[53] Such findings suggest the need for more systematic efforts to measure the effectiveness of alternative remedial structures, both in providing adequate remedies for clients and in improving attorney performance.

E. Malpractice

Three decades ago, legal malpractice claims were so rare and practitioners were so unconcerned about liability that insurance coverage was generally not available on the domestic market. By the late 1990s, the situation had dramatically changed. Recent estimates suggest that ten to twenty percent of attorneys face malpractice exposure in any given year and that insurance payouts total about six billion dollars annually.[54]

What accounts for the recent increase is subject to dispute. Some commentators believe that incompetent practice is growing. As competition within the profession intensifies, profit margins decrease, and billable hour expectations escalate, lawyers are under more pressure to handle matters beyond their expertise. Other commentators believe that the increase in malpractice claims has less to do with increases in the amount of malpractice than with increases in consumer expectations and in other lawyers' willingness to bring such claims. As these observers note, the bar's experience is by no means unique; other professionals have also been subject to rising numbers of malpractice complaints.[55]

The growth in claims against lawyers reflects broader changes in the structure and climate of legal practice. The increasing size and stratification within the legal community have made colleagues less hesitant to challenge each others' conduct in malpractice suits. Financial speculation in the 1980s and 1990s also prompted more civil liability claims. Individuals who lost money in risky ventures looked for deep pockets to sue and targeted lawyers who had brokered the transactions and written opinion letters on which investors relied.[56]

53. Id. at 181.

54. "Figuratively Speaking," ABA J., Oct. 1996, at 12; Manuel R. Ramos, "Legal Malpractice: No Lawyer or Client Is Safe," 47 Fla. L. Rev. 1, 5 (1995); David Z. Webster, "At Issue: Mandatory Malpractice Insurance: Has the Time Come to Require Coverage?—Yes: It's Essential to Public Trust," ABA J., Nov. 1993, at 44.

55. Richard Pérez-Peña, "When Lawyers Go After Their Peers: The Boom in Malpractice Cases," N.Y. Times, Aug. 5, 1994, at A1; Jonathan Gaw, "Lawyers Shed Reluctance to Sue Their Own," L.A. Times, Dec. 14, 1992, at B1; Ramos, supra note 54.

56. ABA Standing Committee on Lawyers' Professional Liability, Legal

Yet despite the escalation of malpractice claims, the barriers to successful actions have remained considerable. Many individuals with grievances against a lawyer are unwilling to incur the costs in time, money, and acrimony involved in filing charges. Unless liability looks clear, damages are substantial, and the defendant has sufficient insurance or legally accessible assets to make a judgment collectible, attorneys who specialize in malpractice litigation will generally decline the case.

The burden of proof necessary to establish liability is also a substantial obstacle. In general, plaintiffs must demonstrate:

- A duty of care arising from an attorney-client relationship or some other relationship giving rise to fiduciary responsibilities;

- A breach of that duty arising from failure to exercise the care that reasonably competent lawyers exercise under similar circumstances; and

- Legally cognizable damages caused by the breach, usually limited to economic injury.

Although the data on malpractice success rates are incomplete and conflicting, the best available evidence suggests that half of all claims cannot meet these requirements and result in no recovery; another quarter result in minimal judgments. Most successful claims involve fairly obvious errors, such as missing deadlines, neglecting to file documents, or failing to consult clients and follow their instructions.[57] In cases presenting less objective proof of error, clients often have difficulty establishing what exactly the attorney did or did not do, and how that conduct fell below average performance standards within the relevant legal community.

Current debates over malpractice liability center on several main issues: how to set performance standards; what proof of causation should be necessary; what should be the role of professional conduct codes; what remedies should be available; who should be entitled to sue; and what prevention strategies are most promising.

Malpractice Claims in the 1990s 12, 16 (1996); John Gibeaut, "Good News, Bad News in Malpractice," ABA J., March 1997, at 100.

57. Ramos, supra note 54; ABA Committee, supra note 56. These suc- cess rates are not, however, significantly lower than malpractice claims against other professionals.

Performance Standards

Courts and commentators have divided over whether "average community" standards are the appropriate benchmark of liability and, if so, how the legal community should be defined. Should the relevant community be the locality, the state, or the legal profession more generally? A leading Vermont decision held that the state, not the locality, should provide the frame of reference. In the court's view, the "minimum knowledge required should not vary with geography. . . . The fact that a lower degree of care or less able practice may be prevalent in a particular local community should not dictate the standard of care."[58] That reasoning, however, raises the question of why state boundaries should be controlling. Some commentators have also objected to making liability depend on prevailing practices in the community, however defined. In their view, it gives the profession the power to dictate its own standard of conduct, a prerogative said to be unavailable to other occupations even in areas involving technical expertise. To these critics, a preferable standard would be reasonable performance under the totality of the circumstances, including clients' legitimate expectations.

As a practical matter, however, cases that are attractive enough to justify prosecution under a contingent fee arrangement (strong liability, large damages, and a financially responsible defendant) usually involve conduct that is (or is alleged to be) grossly abusive. Such misconduct would violate current as well as proposed standards of professional conduct. The difficult problem for most malpractice complainants is not the alleged leniency of the prevailing standard, but factual disputes between client and lawyer (the "he said, she said" problem), and the traditional reluctance of courts to extend lawyer liability to victims beyond immediate clients.

Causation

A further burden for malpractice plaintiffs involves causation. In effect, they must demonstrate not only that the lawyer was negligent or guilty of other misconduct, but also that this breach of professional standards resulted in quantifiable damages. For claims involving malpractice in litigation (which comprise about half of all reported complaints), that burden often requires a trial within a trial; plaintiffs must establish that, but for the lawyer's negligence, they would have prevailed in the original proceeding. This requirement has been subject to considerable criticism. Some commentators advocate an alternative standard modeled on the test applica-

58. Russo v. Griffin, 510 A.2d 436, 438 (Vt.1986).

ble in England and France, and in American medical malpractice cases. Under this test, plaintiffs who demonstrate that the defendant's substandard performance deprived them of a substantial possibility of recovery would be entitled to damages adjusted to reflect the likelihood of success.[59] Many commentators also propose a version of that test for malpractice cases involving criminal defense lawyers. The prevailing standard requires complainants to establish that they were actually innocent, and that their attorneys' substandard performance was responsible for their convictions.[60] That test is almost always impossible to meet even though, as Chapter IX indicated, the performance in many criminal cases falls below acceptable standards.

Professional Conduct Codes

A related issue involves the significance of the bar's ethical codes in establishing attorney malpractice. The Preliminary Statement of the ABA Code disclaims any effort to define standards for civil liability of lawyers for professional conduct. The Scope Note to the Model Rules similarly states that:

> [v]iolation of a rule should not give rise to a cause of action nor should it create any presumption that a legal duty has been breached. The Rules are designed to provide guidance to lawyers and to provide a structure for regulating conduct through disciplinary agencies. They are not designed to be a basis for civil liability. Furthermore, the purpose of the Rules can be subverted when they are invoked by opposing parties as procedural weapons.

In some jurisdictions, violations of ethical rules can serve as evidence of negligence *per se,* or as evidence of failure to meet the proper standard of care. By contrast, other courts disallow any use of the rules, or permit only indirect use (as when an expert refers to them in testifying about the standard of care).[61] This restrictive approach is hard to square with the stated purpose of ethical codes: protecting the public. It is not self-evident why this purpose would be subverted by supplementing the limited resources of bar disciplinary agencies with civil remedies. In any event, even in jurisdictions that are least receptive to admission of bar ethical standards, expert testimony will often incorporate these standards indirectly. For most malpractice cases, such testimony either is a legal require-

---

59. John Leubsdorf, "Legal Malpractice and Professional Responsibility," 48 Rutgers L. Rev. 101, 111–19 (1995).

60. Wiley v. County of San Diego, 966 P.2d 983 (Cal.1998); Wolfram, supra note 21, at 218–27.

61. Gary A. Munneke & Anthony E. Davis, "The Standard of Care in Legal Malpractice: Do the Model Rules of Professional Conduct Define It?" 22 J. Legal Prof., 33, 69 (1998).

ment or a practical necessity to get to the jury. A competent expert is essential to establish that the lawyer's conduct failed to conform to "recognized professional standards." These standards implicitly, and sometimes explicitly, are reflected in the applicable ethical code. In effect, because the codified concept of "competence" generally mirrors prevailing standards of practice, rules restricting the admissibility of codes have limited practical effects.

Remedies

A further issue involves the adequacy of malpractice remedies. One chronic problem concerns the high transaction costs of establishing liability. Unsurprisingly, lawyer defendants are, on the whole, a litigious group when it comes to defending their own conduct. Because many cases are highly contested, less than half of insurance payouts goes to injured victims.[62] A further problem is the high percentage of lawyers who carry no insurance–a number typically ranging between thirty and forty percent, depending on the state.[63] To compensate parties who cannot recover from their attorneys, virtually all state bars provide some assistance from client security funds, which are subsidized by mandatory lawyer contributions. However, most of these funds are too limited to cover more than a small fraction of client grievances. Payouts are available only for intentional misconduct, and are capped at inadequate levels.

To insure more effective remedies, several reform strategies are possible. One option is to expand client security funds, either by increasing bar dues or by imposing fines in disciplinary proceedings. Another possibility noted earlier is to establish low-cost alternative dispute resolution procedures for fee disputes and malpractice claims.

A further strategy, pioneered in Oregon and debated in a growing number of jurisdictions, is to require all attorneys to carry adequate malpractice insurance. Proposals to this effect have attracted strong opposition, particularly among members of the bar who do not practice full-time or who, for other reasons, would find liability premiums to be a substantial hardship. Critics also worry that mandatory coverage would encourage frivolous claims and would fail to distinguish between attorneys with widely varying levels of liability exposure. In opponents' view, a preferable strategy

---

62. Manual R. Ramos, "Legal Malpractice: Reforming Lawyers and Law Professors," 70 Tul. L. Rev. 2583, 2600 (1996).

63. Id. at 2610; Rhode, supra note 16, at 167.

would be to require lawyers to disclose to clients whether they are insured and, if so, at what level.

Supporters of mandatory insurance respond that no increase in claims has occurred in Oregon and that premiums there are quite affordable, at rates below those of comparable jurisdictions. Part of the reason is that Oregon operates a mandatory nonprofit Professional Liability Fund that insures all the state's attorneys, eliminates expensive marketing and brokers' fees, and incorporates effective prevention initiatives. Over four-fifths of the state's attorneys support its malpractice system.[64] Many other nations also require malpractice insurance, and their successful experience suggests that mandatory coverage should be a priority for reform here.

Third Party Obligations

A final area of controversy involves the extent to which non-clients should be able to sue for an attorney's violations of professional rules. The doctrine of privity traditionally blocked such actions, but courts gradually have recognized exceptions to that rule. Some jurisdictions now hold that lawyers who undertake responsibilities that foreseeably affect a third party owe a duty of care to that individual. For example, attorneys may be liable to intended beneficiaries of an estate if errors in drafting the will prevent them from receiving the bequest. Such holdings rely on fiduciary/agency principles, third party beneficiary theories, or a balancing test that considers factors such as the predictability and certainty of harm and the defendant's moral culpability.[65] Underlying this line of cases is a desire to place responsibility on the individual best able to prevent losses and maintain adequate insurance.

By contrast, other courts have concluded that making a lawyer liable to persons apart from clients would "inject undesirable self-protective reservations into the attorney's counseling role," would prevent him from devoting his "entire energies to his client's interests," and would impose an undue financial burden on the profession.[66] A prominent case denying recovery is Schatz v. Weinberg & Green, 943 F.2d 485 (4th Cir.1991). There, the attorneys

---

64. ABA Commission, supra note 5, at 81–82; Rhode, supra note 16, at 163; Harry H. Scheider, Jr., "At Issue: Mandatory Malpractice Insurance: Has the Time Come to Require Coverage?–No: An Invitation to Frivolous Suits," ABA J., Nov., 1993, at 45.

65. Leubsdorf, supra note 59, at 111, 130–35; Geoffrey C. Hazard, Jr., "The

Privity Requirement Reconsidered," 37 S. Tex. L. Rev. 967 (1996); Forest J. Bowman, "Lawyer Liability to Non-Clients," 97 Dick. L. Rev. 267, 276 (1993).

66. Goodman v. Kennedy, 556 P.2d 737 (Cal.1976).

prepared closing documents for the sale of a company that included material misstatements about the client's net worth. When the client declared bankruptcy, the buyers were left with worthless promissory notes that the client had guaranteed as part of the sale. The buyers then sued the law firm, arguing that attorneys should be accountable for information that they knew was false and that was incorporated into a document on which third parties would reasonably rely. In affirming the dismissal of plaintiffs' complaint, the Fourth Circuit reasoned that attorneys owed common law duties only to clients and to direct beneficiaries of the lawyer-client relationship, not to other third parties such as the Schatzes:

> Any other result may prevent a client from reposing complete trust in his lawyer for fear that he might reveal a fact which would trigger the lawyer's duty to the third party. Similarly, if attorneys had a duty to disclose information to third parties, attorneys would have an incentive not to press clients for information. The net result would not be less securities fraud. Instead, attorneys would more often be unwitting accomplices to the fraud as a result of being kept in the dark by their clients or by their own reluctance to obtain information. 943 F.2d at 493.

Under the court's reasoning, only if lawyers had the specific intent to aid fraud should they be liable to third parties.

Critics of the *Schatz* holding note that recent decisions have generally held professionals other than lawyers to a higher standard than the Fourth Circuit's. "Conscious avoidance" of facts indicating fraud will establish federal criminal liability for providers of financial services such as underwriting. Critics believe that attorneys in civil cases should have no greater protection and that, in the long run, third-party liability will serve the profession's interests as well as the public's.[67] Part of what makes lawyers' services valuable in commercial transactions is that preparation of documents serves to corroborate clients' assertions. Decisions like *Schatz* permit negligent or willfully ignorant attorneys to undermine the credibility of the profession and the value of legal assistance.

Such considerations have increased courts' willingness to find third-party liability, particularly where the lawyer knows that the party is an intended beneficiary of the legal services. In a leading case, the Seventh Circuit Court of Appeals reached the opposite

---

67. John M. Freeman & Nathan M. Crystal, "Scienter in Professional Liability Cases," 42 S.C. L. Rev. 783 (1991).

conclusion from *Schatz*. In Greycas v. Proud, 826 F.2d 1560, 1565 (7th Cir.1987), a lawyer was held liable for negligent misrepresentations in a letter on which a third party reasonably relied. In other litigation, such as cases involving failures of savings and loan institutions, lawyers also have been held accountable for failure to make a reasonable investigation.[68] The same approach has been adopted in many states and in §30 of the Restatement (Third) of the Law Governing Lawyers. To many legal ethics experts, the *Schatz* case is out-of-step with prevailing doctrine and sound policy.

Prevention

However these issues concerning the standard and scope of liability are resolved, attorneys have a strong interest in preventing disputes that might trigger malpractice claims. This interest is also shared by insurance companies, who often audit their large policyholders for risky practices and require malpractice prevention systems as a condition of liability coverage. Crucial preventive strategies include systems for identifying conflicts of interest and for reminding lawyers of important deadlines. These systems generally are most effective if they allocate responsibility for monitoring compliance to someone other than the person responsible for performance. An equally important strategy involves communication with clients. Attorneys should provide realistic assessments of costs, fees, delays, and outcomes. Disputes can also be preempted by detailed written retainer agreements and by ongoing reports concerning the status of the case, such as copies of major filings, notices of significant developments, and so forth.

Contrary to conventional wisdom, it is not young, inexperienced attorneys who experience the most malpractice claims. Lawyers practicing over ten years account for a disproportionate share of suits. The same financial and psychological factors that lead to disciplinary charges also contribute to malpractice: unrealistic caseloads, drug and alcohol abuse, and personal stresses such as divorce and burnout. The best protection for both lawyers and their clients is a clear and endlessly reiterated organizational norm of professional integrity, together with comprehensive malpractice insurance, and professional help when personal problems arise.

68. See Stephen Gillers, "Cleaning Up the S & L Mess," ABA J., Feb. 1993, at 93. See generally §§ 30 and 73 of the Restatement (Third) of the Law Governing Lawyers (2000).

EPILOGUE

Professional regulation in the twenty-first century confronts unprecedented challenges. Competition and commercialism are increasing; collegiality and civility are headed in the opposite direction. As the bar grows in size and specialization, its sense of common purpose and its reliance on informal reputational sanctions become harder to sustain. While these changes have intensified the need for formal regulation, other trends in legal markets have made effective enforcement difficult to achieve. As more of lawyers' work crosses jurisdictional boundaries, traditional state-based oversight structures face new constraints. As competition within and across professions grows more intense, the pressure to compromise competing values escalates as well.

These trends in legal practice generate widespread concerns but little consensus on solutions. In a bar that is increasingly diverse in background and practice setting, issues of professional responsibility are increasingly divisive. One result has been a rise of multiple, sometimes inconsistent, forms of regulation. Some states have departed from the ABA's model ethical codes; legislatures and agencies have become more willing to step in where other oversight structures fall short. This lack of uniformity poses further challenges for a profession whose work frequently crosses jurisdictional borders.

Yet the American bar has always adapted to meet the nation's pressing needs, and its own regulatory problems should be no exception. In earlier eras, issues of professional responsibility may have attracted little systematic attention, but contemporary lawyers are acutely conscious of problems in the distribution of legal services and the conditions of legal practice. Today's lawyers are also aware that if they do not actively seek solutions, others may do so for them. If the bar is to justify its regulatory independence, it must address the issues that this book has explored.

Lawyers are surely equal to that task. Leaders of the legal profession have been at the forefront of every major social reform movement in the nation's history. The challenge now is to channel that leadership inward and to make legal ethics a priority, both in principle and in practice.

*

261

TABLE OF CASES

References are to Pages.

---

*

INDEX

References are to pages.

✝